HOW TO BE ALONE

JONATHAN FRANZEN

HOW TO BE ALONE ESSAYS

FARRAR, STRAUS AND GIROUX · PICADOR
NEW YORK

www.picadorusa.com

Picador® is a U.S. registered trademark and is used by Farrar, Straus
and Giroux under license from Pan Books Limited.

For information on Picador Reading Group Guides, as well as ordering,
please contact the Trade Marketing department at St. Martin's Press.
Phone: 1-800-221-7945 extension 763
Fax: 212-677-7456
E-mail: trademarketing@stmartins.com

Earlier versions of most of these essays first appeared in Details, Graywolf Forum,
Harper's, and The New Yorker. The essay "Mr. Difficult" has been added
to this paperback edition, and the essay "Scavenging" has been modified.
The author is extremely grateful to Colin Harrison and Will Dana,
and he is indebted for life to Henry Finder.

Library of Congress Cataloging-in-Publication Data
Franzen, Jonathan.
    How to be alone : essays / Jonathan Franzen.— 1st ed.
    p. cm.
    ISBN 0-312-42216-4
    I. Title.

PS3556.R352   H69   2002
814'.54—dc21

                                                    2002023642
Designed by Abby Kagan

D 30 29 28 27 26 25 24 23

FOR KATHY CHETKOVICH

CONTENTS

CONTENTS

HOW TO BE ALONE

A WORD ABOUT THIS BOOK

MY THIRD NOVEL, *The Corrections*, which I'd worked on for many years, was published a week before the World Trade Center fell. This was a time when it seemed that the voices of self and commerce ought to fall silent—a time when you wanted, in Nick Carraway's phrase, "the world to be in uniform and at a sort of moral attention forever." Nevertheless, business is business. Within forty-eight hours of the calamity, I was giving interviews again.

My interviewers were particularly interested in what they referred to as "the *Harper's* essay." (Nobody used the original title, "Perchance to Dream," that the magazine's editors had given it.) Interviews typically began with the question: "In your *Harper's* essay in 1996, you promised that your third book would be a big social novel that would engage with mainstream culture and rejuvenate American literature; do you think you've kept that promise with *The Corrections*?"

To each succeeding interviewer I explained that, no, to the contrary, I had barely mentioned my third novel in the essay; that the notion of a "promise" had been invented out of thin air by an editor or a headline writer at the *Times* Sunday Magazine; and that, in fact, far from promising to write a big social novel that would bring news to the mainstream, I'd taken the essay as an opportunity to renounce that variety of ambition. Because most interviewers hadn't read the essay, and because the few who had read it seemed to have misunderstood it, I became practiced at giving a clear, concise précis of its argument; by the time I did my hundredth or hundred-tenth interview, in November, I'd worked up a nice little corrective spiel that began, "No, actually, the *Harper's* essay was about *abandoning* my sense of social responsibility as a novelist and learning to write fiction for the fun and entertainment of it . . ." I was puzzled, and more than a little aggrieved, that nobody seemed able to discern this simple, clear idea in the text. How willfully stupid, I thought, these media people were!

In December I decided to pull together an essay collection that would include the complete text of "Perchance to Dream" and make clear what I had and hadn't said in it. But when I opened the April 1996 *Harper's* I found an essay, evidently written by me, that began with a five-thousand-word complaint of such painful stridency and tenuous logic that even *I* couldn't quite follow it. In the five years since I'd written the essay, I'd managed to forget that I used to be a very angry and theory-minded person. I used to consider it apocalyptically worrisome that Americans watch a lot of TV and don't read much Henry James. I used to be the kind of religious nut who convinces himself that, because the world doesn't share his particular faith (for me, a faith in literature), we must be living in End Times. I used to think that our American political economy was a vast cabal whose specific aim was to thwart my artistic ambitions, exterminate all that I found lovely in civilization, and also rape and murder the planet in the process. The first third of the *Harper's* essay was written from this place of anger and despair, in a tone of high theoretical dudgeon that made me cringe a little now.

It's true that, even in 1996, I intended the essay to document a stalled novelist's escape from the prison of his angry thoughts. And so part of me is inclined now to reprint the thing exactly as it first appeared, as a record of my former zealotry. I'm guessing, though, that most readers will have limited appetite for pronouncements such as

> It seemed clear to me that if anybody who mattered in business or government believed there was a future in books, we would not have been witnessing such a frenzy in Washington and on Wall Street to raise half a trillion dollars for an Infobahn whose proponents paid lip service to the devastation it would wreak on reading ("You have to get used to reading on a screen") but could not conceal their indifference to the prospect.

Because a little of this goes a long way, I've exercised my authorial license and cut the essay by a quarter and revised it throughout. (I've also retitled it "Why Bother?") Although it's still very long, my hope is that it's less taxing to read now, more straightforward in its movement. If nothing else, I want to be able to point to it and say, "See, the argument is really quite clear and simple, just like I said!"

What goes for the *Harper's* essay goes for this collection as a whole. I intend this book, in part, as a record of a movement away from an angry and frightened isolation toward an acceptance—even a celebration—of being a reader and a writer. Not that there's not still plenty to be mad and scared about. Our national thirst for petroleum, which has already produced two Bush presidencies and an ugly Gulf War, is now threatening to lead us into an open-ended long-term conflict in Central Asia. Although you wouldn't have thought it possible, Americans seem to be asking even fewer questions about their government today than in 1991, and the major media sound even more monolithically jingoistic. While Congress yet again votes against applying easily achievable fuel-efficiency standards to SUVs, the president of Ford Motor Company can be seen patriotically defending these vehicles in a TV ad, avowing that Americans *must never accept* "boundaries of any kind."

With so much fresh outrageousness being manufactured daily, I've chosen to do only minimal tinkering with the other essays in this book. "First City" reads a little differently without the World Trade Center; "Imperial Bedroom" was written before John Ashcroft came to power with his seeming indifference to personal liberties; anthrax has lent further poignancy to the woes of the United States Postal Service, as described in "Lost in the Mail"; and Oprah Winfrey's disinvitation of me from her Book Club makes the descriptive word "elitist" fluoresce in the several essays where it appears. But the local particulars of content matter less to me than the underlying investigation in all these essays: the problem of preserving individuality and complexity in a noisy and distracting mass culture: the question of how to be alone.

[2002]

MY FATHER'S BRAIN

H ERE'S A MEMORY. On an overcast morning in February 1996, I received in the mail from my mother, in St. Louis, a Valentine's package containing one pinkly romantic greeting card, two four-ounce Mr. Goodbars, one hollow red filigree heart on a loop of thread, and one copy of a neuropathologist's report on my father's brain autopsy.

I remember the bright gray winter light that morning. I remember leaving the candy, the card, and the ornament in my living room, taking the autopsy report into my bedroom, and sitting down to read it. *The brain* (it began) *weighed 1,255 gm and showed parasagittal atrophy with sulcal widening.* I remember translating grams into pounds and pounds into the familiar shrink-wrapped equivalents in a supermarket meat case. I remember putting the report back into its envelope without reading any further.

Some years before he died, my father had participated

in a study of memory and aging sponsored by Washington University, and one of the perks for participants was a postmortem brain autopsy, free of charge. I suspect that the study offered other perks of monitoring and treatment which had led my mother, who loved freebies of all kinds, to insist that my father volunteer for it. Thrift was also probably her only conscious motive for including the autopsy report in my Valentine's package. She was saving thirty-two cents' postage.

My clearest memories of that February morning are visual and spatial: the yellow Mr. Goodbar, my shift from living room to bedroom, the late-morning light of a season as far from the winter solstice as from spring. I'm aware, however, that even these memories aren't to be trusted. According to the latest theories, which are based on a wealth of neurological and psychological research in the last few decades, the brain is not an album in which memories are stored discretely like unchanging photographs. A memory is, instead, in the phrase of the psychologist Daniel L. Schachter, a "temporary constellation" of activity—a necessarily approximate excitation of neural circuits that bind a set of sensory images and semantic data into the momentary sensation of a remembered whole. These images and data are seldom the exclusive property of one particular memory. Indeed, even as my experience on that Valentine's morning was unfolding, my brain was relying on pre-existing categories of "red" and "heart" and "Mr. Goodbar"; the gray sky in my windows was familiar from a thousand other winter mornings; and I already had millions of neurons devoted to a picture of my mother—her stinginess with postage, her romantic attachments to her children, her lingering anger toward my father, her weird lack of tact, and so on. What my memory of that morning therefore consists of, according to the latest models, is a set of hardwired neuronal connections among the pertinent regions of the brain, and a predisposition for the entire constellation to light up—chemically, electrically—when any one part of the circuit is stimulated. Speak the words "Mr. Goodbar" and ask me to free-associate, and if I don't say "Diane Keaton" I will surely say "brain autopsy."

My Valentine's memory would work this way even if I were dredging it up now for the first time ever. But the fact is that I've re-remembered that February morning countless times since then. I've told the story to my brothers. I've offered it as an Outrageous Mother Incident to friends of mine who enjoy that kind of thing. I've even, shameful to report, told people I hardly know at all. Each succeeding recollection and retelling reinforces the constellation of images and knowledge that constitute the memory. At the cellular level, according to neuroscientists, I'm burning the memory in a little deeper each time, strengthening the dendritic connections among its components, further encouraging the firing of that specific set of synapses. One of the great adaptive virtues of our brains, the feature that makes our gray matter so much smarter than any machine yet devised (my laptop's cluttered hard drive or a World Wide Web that insists on recalling, in pellucid detail, a *Beverly Hills 90210* fan site last updated on 11/20/98), is our ability to forget almost everything that has ever happened to us. I retain general, largely categorical memories of the past (a year spent in Spain; various visits to Indian restaurants on East Sixth Street) but relatively few specific episodic memories. Those memories that I do retain I tend to revisit and, thereby, strengthen. They become literally—morphologically, electrochemically—part of the architecture of my brain.

This model of memory, which I've presented here in a rather loose layperson's summary, excites the amateur scientist in me. It feels true to the twinned fuzziness and richness of my own memories, and it inspires awe with its image of neural networks effortlessly self-coordinating, in a massively parallel way, to create my ghostly consciousness and my remarkably sturdy sense of self. It seems to me lovely and postmodern. The human brain is a web of a hundred billion neurons, maybe as many as two hundred billion, with trillions of axons and dendrites exchanging quadrillions of messages by way of at least fifty different chemical transmitters. The organ with which we observe and make sense of the universe is, by a comfortable margin, the most complex object we know of in that universe.

And yet it's also a lump of meat. At some point, maybe later on that same Valentine's Day, I forced myself to read the entire pathology report. It included a "Microscopic Description" of my father's brain:

Sections of the frontal, parietal, occipital, and temporal cerebral cortices showed numerous senile plaques, prominently diffuse type, with minimal numbers of neurofibrillary tangles. Cortical Lewy bodies were easily detected in H&E stained material. The amygdala demonstrated plaques, occasional tangles and mild neuron loss.

In the notice that we had run in local newspapers nine months earlier, my mother insisted that we say my father had died "after long illness." She liked the phrase's formality and reticence, but it was hard not to hear her grievance in it as well, her emphasis on *long*. The pathologist's identification of senile plaques in my father's brain served to confirm, as only an autopsy could, the fact with which she'd struggled daily for many years: like millions of other Americans, my father had had Alzheimer's disease.

This was his disease. It was also, you could argue, his story. But you have to let me tell it.

ALZHEIMER'S IS A DISEASE of classically "insidious onset." Since even healthy people become more forgetful as they age, there's no way to pinpoint the first memory to fall victim to it. The problem was especially vexed in the case of my father, who not only was depressive and reserved and slightly deaf but also was taking strong medicines for other ailments. For a long time it was possible to chalk up his non sequiturs to his hearing impairment, his forgetfulness to his depression, his hallucinations to his medicines; and chalk them up we did.

My memories of the years of my father's initial decline are vividly about things other than him. Indeed, I'm somewhat appalled by how large I loom in my own memories, how peripheral my parents are. But I was living far from home in those years. My information came mainly from my mother's complaints about my father, and these complaints I took with a grain of salt; she'd been complaining to me pretty much all my life.

My parents' marriage was, it's safe to say, less than happy. They stayed together for the sake of their children and for want of hope that divorce would make them any happier. As long as my father was working, they enjoyed autonomy in their respective fiefdoms of home and workplace, but after he retired, in 1981, at the age of sixty-six, they commenced a round-the-clock performance of *No Exit* in their comfortably furnished suburban house. I arrived for brief visits like a U.N. peacekeeping force to which each side passionately presented its case against the other.

Unlike my mother, who was hospitalized nearly thirty times in her life, my father had perfect health until he retired. His parents and uncles had lived into their eighties and nineties, and he, Earl Franzen, fully expected to be around at ninety "to see," as he liked to say, "how things turn out." (His anagramatic namesake Lear imagined his last years in similar terms: listening to "court news," with Cordelia, to see "who loses and who wins, who's in, who's out.") My father had no hobbies and few pleasures besides eating meals, seeing his children, and playing bridge, but he did take a *narrative* interest in life. He watched a staggering amount of TV news. His ambition for old age was to follow the unfolding histories of the nation and his children for as long as he could.

The passivity of this ambition, the sameness of his days, tended to make him invisible to me. From the early years of his mental decline I can dredge up exactly one direct memory: watching him, toward the end of the eighties, struggle and fail to calculate the tip on a restaurant bill.

Fortunately, my mother was a great writer of letters. My father's passivity, which I regarded as regrettable but not really any of my business, was a source of bitter disappointment to her. As late as the fall of 1989—a season in which, according to her letters, my father was still playing golf and undertaking major home repairs—the terms of her complaints remained strictly personal:

> It is extremely difficult living with a very unhappy person when you know you must be the major cause of the unhappiness. *Decades* ago when Dad told me he didn't believe

there is such a thing as love (that sex is a "trap") and that he was not cut out to be a "happy" person I should have been smart enough to realize there was no hope for a relationship satisfactory to *me*. But I was busy & involved with my children and friends I loved and I guess, like Scarlett O'Hara, I told myself I would "worry about that tomorrow."

This letter dates from a period during which the theater of my parents' war had shifted to the issue of my father's hearing impairment. My mother maintained that it was inconsiderate not to wear a hearing aid; my father complained that other people lacked the consideration to "speak up." The battle culminated Pyrrhically in his purchase of a hearing aid that he then declined to wear. Here again, my mother constructed a moral story of his "stubbornness" and "vanity" and "defeatism"; but it's hard not to suspect, in hindsight, that his faulty ears were already serving to camouflage more serious trouble.

A letter from January 1990 contains my mother's first written reference to this trouble:

Last week one day he had to skip his breakfasttime medication in order to take some motor skills tests at Wash U. where he is in the Memory & Ageing study. That night I awakened to the sound of his electric razor, looked at the clock & he was in the bathroom shaving at 2:30 AM.

Within a few months my father was making so many mistakes that my mother was forced to entertain other explanations:

Either he's stressed or not concentrating or having some mental deterioration but there have been quite a few incidents recently that really worry me. He keeps leaving the car door open or the lights on & twice in one week we had to call triple A & have them come out & charge the battery (now I've posted signs in the garage & that seems to have helped) . . . I really don't like the idea of leaving him in the house alone for more than a short while.

My mother's fear of leaving him alone assumed greater urgency as the year wore on. Her right knee was worn out, and, because she already had a steel plate in her leg from an earlier fracture, she was facing complicated surgery followed by prolonged recovery and rehab. Her letters from late 1990 and early 1991 are marked by paragraphs of agonizing over whether to have surgery and how to manage my father if she did.

Were he in the house alone more than overnight with me in the hospital I would be an absolute basket case as he leaves the water running, the stove on at times, lights on every-where, etc. . . . I check & recheck as much as I can on most things lately but even so many of our affairs are in a state of confusion & what really is hardest is his resentment of my intrusion—"stay out of my affairs!!!" He does not accept or realize my *wanting* to be *helpful* & that is the hardest thing of all for me.

At the time, I'd recently finished my second novel, and so I offered to stay with my father while my mother had her operation. To steer clear of his pride, she and I agreed to pretend that I was coming for her sake, not his. What's odd, though, is that I was only half-pretending. My mother's characterization of my father's incapacity was compelling, but so was my father's portrayal of my mother as an alarmist nag. I went to St. Louis because, for her, his incapacity was absolutely real; once there, I behaved as if, for me, it absolutely wasn't.

Just as she'd feared, my mother was in the hospital for nearly five weeks. Strangely, although I'd never lived alone with my father for so long and never would again, I can now remember almost nothing specific about my stay with him; I have a general impression that he was somewhat quiet, maybe, but otherwise completely normal. Here, you might think, was a direct contradiction of my mother's earlier reports. And yet I have no memory of being bothered by the contradiction. What I do have is a copy of a letter that I wrote to a friend while in St. Louis. In the letter, I mention that my father has had his medication adjusted and now everything is fine.

Wishful thinking? Yes, to some extent. But one of the basic features of the mind is its keenness to construct wholes out of fragmentary parts. We all have a literal blind spot in our vision where the optic nerve attaches to the retina, but our brain unfailingly registers a seamless world around us. We catch part of a word and hear the whole. We see expressive faces in floral-pattern upholstery; we constantly fill in blanks. In a similar way, I think I was inclined to interpolate across my father's silences and mental absences and to persist in seeing him as the same old wholly whole Earl Franzen. I still needed him to be an actor in my story of myself. In my letter to my friend, I describe a morning rehearsal of the St. Louis Symphony that my mother insisted that my father and I attend so as not to waste her free tickets to it. After the first half of the session, in which the very young Midori *nailed* the Sibelius violin concerto, my father sprang from his seat with miserable geriatric agitation. "So," he said, "we'll go now." I knew better than to ask him to sit through the Charles Ives symphony that was coming, but I hated him for what I took to be his philistinism. On the drive home, he had one comment about Midori and Sibelius. "I don't understand that music," he said. "What do they do—memorize it?"

LATER THAT SPRING, my father was diagnosed with a small, slow-growing cancer in his prostate. His doctors recommended that he not bother treating it, but he insisted on a course of radiation. With a kind of referred wisdom about his own mental state, he became terrified that something was dreadfully wrong with him: that he would not, after all, survive into his nineties. My mother, whose knee continued to bleed internally six months after her operation, had little patience with what she considered his hypochondria. In September 1991 she wrote:

> I'm relieved to have Dad started on his radiation therapy & it forces him to get out of the house *every day* [inserted, here, a smiley face]—a big plus. He got to the point where he was *so nervous, so worried*, so depressed I knew he had to make some decision. Actually, being so sedentary now (content to do nothing), he has had too much time to worry & think about himself—he NEEDS distractions! . . . More & more I feel the greatest attributes anyone can have are (1), a positive attitude & (2), a sense of humor—wish Dad had them.

There ensued some months of relative optimism. The cancer was eradicated, my mother's knee finally improved, and her native hopefulness returned to her letters. She reported that my father had taken first place in a game of bridge: "With his confusion cleared up & his less conservative approach to the game he is doing remarkably well & it's about the only thing he enjoys (& can stay awake for!)." But my father's anxiety about his health did not abate; he had stomach pains that he was convinced were caused by cancer. Gradually, the import of the story my mother was telling me migrated from the personal and the moral toward the psychiatric. "The past six months we have lost so many friends it is very unsettling—part of Dad's nervousness & depression I'm sure," she wrote in February 1992. The letter continued:

> Dad's internist, Dr. Rouse, has about concluded what I have felt all along regarding Dad's stomach discomfort (he's ruled out all clinical possibilities). Dad is (1) terribly nervous, (2) terribly depressed & I hope Dr. Rouse will put him on an anti-depressant. I *know* there has to be help for this . . . There have been disturbing, distressing things in our lives the past year, I know that very well, but Dad's mental condition is hurting him physically & if he won't go for counseling (suggested by Dr. Weiss) perhaps he now will accept pills or whatever it takes for nervousness & depression.

For a while, the phrase "nervousness & depression" was a fixture of her letters. Prozac briefly seemed to lift my father's spirits, but the effects were short-lived. Finally, in July 1992, to my surprise, he agreed to see a psychiatrist.

My father had always been supremely suspicious of psychiatry. He viewed therapy as an invasion of privacy, mental health as a matter of self-discipline, and my mother's increasingly pointed suggestions that he "talk to someone" as acts of aggression—little lobbed grenades of blame for their unhappiness as a couple. It was a measure of his desperation that he voluntarily set foot in a psychiatrist's office.

In October, when I stopped in St. Louis on my way to Italy, I asked him about his sessions with the doctor. He made a hopeless gesture with his hands. "He's extremely able," he said. "But I'm afraid he's written me off."

The idea of anybody writing my father off was more than I could stand. From Italy I sent the psychiatrist a three-page appeal for reconsideration, but even as I was writing it the roof was caving in at home. "Much as I dislike telling you," my mother wrote in a letter faxed to Italy, "Dad has regressed terribly. Medicine for the urinary problem a urologist is treating in combination with medication for depression and nervousness blew his mind again and the hallucinating, etc. was terrible." There had been a weekend with my Uncle Erv in Indiana, where my father, removed from his familiar surroundings, unleashed a night of madness that culminated in my uncle's shouting into his face, *"Earl, my God, it's your brother, Erv, we slept in the same bed!"* Back in St. Louis, my father had begun to rage against the retired lady, Mrs. Pryble, whom my mother had engaged to sit with him two mornings a week while she ran errands. He didn't see why he needed sitting, and, even assuming that he did need sitting, he didn't see why a stranger, rather than his wife, should be doing it. He'd become a classic "sundowner," dozing through the day and rampaging in the wee hours.

There followed a dismal holiday visit during which my wife and I finally intervened on my mother's behalf and put her in touch with a geriatric social worker, and my mother urged my wife and me to tire my father out so that he would sleep through the night without psychotic incident, and my father sat stone-faced by the fireplace or told grim stories of his childhood while my mother fretted about the expense, the prohibitive expense, of sessions with a social worker. But even then, as far as I can remember, nobody ever said "dementia." In all my mother's letters to me, the word "Alzheimer's" appears exactly once, in reference to an old German woman I worked for as a teenager.

I REMEMBER my suspicion and annoyance, fifteen years ago, when the term "Alzheimer's disease" was first achieving currency. It seemed to me another instance of the medicalization of human experience, the latest entry in the ever-expanding nomenclature of victimhood. To my mother's news about my old employer I replied: "What you describe sounds like the same old Erika, only quite a bit worse, and that's not how Alzheimer's is supposed to work, is it? I spend a few minutes every month fretting about ordinary mental illness being trendily misdiagnosed as Alzheimer's."

From my current vantage, where I spend a few minutes every month fretting about what a self-righteous thirty-year-old I was, I can see my reluctance to apply the term "Alzheimer's" to my father as a way of protecting the specificity of Earl Franzen from the generality of a nameable condition. Conditions have symptoms; symptoms point to the organic basis of everything we are. They point to the brain as meat. And, where I ought to recognize that, yes, the brain is meat, I seem instead to maintain a blind spot across which I then interpolate stories that emphasize the more soul-like aspects of the self. Seeing my afflicted father as a set of organic symptoms would invite me to understand the *healthy* Earl Franzen (and the healthy me) in symptomatic terms as well—to reduce our beloved personalities to finite sets of neurochemical coordinates. Who wants a story of life like that?

Even now, I feel uneasy when I gather facts about Alzheimer's. Reading, for example, David Shenk's book *The Forgetting: Alzheimer's: Portrait of an Epidemic*, I'm reminded that when my father got lost in his own neighborhood, or forgot to flush the toilet, he was exhibiting symptoms identical to those of millions of other afflicted people. There can be comfort in having company like this, but I'm sorry to see the personal significance drained from certain mistakes of my father's, like his confusion of my mother with her mother, which struck me at the time as singular and orphic, and from which I gleaned all manner of important new insights into my parents' marriage. My sense of private selfhood turns out to have been illusory.

Senile dementia has been around for as long as people have had the means of recording it. While the average human life span remained short and old age was a comparative rarity, senility was considered a natural by-product of aging—perhaps the result of sclerotic cerebral arteries. The young German neuropathologist Alois Alzheimer believed he was witnessing an entirely new variety of mental illness when, in 1901, he admitted to his clinic a fifty-one-year-old woman, Auguste D., who was suffering from bizarre mood swings and severe memory loss and who, in Alzheimer's initial examination of her, gave problematic answers to his questions:

"What is your name?"
"Auguste."
"Last name?"

"Auguste."

"What is your husband's name?"

"Auguste, I think."

When Auguste D. died in an institution, four years later, Alzheimer availed himself of recent advances in microscopy and tissue-staining and was able to discern, in slides of her brain tissue, the striking dual pathology of her disease: countless sticky-looking globs of "plaque" and countless neurons engulfed by "tangles" of neuronal fibrils. Alzheimer's findings greatly interested his patron Emil Kraepelin, then the dean of German psychiatry, who was engaged in a fierce scientific battle with Sigmund Freud and Freud's psycholiterary theories of mental illness. To Kraepelin, Alzheimer's plaques and tangles provided welcome clinical support for his contention that mental illness was fundamentally organic. In his *Handbook of Psychiatry* he dubbed Auguste D.'s condition *Morbus Alzheimer*.

For six decades after Alois Alzheimer's autopsy of Auguste D., even as breakthroughs in disease prevention and treatment were adding fifteen years to life expectancy in developed nations, Alzheimer's continued to be viewed as a medical rarity à la Huntington's disease. David Shenk tells the story of an American neuropathologist named Meta Naumann who, in the early fifties, autopsied the brains of 210 victims of senile dementia and found sclerotic arteries in few of them, plaques and tangles in the majority. Here was ironclad evidence that Alzheimer's was far more common than anyone had guessed; but Naumann's work appears to have persuaded no one. "They felt that Meta was talking nonsense," her husband recalled.

The scientific community simply wasn't ready to consider that senile dementia might be more than a natural consequence of aging. In the early fifties there was no self-conscious category of "seniors," no explosion of Sun Belt retirement communities, no AARP, no Early Bird tradition at low-end restaurants; and scientific thinking reflected these social realities. Not until the seventies did conditions become ripe for a reinterpretation of senile dementia. By then, as Shenk says, "so many people were living so long that senility didn't feel so normal or acceptable anymore." Congress passed the Research on Aging Act in 1974, and established the National Institute on Aging, for which funding soon mushroomed. By the end of the eighties, at the crest of my annoyance with the clinical term and its sudden ubiquity, Alzheimer's had achieved the same social and medical standing as heart disease or cancer—and had the research funding levels to show for it.

What happened with Alzheimer's in the seventies and eighties wasn't simply a diagnostic paradigm shift. The number of new cases really is soaring. As fewer and fewer people drop dead of heart attacks or die of infections, more and more survive to become demented. Alzheimer's patients in nursing homes live much longer than other patients, at a cost of at least forty thousand dollars annually per patient; until they're institutionalized, they increasingly derange the lives of family members charged with caring for them. Already, five million Americans have the disease, and the number could rise to fifteen million by 2050.

Because there's so much money in chronic illness, drug companies are investing feverishly in proprietary Alzheimer's research while publicly funded scientists file for patents on the side. But because the science of the disease remains cloudy (a functioning brain is not a lot more accessible than the center of the earth or the edge of the universe), nobody can be sure which avenues of research will lead to effective treatments. Overall, the feeling in the field seems to be that if you're under fifty you can reasonably expect to be offered effective drugs for Alzheimer's by the time you need them. Then again, twenty years ago, many cancer researchers were predicting a cure within twenty years.

David Shenk, who is comfortably under fifty, makes the case in *The Forgetting* that a cure for senile dementia might not be an entirely unmitigated blessing. He notes, for example, that one striking peculiarity of the disease is that its "sufferers" often suffer less and less as it progresses. Caring for an Alzheimer's patient is gruelingly repetitious precisely because the patient himself has lost the cerebral equipment to experience anything as a repetition. Shenk quotes patients who speak of "something delicious in oblivion" and who report an enhancement of their sensory pleasures as they come to dwell in an eternal, pastless Now. If your short-term memory is shot, you don't remember, when you stoop to smell a rose, that you've been stooping to smell the same rose all morning.

As the psychiatrist Barry Reisberg first observed twenty years ago, the decline of an Alzheimer's patient mirrors in reverse the neurological development of a child. The earliest capacities a child develops—raising the head (at one to three months), smiling (two to four months), sitting up unassisted (six to ten months)—are the last capacities an Alzheimer's patient loses. Brain development in a growing child is consolidated through a process called myelinization, wherein the axonal connections among neurons are gradually strengthened by sheathings of the fatty substance myelin. Apparently, since the last regions of the child's brain to mature remain the least myelinated, they're the regions most vulnerable to the insult of Alzheimer's. The hippocampus, which processes short-term memories into long-term, is very slow to myelinate. This is why we're unable to form permanent episodic memories before the age of three or four, and why the hippocampus is where the plaques and tangles of Alzheimer's first appear. Hence the ghostly apparition of the middle-stage patient who continues to be able to walk and feed herself even as she remembers nothing from hour to hour. The inner child isn't inner anymore. Neurologically speaking, we're looking at a one-year-old.

Although Shenk tries valiantly to see a boon in the Alzheimer's patient's childish relief from responsibility and childlike focus on the Now, I'm mindful that becoming a baby again was the last thing my father wanted. The stories he told from his childhood in northern Minnesota were mainly (as befits a depressive's recollections) horrible: brutal father, unfair mother, endless chores, backwoods poverty, family betrayals, hideous accidents. He told me more than once, after his retirement, that his greatest pleasure in life had been going to work as an adult in the company of other men who valued his abilities. My father was an intensely private person, and privacy for him had the connotation of keeping the shameful content of one's interior life out of public sight. Could there have been a worse disease for him than Alzheimer's? In its early stages, it worked to dissolve the personal connections that had saved him from the worst of his depressive isolation. In its later stages it robbed him of the sheathing of adulthood, the means to hide the child inside him. I wish he'd had a heart attack instead.

Still, shaky though Shenk's arguments for the brighter side of Alzheimer's may be, his core contention is harder to dismiss: senility is not merely an erasure of meaning but a source of meaning. For my mother, the losses of Alzheimer's both amplified and reversed long-standing patterns in her marriage. My father had always refused to open himself to her, and now, increasingly, he *couldn't* open himself. To my mother, he remained the same Earl Franzen napping in the den and failing to hear. She, paradoxically, was the one who slowly and surely lost her self, living with a man who mistook her for her mother, forgot every fact he'd ever known about her, and finally ceased to speak her name. He, who had always insisted on being the boss in the marriage, the maker of decisions, the adult protector of the childlike wife, now couldn't help behaving like the child. Now the unseemly outbursts were his, not my mother's. Now she ferried him around town the way she'd once ferried me and my brothers. Task by task, she took charge of their life. And so, although my father's "long illness" was a crushing strain and disappointment to her, it was also an opportunity to grow slowly into an autonomy she'd never been allowed: to settle some very old scores.

As for me, once I accepted the scope of the disaster, the sheer duration of Alzheimer's forced me into unexpectedly welcome closer contact with my mother. I learned, as I might not have otherwise, that I could seriously rely on my brothers and that they could rely on me. And, strangely, although I'd always prized my intelligence and sanity and self-consciousness, I found that watching my father lose all three made me less afraid of losing them myself. I became a little less afraid in general. A bad door opened, and I found I was able to walk through it.

THE DOOR in question was on the fourth floor of Barnes Hospital, in St. Louis. About six weeks after my wife and I had put my mother in touch with the social worker and gone back east, my oldest brother and my father's doctors persuaded him to enter the hospital for testing. The idea was to get all the medications out of his bloodstream and see what we were dealing with underneath. My mother helped him check in and spent the afternoon settling him into his room. He was still his usual, semipresent self when she left for dinner, but that evening, at home, she began to get calls from the hospital, first from my father, who demanded that she come and remove him from "this hotel," and then from nurses who reported that he'd become belligerent. When she returned to the hospital in the morning, she found him altogether gone—raving mad, profoundly disoriented.

I flew back to St. Louis a week later. My mother took me straight from the airport to the hospital. While she spoke to the nurses, I went to my father's room and found him in bed, wide awake. I said hello. He made frantic shushing gestures and beckoned me to his pillow. I leaned over him and he asked me, in a husky whisper, to keep my voice down because "they" were "listening." I asked him who "they" were. He couldn't tell me, but his eyes rolled fearfully to scan the room, as if he'd lately seen "them" everywhere and were puzzled by "their" disappearance. When my mother appeared in the doorway, he confided to me, in an even lower whisper, "I think they've gotten to your mother."

My memories of the week that followed are mainly a blur, punctuated by a couple of life-changing scenes. I went to the hospital every day and sat with my father for as many hours as I could stand. At no point did he string together two coherent sentences. The memory that appears to me most significant in hindsight is a very peculiar one. It's lit by a dreamlike indoor twilight, it's set in a hospital room whose orientation and cramped layout are unfamiliar from any of my other memories, and it returns to me now without any of the chronological markers that usually characterize my memories. I'm not sure it even dates from that first week I saw my father in the hospital. And yet I'm sure that I'm not remembering a dream. All memories, the neuroscientists say, are actually memories of memory, but usually they don't feel that way. Here's one that does. I remember remembering: my father in bed, my mother sitting beside it, me standing near the door. We've been having an anguished family conversation, possibly about where to move my father after his discharge from the hospital. It's a conversation that my father, to the slight extent that he can follow it, is hating. Finally he cries out with passionate emphasis, as if he's had enough of all the nonsense, "I have *always* loved your mother. *Always*." And my mother buries her face in her hands and sobs.

This was the only time I ever heard my father say he loved her. I'm certain the memory is legitimate because the scene seemed to me immensely significant even at the time, and I then described it to my wife and brothers and incorporated it into the story I was telling myself about my parents. In later years, when my mother insisted that my father had never said he loved her, not even once, I asked if she remembered that time in the hospital. I repeated what he'd said, and she shook her head uncertainly. "Maybe," she said. "Maybe he did. I don't remember that."

My brothers and I took turns going to St. Louis every few months. My father never failed to recognize me as someone he was happy to see. His life in a nursing home appeared to be an endless troubled dream populated by figments from his past and by his deformed and brain-damaged fellow inmates; his nurses were less like actors in the dream than like unwelcome intruders on it. Unlike many of the female inmates, who at one moment were wailing like babies and at the next moment glowing with pleasure while someone fed them ice cream, I never saw my father cry, and the pleasure he took in ice cream never ceased to look like an adult's. He gave me significant nods and wistful smiles as he confided to me fragments of nonsense to which I nodded as if I understood. His most consistently near-coherent theme was his wish to be removed from "this hotel" and his inability to understand why he couldn't live in a little apartment and let my mother take care of him.

For Thanksgiving that year, my mother and my wife and I checked him out of the nursing home and brought him home with a wheelchair in my Volvo station wagon. He hadn't been in the house since he'd last been living there, ten months earlier. If my mother had been hoping for a gratifying show of pleasure from him, she was disappointed; by then, a change of venue no more impressed my father than it does a one-year-old. We sat by the fireplace and, out of unthinking, wretched habit, took pictures of a man who, if he knew nothing else, seemed full of unhappy knowledge of how dismal a subject for photographs he was. The images are awful to me now: my father listing in his wheelchair like an unstrung marionette, eyes mad and staring, mouth sagging, glasses smeared with strobe light and nearly falling off his nose; my mother's face a mask of reasonably well-contained despair; and my wife and I flashing grotesquely strained smiles as we reach to touch my father. At the dinner table my mother spread a bath towel over my father and cut his turkey into little bites. She kept asking him if he was happy to be having Thanksgiving dinner at home. He responded with silence, shifting eyes, sometimes a faint shrug. My brothers called to wish him a happy holiday; and here, out of the blue, he mustered a smile and a hearty voice, he was able to answer simple questions, he thanked them both for calling.

This much of the evening was typically Alzheimer's. Because children learn social skills very early, a capacity for gestures of courtesy and phrases of vague graciousness survives in many Alzheimer's patients long after their memories are shot. It wasn't so remarkable that my father was able to handle (sort of) my brothers' holiday calls. But consider what happened next, after dinner, outside the nursing home. While my wife ran inside for a geri chair, my father sat beside me and studied the institutional portal that he was about to reenter. "Better not to leave," he told me in a clear, strong voice, "than to have to come back." This was not a vague phrase; it pertained directly to the situation at hand, and it strongly suggested an awareness of his larger plight and his connection to the past and future. He was requesting that he be spared the pain of being dragged back toward consciousness and memory. And, sure enough, on the morning after Thanksgiving, and for the remainder of our visit, he was as crazy as I ever saw him, his words a hash of random syllables, his body a big flail of agitation.

For David Shenk, the most important of the "windows onto meaning" afforded by Alzheimer's is its slowing down of death. Shenk likens the disease to a prism that refracts death into a spectrum of its otherwise tightly conjoined parts—death of autonomy, death of memory, death of self-consciousness, death of personality, death of body—and he subscribes to the most common trope of Alzheimer's: that its particular sadness and horror stem from the sufferer's loss of his or her "self" long before the body dies.

This seems mostly right to me. By the time my father's heart stopped, I'd been mourning him for years. And yet, when I consider his story, I wonder whether the various deaths can ever really be so separated, and whether memory and consciousness have such secure title, after all, to the seat of selfhood. I can't stop looking for meaning in the two years that followed his loss of his supposed "self," and I can't stop finding it.

I'm struck, above all, by the apparent persistence of his *will*. I'm powerless not to believe that he was exerting some bodily remnant of his self-discipline, some reserve of strength in the sinews beneath both consciousness and memory, when he pulled himself together for the request he made to me outside the nursing home. I'm powerless as well not to believe that his crash on the following morning, like his crash on his first night alone in a hospital, amounted to a relinquishment of that will, a letting-go, an embrace of madness in the face of unbearable emotion. Although we can fix the starting point of his decline (full consciousness and sanity) and the end point (oblivion and death), his brain wasn't simply a computational device running gradually and inexorably amok. Where the subtractive progress of Alzheimer's might predict a steady downward trend like this—

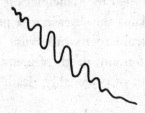

what I saw of my father's fall looked more like this:

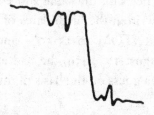

He held himself together longer, I suspect, than it might have seemed he had the neuronal wherewithal to do. Then he collapsed and fell lower than his pathology may have strictly dictated, and he chose to stay low, ninety-nine percent of the time. What he *wanted* (in the early years, to stay clear; in the later years, to let go) was integral to what he *was*. And what *I* want (stories of my father's brain that are not about meat) is integral to what I choose to remember and retell.

One of the stories I've come to tell, then, as I try to forgive myself for my long blindness to his condition, is that he was bent on concealing that condition and, for a remarkably long time, retained the strength of character to bring it off. My mother used to swear that this was so. He couldn't fool the woman he lived with, no matter how he bullied her, but he could pull himself together as long as he had sons in town or guests in the house. The true solution of the conundrum of my stay with him during my mother's operation probably has less to do with my blindness than with the additional will he was exerting.

After the bad Thanksgiving, when we knew he was never coming home again, I helped my mother sort through his desk. (It's the kind of liberty you take with the desk of a child or a dead person.) In one of his drawers we found evidence of small, covert endeavors not to forget. There was a sheaf of papers on which he'd written the addresses of his children, one address per slip, the same address on several. On another slip he'd written the birth dates of his older sons—"Bob 1-13-48" and "TOM 10-15-50"—and then, in trying to recall mine (August 17, 1959), he had erased the month and day and made a guess on the basis of my brothers' dates: "JON 10-13-49."

Consider, too, what I believe are the last words he ever spoke to me, three months before he died. For a couple of days, I'd been visiting the nursing home for a dutiful ninety minutes and listening to his mutterings about my mother and to his affable speculations about certain tiny objects that he persisted in seeing on the sleeves of his sweater and the knees of his pants. He was no different when I dropped by on my last morning, no different when I wheeled him back to his room and told him I was heading out of town. But then he raised his face toward mine and—again, out of nowhere, his voice was clear and strong—he said: "Thank you for coming. I appreciate your taking the time to see me."

Set phrases of courtesy? A window on his fundamental self? I seem to have little choice about which version to believe.

IN RELYING ON MY MOTHER'S LETTERS to reconstruct my father's disintegration, I feel the shadow of the undocumented years after 1992, when she and I talked on the phone at greater length and ceased to write all but the briefest notes. Plato's description of writing, in the *Phaedrus*, as a "crutch of memory" seems to me fully accurate: I couldn't tell a clear story of my father without those letters. But, where Plato laments the decline of the oral tradition and the atrophy of memory which writing induces, I at the other end of the Age of the Written Word am impressed by the sturdiness and reliability of words on paper. My mother's letters are truer and more complete than my self-absorbed and biased memories; she's more alive to me in the written phrase "he NEEDS distractions!" than in hours of videotape or stacks of pictures of her.

The will to record indelibly, to set down stories in permanent words, seems to me akin to the conviction that we are larger than our biologies. I wonder if our current cultural susceptibility to the charms of materialism—our increasing willingness to see psychology as chemical, identity as genetic, and behavior as the product of bygone exigencies of human evolution—isn't intimately related to the postmodern resurgence of the oral and the eclipse of the written: our incessant telephoning, our ephemeral e-mailing, our steadfast devotion to the flickering tube.

Have I mentioned that my father, too, wrote letters? Usually typewritten, usually prefaced with an apology for misspellings, they came much less frequently than my mother's. One of the last is from December 1987:

This time of the year is always difficult for me. I'm ill at ease with all the gift-giving, as I would love to get things for people but lack the imagination to get the right things. I dread the shopping for things that are the wrong size or the wrong color or something not needed, and anticipate the problems of returning or exchanging. I like to buy tools, but Bob pointed out a problem with this category, when for some occasion I gave him a nice little hammer with good balance, and his comment was that this was the second or third hammer and I don't need any more, thank you. And then there is the problem of gifts for your mother. She is so sentimental that it hurts me not to get her something nice, but she has access to my checking account with no restrictions. I have told her to buy something for herself, and say it is from me, so she can compete with the after-Christmas comment: "See what I got from my husband!" But she won't participate in that fraud. So I suffer through the season.

In 1989, as his powers of concentration waned with his growing "nervousness & depression," my father stopped writing letters altogether. My mother and I were therefore amazed to find, in the same drawer in which he'd left those addresses and birth dates, an unsent letter dated January 22, 1993—unimaginably late, a matter of weeks before his final breakdown. The letter was in an envelope addressed to my nephew Nick, who, at age six, had just begun to write letters himself. Possibly my father was ashamed to send a letter that he knew wasn't fully coherent; more likely, given the state of his hippocampal health, he simply forgot. The letter, which for me has become an emblem of invisibly heroic exertions of the will, is written in a tiny penciled script that keeps veering away from the horizontal:

Dear Nick,

We got your letter a couple days ago and were pleased to see how well you were doing in school, particularly in math. It is important to write well, as the ability to exchange ideas will govern the use that one country can make of another country's ideas.

Most of your nearest relatives are good writers, and thereby took the load off me. I should have learned better how to write, but it is so easy to say, Let Mom do it.

I know that my writing will not be easy to read, but I have a problem with the nerves in my legs and tremors in my hands. In looking at what I have written, I expect you will have difficulty to understand, but with a little luck, I may keep up with you.

We have had a change in the weather from cold and wet to dry with fair blue skies. I hope it stays this way. Keep up the good work.

Love, Grandpa

P.S. Thank you for the gifts.

MY FATHER'S HEART and lungs were very strong, and my mother was bracing herself for two or three more years of endgame when, one day in April 1995, he stopped eating. Maybe he was having trouble swallowing, or maybe, with his remaining shreds of will, he'd resolved to put an end to his unwanted second childhood.

His blood pressure was seventy over palpable when I flew into town. Again, my mother took me straight to the nursing home from the airport. I found him curled up on his side under a thin sheet, breathing shallowly, his eyes shut loosely. His muscle had wasted away, but his face was smooth and calm and almost entirely free of wrinkles, and his hands, which had changed not at all, seemed curiously large in comparison to the rest of him. There's no way to know if he recognized my voice, but within minutes of my arrival his blood pressure climbed to 120/90. I worried then, worry even now, that I made things harder for him by arriving: that he'd reached the point of being ready to die but was ashamed to perform such a private or disappointing act in front of one of his sons.

My mother and I settled into a rhythm of watching and waiting, one of us sleeping while the other sat in vigil. Hour after hour, my father lay unmoving and worked his way toward death; but when he yawned, the yawn was *his*. And his body, wasted though it was, was likewise still radiantly *his*. Even as the surviving parts of his self grew ever smaller and more fragmented, I persisted in seeing a whole. I still loved, specifically and individually, the man who was yawning in that bed. And how could I not fashion stories out of that love—stories of a man whose will remained intact enough to avert his face when I tried to clear his mouth out with a moist foam swab? I'll go to my own grave insisting that my father was determined to die and to die, as best he could, on his own terms.

We, for our part, were determined that he not be alone when he died. Maybe this was exactly wrong, maybe all he was waiting for was to be left alone. Nevertheless, on my sixth night in town, I stayed up and read a light novel cover to cover while he lay and breathed and loosed his great yawns. A nurse came by, listened to his lungs, and told me he must never have been a smoker. She suggested that I go home to sleep, and she offered to send in a particular nurse from the floor below to visit him. Evidently, the nursing home had a resident angel of death with a special gift for persuading the nearly dead, after their relatives had left for the night, that it was OK for them to die. I declined the nurse's offer and performed this service myself. I leaned over my father, who smelled faintly of acetic acid but was otherwise clean and warm. Identifying myself, I told him that whatever he needed to do now was fine by me, he should let go and do what he needed to do.

Late that afternoon, a big early-summer St. Louis wind

kicked up. I was scrambling eggs when my mother called from the nursing home and told me to hurry over. I don't know why I thought I had plenty of time, but I ate the eggs with some toast before I left, and in the nursing-home parking lot I sat in the car and turned up the radio, which was playing the Blues Traveler song that was all the rage that season. No song has ever made me happier. The great white oaks all around the nursing home were swaying and turning pale in the big wind. I felt as though I might fly away with happiness.

And still he didn't die. The storm hit the nursing home in the middle of the evening, knocking out all but the emergency lighting, and my mother and I sat in the dark. I don't like to remember how impatient I was for my father's breathing to stop, how ready to be free of him I was. I don't like to imagine what he was feeling as he lay there, what dim or vivid sensory or emotional forms his struggle took inside his head. But I also don't like to believe that there was nothing.

Toward ten o'clock, my mother and I were conferring with a nurse in the doorway of his room, not long after the lights came back on, when I noticed that he was drawing his hands up toward his throat. I said, "I think something is happening." It was agonal breathing: his chin rising to draw air into his lungs after his heart had stopped beating. He seemed to be nodding very slowly and deeply in the affirmative. And then nothing.

After we'd kissed him goodbye and signed the forms that authorized the brain autopsy, after we'd driven through flooding streets, my mother sat down in our kitchen and uncharacteristically accepted my offer of undiluted Jack Daniel's. "I see now," she said, "that when you're dead you're really dead." This was true enough. But, in the slow-motion way of Alzheimer's, my father wasn't much deader now than he'd been two hours or two weeks or two months ago. We'd simply lost the last of the parts out of which we could fashion a living whole. There would be no new memories of him. The only stories we could tell now were the ones we already had.

[2001]

IMPERIAL BEDROOM

PRIVACY, privacy, the new American obsession: espoused as the most fundamental of rights, marketed as the most desirable of commodities, and pronounced dead twice a week.

Even before Linda Tripp pressed the "Record" button on her answering machine, commentators were warning us that "privacy is under siege," that "privacy is in a dreadful state," that "privacy as we now know it may not exist in the year 2000." They say that both Big Brother and his little brother, John Q. Public, are shadowing me through networks of computers. They tell me that security cameras no bigger than spiders are watching from every shaded corner, that dour feminists are monitoring bedroom behavior and water-cooler conversations, that genetic sleuths can decoct my entire being from a droplet of saliva, that voyeurs can retrofit ordinary camcorders with a filter that lets them *see through people's clothing.* Then comes the flood of dirty suds from the Office of the Independent Counsel, oozing forth through official and commercial channels to saturate the national consciousness. The Monica Lewinsky scandal marks, in the words of the philosopher Thomas Nagel, "the culmination of a disastrous erosion" of privacy; it represents, in the words of the author Wendy Kaminer, "the utter disregard for privacy and individual autonomy that exists in totalitarian regimes." In the person of Kenneth Starr, the "public sphere" has finally overwhelmed—shredded, gored, trampled, invaded, run roughshod over—"the private."

The panic about privacy has all the finger-pointing and paranoia of a good old American scare, but it's missing one vital ingredient: a genuinely alarmed public. Americans care about privacy mainly in the abstract. Sometimes a well-informed community unites to defend itself, as when Net users bombarded the White House with e-mails against the "clipper chip," and sometimes an especially outrageous piece of news provokes a national outcry, as when the Lotus Development Corporation tried to market a CD-ROM containing financial profiles of nearly half the people in the country. By and large, though, even in the face of wholesale infringements like the war on drugs, Americans remain curiously passive. I'm no exception. I read the editorials and try to get excited, but I can't. More often than not, I find myself feeling the opposite of what the privacy mavens want me to. It's happened twice in the last month alone.

On the Saturday morning when the *Times* came carrying the complete text of the Starr report, what I felt as I sat alone in my apartment and tried to eat my breakfast was that my own privacy—not Clinton's, not Lewinsky's—was being violated. I love the distant pageant of public life. I love both the pageantry and the distance. Now a President was facing impeachment, and as a good citizen I had a duty to stay informed about the evidence, but the evidence here consisted of two people's groping, sucking, and mutual self-deception. What I felt, when this evidence landed beside my toast and coffee, wasn't a pretend revulsion to camouflage a secret interest in the dirt; I wasn't offended by the sex qua sex; I wasn't worrying about a potential future erosion of my own rights; I didn't feel the President's pain in the empathic way he'd once claimed to feel mine; I wasn't repelled by the revelation that public officials do bad things; and, although I'm a registered Democrat, my disgust was of a different order from my partisan disgust at the news that the Giants have blown a fourth-quarter lead. What I felt I felt personally. I was being intruded on.

A couple of days later, I got a call from one of my credit-card providers, asking me to confirm two recent charges at a gas station and one at a hardware store. Queries like this are common nowadays, but this one was my first, and for a moment I felt eerily exposed. At the same time, I was perversely flattered that someone, somewhere, had taken an interest in me and had bothered to phone. Not that the young male operator seemed to care about me personally. He sounded like he was reading his lines from a laminated booklet. The strain of working hard at a job he almost certainly didn't enjoy seemed to thicken his tongue. He tried to rush his words out, to speed through them as if in embarrassment or vexation at how nearly worthless they were, but they kept bunching up in his teeth, and he had to stop and extract them with his lips, one by one. It was the computer, he said, the computer that routinely, ah, scans the, you know, the pattern of charges . . . and was there something else he could help me with tonight? I decided that if this young person wanted to scroll through my charges and ponder the significance of my two fill-ups and my gallon of latex paint, I was fine with it.

So here's the problem. On the Saturday morning the Starr Report came out, my privacy was, in the classic liberal view, absolute. I was alone in my home and unobserved, unbothered by neighbors, unmentioned in the news, and perfectly free, if I chose, to ignore the report and do the pleasantly *al dente* Saturday crossword; yet the report's mere existence so offended my sense of privacy that I could hardly bring myself to touch the thing. Two days later, I was disturbed in my home by a ringing phone, asked to cough up my mother's maiden name, and made aware that the digitized minutiae of my daily life were being scrutinized by strangers; and within five minutes I'd put the entire episode out of my mind. I felt encroached on when I was ostensibly safe, and I felt safe when I was ostensibly encroached on. And I didn't know why.

THE RIGHT to privacy—defined by Louis Brandeis and Samuel Warren, in 1890, as "the right to be let alone"—seems at first glance to be an elemental principle in American life. It's the rallying cry of activists fighting for reproductive rights, against stalkers, for the right to die, against a national health-care database, for stronger data-encryption standards, against paparazzi, for the sanctity of employee e-mail, and against employee drug testing. On closer examination, though, privacy proves to be the Cheshire cat of values: not much substance, but a very winning smile.

Legally, the concept is a mess. Privacy violation is the emotional core of many crimes, from stalking and rape to

Peeping Tommery and trespass, but no criminal statute forbids it in the abstract. Civil law varies from state to state but generally follows a forty-year-old analysis by the legal scholar Dean William Prosser, who dissected the invasion of privacy into four torts: *intrusion* on my solitude, the publishing of *private facts* about me which are not of legitimate public concern, publicity that puts my character in a *false light*, and *appropriation* of my name or likeness without my consent. This is a crumbly set of torts. Intrusion looks a lot like criminal trespass, false light like defamation, and appropriation like theft; and the harm that remains when these extraneous offenses are subtracted is so admirably captured by the phrase "infliction of emotional distress" as to render the tort of privacy invasion all but superfluous. What really undergirds privacy is the classical liberal conception of personal autonomy or liberty. In the last few decades, many judges and scholars have chosen to speak of a "zone of privacy," rather than a "sphere of liberty," but this is a shift in emphasis, not in substance: not the making of a new doctrine but the repackaging and remarketing of an old one.

Whatever you're trying to sell, whether it's luxury real estate or Esperanto lessons, it helps to have the smiling word "private" on your side. Last winter, as the owner of a Bank One Platinum Visa Card, I was offered enrollment in a program called PrivacyGuard®, which, according to the literature promoting it, "*puts you in the know* about the very personal records available to your employer, insurers, credit card companies, and government agencies." The first three months of PrivacyGuard® were free, so I signed up. What came in the mail then was paperwork: envelopes and request forms for a Credit Record Search and other searches, also a disappointingly undeluxe logbook in which to jot down the search results. I realized immediately that I didn't care enough about, say, my driving records to wait a month to get them; it was only when I called PrivacyGuard® to cancel my membership, and was all but begged not to, that I realized that the whole point of this "service" was to harness my time and energy to the task of reducing Bank One Visa's fraud losses.

Even issues that legitimately touch on privacy are rarely concerned with the actual emotional harm of unwanted exposure or intrusion. A proposed national Genetic Privacy Act, for example, is premised on the idea that my DNA reveals more about my identity and future health than other medical data do. In fact, DNA is as yet no more intimately revealing than a heart murmur, a family history of diabetes, or an inordinate fondness for Buffalo chicken wings. As with any medical records, the potential for abuse of genetic information by employers and insurers is chilling, but this is only tangentially a privacy issue; the primary harm consists of things like job discrimination and higher insurance premiums.

In a similar way, the problem of online security is mainly about nuts and bolts. What American activists call "electronic privacy" their European counterparts call "data protection." Our term is exciting; theirs is accurate. If someone is out to steal your Amex number and expiration date, or if an evil ex-boyfriend is looking for your new address, you need the kind of hard-core secrecy that encryption seeks to guarantee. If you're talking to a friend on the phone, however, you need only a *feeling* of privacy.

The social drama of data protection goes something like this: a hacker or an insurance company or a telemarketer gains access to a sensitive database, public-interest watchdogs bark loudly, and new firewalls go up. Just as most people are moderately afraid of germs but leave virology to the Centers for Disease Control, most Americans take a reasonable interest in privacy issues but leave the serious custodial work to experts. Our problem now is that the custodians have started speaking a language of panic and treating privacy not as one of many competing values but as the one value that trumps all others.

The novelist Richard Powers recently declared in a *Times* op-ed piece that privacy is a "vanishing illusion" and that the struggle over the encryption of digital communications is therefore as "great with consequence" as the Cold War. Powers defines "the private" as "that part of life that goes unregistered," and he sees in the digital footprints we leave whenever we charge things the approach of "that moment when each person's every living day will become a Bloomsday, recorded in complete detail and reproducible with a few deft keystrokes." It is scary, of course, to think that the mystery of our identities might be reducible to finite data sequences. That Powers can seriously compare credit-card fraud and intercepted cell-phone calls to thermonuclear incineration, however, speaks mainly to the infectiousness of privacy panic. Where, after all, is it "registered" what Powers or anybody else is thinking, seeing, saying, wishing, planning, dreaming, and feeling ashamed of? A digital *Ulysses* consisting of nothing but a list of its hero's purchases and other recordable transactions might run, at most, to four pages: was there really nothing more to Bloom's day?

When Americans do genuinely sacrifice privacy, moreover, they do so for tangible gains in health or safety or efficiency. Most legalized infringements—HIV notification, airport X-rays, Megan's Law, Breathalyzer roadblocks, the drug-testing of student athletes, laws protecting fetuses, laws protecting the vegetative, remote monitoring of automobile emissions, county-jail strip searches, even Ken Starr's exposure of presidential corruption—are essentially public health measures. I resent the security cameras in Washington Square, but I appreciate the ones on a subway platform. The risk that someone is abusing my E-ZPass toll records seems to me comfortably low in comparison with my gain in convenience. Ditto the risk that some gossip rag will make me a victim of the First Amendment; with two hundred and seventy million people in the country, any individual's chances of being nationally exposed are next to nil.

The legal scholar Lawrence Lessig has characterized Americans as "bovine" for making calculations like this and for thereby acquiescing in what he calls the "Sovietization" of personal life. The curious thing about privacy, though, is that simply by expecting it we can usually achieve it. One of my neighbors in the apartment building across the street spends a lot of time at her mirror examining her pores, and I can see her doing it, just as she can undoubtedly see me sometimes. But our respective privacies remain intact as long as neither of us *feels* seen. When I send a postcard through the U.S. mail, I'm aware in the abstract that mail handlers may be reading it, may be reading it aloud, may even be laughing at it, but I'm safe from all harm unless, by sheer bad luck, the one handler in the country whom I actually know sees the postcard and slaps his forehead and says, "Oh, jeez, I know this guy."

OUR PRIVACY panic isn't merely exaggerated. It's founded on a fallacy. Ellen Alderman and Caroline Kennedy, in *The*

Right to Privacy, sum up the conventional wisdom of privacy advocates like this: "There is less privacy than there used to be." The claim has been made or implied so often, in so many books and editorials and talk-show dens, that Americans, no matter how passive they are in their behavior, now dutifully tell pollsters that they're very much worried about privacy. From almost any historical perspective, however, the claim seems bizarre.

In 1890, an American typically lived in a small town under conditions of near-panoptical surveillance. Not only did his every purchase "register," but it registered in the eyes and the memory of shopkeepers who knew him, his parents, his wife, and his children. He couldn't so much as walk to the post office without having his movements tracked and analyzed by neighbors. Probably he grew up sleeping in the same bed with his siblings and possibly with his parents, too. Unless he was well off, his transportation—a train, a horse, his own two feet—either was communal or exposed him to the public eye.

In the suburbs and exurbs where the typical American lives today, tiny nuclear families inhabit enormous houses, in which each person has his or her own bedroom and, sometimes, bathroom. Compared even with suburbs in the sixties and seventies, when I was growing up, the contemporary condominium development or gated community offers a striking degree of anonymity. It's no longer the rule that you know your neighbors. Communities increasingly tend to be virtual, the participants either faceless or firmly in control of the face they present. Transportation is largely private: the latest SUVs are the size of living rooms and come with onboard telephones, CD players, and TV screens; behind the tinted windows of one of these high-riding I-see-you-but-you-can't-see-me mobile PrivacyGuard® units, a person can be wearing pajamas or a licorice bikini, for all anybody knows or cares. Maybe the government intrudes on the family a little more than it did a hundred years ago (social workers look in on the old and the poor, health officials require inoculations, the police inquire about spousal battery), but these intrusions don't begin to make up for the small-town snooping they've replaced.

The "right to be left alone"? Far from disappearing, it's exploding. It's the *essence* of modern American architecture, landscape, transportation, communication, and mainstream political philosophy. The real reason that Americans are apathetic about privacy is so big as to be almost invisible: we're flat-out *drowning* in privacy.

What's threatened, then, isn't the private sphere. It's the public sphere. Much has been made of the discouraging effect that the Starr investigation may have on future aspirants to public office (only zealots and zeros need apply), but that's just half of it. The public world of Washington, because it's public, belongs to everyone. We're all invited to participate with our votes, our patriotism, our campaigning, and our opinions. The collective weight of a population makes possible our faith in the public world as something larger and more enduring and more dignified than any messy individual can be in private. But, just as one sniper in a church tower can keep the streets of an entire town empty, one real grossout scandal can undermine that faith.

If privacy depends upon an expectation of invisibility, the expectation of *visibility* is what defines a public space. My "sense of privacy" functions to keep the public out of the private *and* to keep the private out of the public. A kind of mental Border collie yelps in distress when I feel that the line between the two has been breached. This is why the violation of a public space is so similar, as an experience, to the violation of privacy. I walk past a man taking a leak on a sidewalk in broad daylight (delivery-truck drivers can be especially self-righteous in their "Ya gotta go, ya gotta go" philosophy of bladder management), and although the man with the yawning fly is ostensibly the one whose privacy is compromised by the leak, I'm the one who feels the impingement. Flashers and sexual harassers and fellators on the pier and self-explainers on the crosstown bus all similarly assault our sense of the "public" by exposing themselves.

Since really serious exposure in public today is assumed to be synonymous with being seen on television, it would seem to follow that televised space is the premier public space. Many things that people say to me on television, however, would never be tolerated in a genuine public space—in a jury box, for example, or even on a city sidewalk. TV is an enormous, ramified extension of the billion living rooms and bedrooms in which it's consumed. You rarely hear a person on the subway talking loudly about, say, incontinence, but on television it's been happening for years. TV is devoid of shame, and without shame there can be no distinction between public and private. Last winter, an anchorwoman looked me in the eye and, in the tone of a close female relative, referred to a litter of babies in Iowa as "America's seven little darlin's." It was strange enough, twenty-five years ago, to get Dan Rather's reports on Watergate between spots for Geritol and Bayer aspirin, as if Nixon's impending resignation were somehow located in my medicine chest. Now, shelved between ads for Promise margarine and Celebrity Cruises, the news itself is a soiled cocktail dress—TV the bedroom floor and nothing but.

Reticence, meanwhile, has become an obsolete virtue. People now readily name their diseases, rents, antidepressants. Sexual histories get spilled on first dates, Birkenstocks and cutoffs infiltrate the office on casual Fridays, telecommuting puts the boardroom in the bedroom, "softer" modern office design puts the bedroom in the boardroom, salespeople unilaterally address customers by their first name, waiters won't bring me food until I've established a personal relationship with them, voice-mail machinery stresses the "I" in "*I'm* sorry, but *I* don't understand what you dialed," and cyberenthusiasts, in a particularly grotesque misnomer, designate as "public forums" pieces of etched silicon with which a forum's unshaved "participant" may communicate while sitting crosslegged in tangled sheets. The networked world as a threat to privacy? It's the ugly spectacle of a privacy triumphant.

A genuine public space is a place where every citizen is welcome to be present and where the purely private is excluded or restricted. One reason that attendance at art museums has soared in recent years is that museums still feel public in this way. After those tangled sheets, how delicious the enforced decorum and the hush, the absence of in-your-face consumerism. How sweet the promenading, the seeing and being seen. Everybody needs a promenade sometimes— a place to go when you want to announce to the world (not the little world of friends and family but the big world, the real world) that you have a new suit, or that you're in love, or that you suddenly realize you stand a full inch taller when you don't hunch your shoulders.

Unfortunately, the fully public place is a nearly extinct category. We still have courtrooms and the jury pool, commuter trains and bus stations, here and there a small-town Main Street that really is a main street rather than a strip mall, certain coffee bars, and certain city sidewalks. Otherwise, for American adults, the only halfway public space is the world of work. Here, especially in the upper echelons of business, codes of dress and behavior are routinely enforced, personal disclosures are penalized, and formality is still the rule. But these rituals extend only to the employees of the firm, and even they, when they become old, disabled, obsolete, or outsourceable, are liable to be expelled and thereby relegated to the tangled sheets.

The last big, steep-walled bastion of public life in America is Washington, D.C. Hence the particular violation I felt when the Starr Report crashed in. Hence the feeling of being intruded on. It was privacy invasion, all right: private life brutally invading the most public of public spaces. I don't want to see sex on the news from Washington. There's sex everywhere else I look—on sitcoms, on the Web, on dust jackets, in car ads, on the billboards at Times Square. Can't there be one thing in the national landscape that isn't about the bedroom? We all know there's sex in the cloakrooms of power, sex behind the pomp and circumstance, sex beneath the robes of justice; but can't we act like grownups and pretend otherwise? Pretend not that "no one is looking" but that *everyone* is looking?

For two decades now, business leaders and politicians across much of the political spectrum, both Gingrich Republicans and Clinton Democrats, have extolled the virtues of privatizing public institutions. But what better word can there be for Lewinskygate and the ensuing irruption of disclosures (the infidelities of Helen Chenoweth, of Dan

Burton, of Henry Hyde) than "privatization"? Anyone who wondered what a privatized presidency might look like may now, courtesy of Mr. Starr, behold one.

IN DENIS JOHNSON'S SHORT STORY "Beverly Home," the young narrator spends his days working at a nursing home for the hopelessly disabled, where there is a particularly unfortunate patient whom no one visits:

> A perpetual spasm forced him to perch sideways on his wheelchair and peer down along his nose at his knotted fingers. This condition had descended on him suddenly. He got no visitors. His wife was divorcing him. He was only thirty-three, I believe he said, but it was hard to guess what he told about himself because he really couldn't talk anymore, beyond clamping his lips repeatedly around his protruding tongue while groaning.
>
> No more pretending for him! He was completely and openly a mess. Meanwhile the rest of us go on trying to fool each other.

In a coast-to-coast, shag-carpeted imperial bedroom, we could all just be messes and save ourselves the trouble of pretending. But who wants to live in a pajama-party world? Privacy loses its value unless there's something it can be defined against. "Meanwhile the rest of us go on trying to fool each other"—and a good thing, too. The need to put on a public face is as basic as the need for the privacy in which to take it off. We need both a home that's not like a public space and a public space that's not like home.

Walking up Third Avenue on a Saturday night, I feel

bereft. All around me, attractive young people are hunched over their StarTacs and Nokias with preoccupied expressions, as if probing a sore tooth, or adjusting a hearing aid, or squeezing a pulled muscle; personal technology has begun to look like a personal handicap. All I really want from a sidewalk is that people see me and let themselves be seen, but even this modest ideal is thwarted by cell-phone users and their unwelcome privacy. They say things like "Should we have couscous with that?" and "I'm on my way to Blockbuster." They aren't breaking any law by broadcasting these breakfast-nook conversations. There's no PublicityGuard that I can buy, no expensive preserve of public life to which I can flee. Seclusion, whether in a suite at the Plaza or in a cabin in the Catskills, is comparatively effortless to achieve. Privacy is protected as both commodity and right; public forums are protected as neither. Like old-growth forests, they're few and irreplaceable and should be held in trust by everyone. The work of maintaining them gets only harder as the private sector grows ever more demanding, distracting, and disheartening. Who has the time and energy to stand up for the public sphere? What rhetoric can possibly compete with the American love of "privacy"?

When I return to my apartment after dark, I don't immediately turn my lights on. Over the years, it's become a reflexive precaution on my part not to risk spooking exposed neighbors by flooding my living room with light, although the only activity I ever seem to catch them at is watching TV.

My skin-conscious neighbor is home with her husband tonight, and they seem to be dressing for a party. The woman, a vertical strip of whom is visible between the Levelors and the window frame, is wearing a bathrobe and a barrette and sitting in front of a mirror. The man, slick-haired, wearing suit pants and a white T-shirt, stands by the sofa in the other room and watches television in a posture that I recognize as uncommitted. Finally the woman disappears into the bedroom. The man puts on a white shirt and a necktie and perches sidesaddle on the arm of the sofa, still watching television, more involved with it now. The woman returns wearing a strapless yellow dress and looking like a whole different species of being. Happy the transformation! Happy the distance between private and public! I see a rapid back-and-forth involving jewelry, jackets, and a clutch purse, and then the couple, dressed to the nines, ventures out into the world.

[1998]

WHY BOTHER?

(The *Harper's* Essay)

M Y DESPAIR about the American novel began in the winter of 1991, when I fled to Yaddo, the artists' colony in upstate New York, to write the last two chapters of my second book. My wife and I had recently separated, and I was leading a life of self-enforced solitude in New York City, working long days in a small white room, packing up ten years' worth of communal property, and taking nighttime walks on avenues where Russian, Hindi, Korean, and Spanish were spoken in equal measure. Even deep in my Queens neighborhood, however, news could reach me through my TV set and my *Times* subscription. The country was preparing for war ecstatically, with rhetoric supplied by George Bush: "Vital issues of principle are at stake." In Bush's eighty-nine-percent approval rating, as in the near-total absence of public skepticism about the war, the United States seemed to me hopelessly unmoored from reality—dreaming of glory in the massacre of faceless Iraqis, dreaming of infinite oil for hour-long commutes, dreaming of exemption from the rules of history. And so I, too, was dreaming of escape. I wanted to hide from America. But when I got to Yaddo and realized that it was no haven—the *Times* came there daily, and my fellow colonists kept talking about Patriot missiles and yellow ribbons—I began to think that what I really needed was a monastery.

Then one afternoon, in Yaddo's little library, I picked up and read Paula Fox's short novel *Desperate Characters*. "She was going to get away with everything!" is the hope that seizes the novel's main character, Sophie Bentwood, a child-less Brooklynite who's unhappily married to a conservative lawyer. Sophie used to translate French novels; now she's so depressed that she can hardly even read them. Against the advice of the husband, Otto, she has given milk to a home-less cat, and the cat has repaid the kindness by biting her hand. Sophie immediately feels "vitally wounded"—she's been bitten for "no reason" just as Josef K. is arrested for "no reason" in *The Trial*—but when the swelling in her hand subsides she becomes giddy with the hope of being spared rabies shots.

The "everything" Sophie wants to get away with, how-ever, is more than her liberal self-indulgence with the cat. She wants to get away with reading Goncourt novels and eating *omelettes aux fines herbes* on a street where derelicts lie sprawled in their own vomit and in a country that's fighting a dirty war in Vietnam. She wants to be spared the pain of confronting a future beyond her life with Otto. She wants to keep dreaming. But the novel's logic won't let her. She's compelled, instead, to this equation of the personal and the social:

> *"God, if I am rabid, I am equal to what is outside,"* she said out loud, and felt an extraordinary relief as though, at last, she'd discovered what it was that could create a balance between the quiet, rather vacant progression of the days she spent in this house, and those portents that lit up the dark at the edge of her own existence.

Desperate Characters, which was first published in 1970, ends with an act of prophetic violence. Breaking under the strain of his collapsing marriage, Otto Bentwood grabs a bottle of ink from Sophie's escritoire and smashes it against their bedroom wall. The ink in which his law books and Sophie's translations have been printed now forms an unreadable blot. The black lines on the wall are both a mark of doom and the harbinger of an extraordinary relief, the end to a fevered isolation.

With its equation of a crumbling marriage with a crumbling social order, *Desperate Characters* spoke directly to the ambiguities that I was experiencing that January. Was it a great thing or a horrible thing that my marriage was coming apart? And did the distress I was feeling derive from some internal sickness of the soul, or was it imposed on me by the sickness of society? That someone besides me had suffered from these ambiguities and had seen light on their far side—that Fox's book had been published and preserved; that I could find company and consolation and hope in an object pulled almost at random from a bookshelf—felt akin to an instance of religious grace.

Yet even while I was being saved as a reader by *Desperate Characters* I was succumbing, as a novelist, to despair about the possibility of connecting the personal and the social. The reader who happens on *Desperate Characters* today will be as struck by the foreignness of the Bentwoods' world as by its familiarity. A quarter-century has only broadened and confirmed the sense of cultural crisis that Fox was registering. But what now feels like the locus of that crisis—the banal ascendancy of television, the electronic fragmentation of public discourse—is nowhere to be seen in the novel. Communication for the Bentwoods meant books, a telephone, and letters. Portents didn't stream uninterruptedly through a cable converter or a modem; they were only dimly glimpsed, on the margins of existence. An ink bottle, which now seems impossibly quaint, was still thinkable as a symbol in 1970.

In a winter when every house in the nation was haunted by the ghostly telepresences of Peter Arnett in Baghdad and Tom Brokaw in Saudi Arabia—a winter when the inhabitants of those houses seemed less like individuals than a collective algorithm for the conversion of media jingoism into an eighty-nine-percent approval rating—I was tempted to think that if a contemporary Otto Bentwood were breaking down, he would kick in the screen of his bedroom TV. But this would have missed the point. Otto Bentwood, if he existed in the nineties, would not break down, because the world would no longer even bear on him. As an unashamed elitist, an avatar of the printed word, and a genuinely solitary man, he belongs to a species so endangered as to be all but irrelevant in an age of electronic democracy. For centuries, ink in the form of printed novels has fixed discrete, subjective individuals within significant narratives. What Sophie and Otto were glimpsing, in the vatic black mess on their bedroom wall, was the disintegration of the very notion of a literary character. Small wonder they were desperate. It was still the sixties, and they had no idea what had hit them.

> *There was a siege going on: it had been going on for a long time, but the besieged themselves were the last to take it seriously.*
>
> —*from* Desperate Characters

WHEN I GOT OUT OF COLLEGE, in 1981, I hadn't heard the news about the social novel's death. I didn't know that Philip Roth had long ago performed the autopsy, describing "American reality" as a thing that "stupefies . . . sickens . . . infuriates, and finally . . . is even a kind of embarrassment to one's own meager imagination. The actuality is continually outdoing our talents . . ." I was in love with literature and with a woman to whom I'd been attracted in part because she was a brilliant reader. I had lots of models for the kind of uncompromising novel I wanted to write. I even had a model for an uncompromising novel that had found a big audience: *Catch-22*. Joseph Heller had figured out a way of outdoing the actuality, employing the illogic of modern warfare as a metaphor for the more general denaturing of American reality. His book had seeped into the national imagination so thoroughly that my *Webster's Ninth Collegiate* gave no fewer than five shades of meaning for the title. That no challenging novel since *Catch-22* had affected the culture anywhere near as deeply, just as no issue since the Vietnam War had galvanized so many alienated young Americans, was easily overlooked. In college my head had been turned by Marxism, and I believed that "monopoly capitalism" (as we called it) abounded with "negative moments" (as we called them) that a novelist could trick Americans into confronting if only he could package his subversive bombs in a sufficiently seductive narrative.

I began my first book as a twenty-two-year-old dreaming of changing the world. I finished it six years older. The one tiny world-historical hope I still clung to was to appear on KMOX Radio, "the Voice of St. Louis," whose long, thoughtful author interviews I'd grown up listening to in my mother's kitchen. My novel, *The Twenty-Seventh City*, was about the innocence of a Midwestern city—about the poignancy of St. Louis's municipal ambitions in an age of apathy and distraction—and I looked forward to forty-five minutes with one of KMOX's afternoon talk-show hosts, whom I imagined teasing out of me the themes that I'd left latent in the book itself. To the angry callers demanding to know why I hated St. Louis I would explain, in the brave voice of someone who had lost his innocence, that what looked to them like hate was in fact tough love. In the listening audience would be my family: my mother, who considered fiction-writing a socially irresponsible career, and my father, who hoped that one day he would pick up *Time* magazine and find me reviewed in it.

It wasn't until *The Twenty-Seventh City* was published, in 1988, that I discovered how innocent I still was. The media's obsessive interest in my youthfulness surprised me. So did the money. Boosted by the optimism of publishers who imagined that an essentially dark, contrarian entertainment might somehow sell a zillion copies, I made enough to fund the writing of my next book. But the biggest surprise—the true measure of how little I'd heeded my own warning in

The Twenty-Seventh City—was the failure of my culturally engaged novel to engage with the culture. I'd intended to provoke; what I got instead was sixty reviews in a vacuum.

My appearance on KMOX was indicative. The announcer was a journeyman with a whiskey sunburn and a heartrending comb-over who clearly hadn't read past chapter two. Beneath his boom mike he brushed at the novel's pages as though he hoped to absorb the plot transdermally. He asked me the questions that everybody asked me: How did it feel to get such good reviews? (It felt great, I said.) Was the novel autobiographical? (It was not, I said.) How did it feel to be a local kid returning to St. Louis on a fancy book tour? It felt obscurely disappointing. But I didn't say this. I'd already realized that the money, the hype, the limo ride to a *Vogue* shoot weren't simply fringe benefits. They were the main prize, the consolation for no longer mattering to a culture.

EXACTLY HOW MUCH LESS novels now matter to the American mainstream than they did when *Catch-22* was published is impossible to judge. But the ambitious young fiction writer can't help noting that, in a recent *USA Today* survey of twenty-four hours in the life of American culture, there were twenty-one references to television, eight to film, seven to popular music, four to radio, and one to fiction (*The Bridges of Madison County*). Or that magazines like *The Saturday Review*, which in Joseph Heller's heyday still vetted novels by the bushel, have entirely disappeared. Or that the *Times Book Review* nowadays runs as few as two full fiction reviews a week (fifty years ago, the fiction-to-nonfiction ratio was one to one).

The only mainstream American household I know well is

the one I grew up in, and I can report that my father, who was not a reader, nevertheless had some acquaintance with James Baldwin and John Cheever, because *Time* magazine put them on its cover and *Time*, for my father, was the ultimate cultural authority. In the last decade, the magazine whose red border twice enclosed the face of James Joyce has devoted covers to Scott Turow and Stephen King. These are honorable writers; but no one doubts it was the size of their contracts that won them covers. The dollar is now the yardstick of cultural authority, and an organ like *Time*, which not long ago aspired to shape the national taste, now serves mainly to reflect it.

The literary America in which I found myself after I published *The Twenty-Seventh City* bore a strange resemblance to the St. Louis I'd grown up in: a once-great city that had been gutted and drained by white flight and superhighways. Ringing the depressed urban core of serious fiction were prosperous new suburbs of mass entertainments. Much of the inner city's remaining vitality was concentrated in the black, Hispanic, Asian, gay, and women's communities that had taken over the structures vacated by fleeing straight white males. MFA programs offered housing and workfare to the underemployed; a few crackpot city-loving artists continued to hole up in old warehouses; and visiting readers could still pay weekend visits to certain well-policed cultural monuments—the temple of Toni Morrison, the orchestra of John Updike, the Faulkner House, the Wharton Museum, and Mark Twain Park.

By the early nineties I was as depressed as the inner city of fiction. My second novel, *Strong Motion*, was a long, complicated story about a Midwestern family in a world of moral upheaval, and this time, instead of sending my bombs in a

Jiffy-Pak mailer of irony and understatement, as I had with *The Twenty-Seventh City*, I'd come out throwing rhetorical Molotov cocktails. But the result was the same: another report card with A's and B's from the reviewers who had replaced the teachers whose approval, when I was younger, I had both craved and taken no satisfaction from; decent money; and the silence of irrelevance. Meanwhile, my wife and I had reunited in Philadelphia. For two years we'd bounced around in three time zones, trying to find a pleasant, inexpensive place in which we didn't feel like strangers. Finally, after exhaustive deliberation, we'd rented a too-expensive house in yet another depressed city. That we then proceeded to be miserable seemed to confirm beyond all doubt that there was *no* place in the world for fiction writers.

In Philadelphia I began to make unhelpful calculations, multiplying the number of books I'd read in the previous year by the number of years I might reasonably be expected to live, and perceiving in the three-digit product not so much an intimation of mortality (though the news on that front wasn't cheering) as a measure of the incompatibility of the slow work of reading and the hyperkinesis of modern life. All of a sudden it seemed as if the friends of mine who used to read no longer even apologized for having stopped. A young acquaintance who had been an English major, when I asked her what she was reading, replied: "You mean *linear* reading? Like when you read a book from start to finish?"

There's never been much love lost between literature and the marketplace. The consumer economy loves a product that sells at a premium, wears out quickly or is susceptible to regular improvement, and offers with each improvement some marginal gain in usefulness. To an economy like this, news that stays news is not merely an inferior product; it's an *antithetical* product. A classic work of literature is inexpensive, infinitely reusable, and, worst of all, unimprovable.

After the collapse of the Soviet Union, the American political economy had set about consolidating its gains, enlarging its markets, securing its profits, and demoralizing its few remaining critics. In 1993 I saw signs of the consolidation everywhere. I saw it in the swollen minivans and broad-beamed trucks that had replaced the automobile as the suburban vehicle of choice—these Rangers and Land Cruisers and Voyagers that were the true spoils of a war waged to keep American gasoline cheaper than dirt, a war that had played like a thousand-hour infomercial for high technology, a consumer's war dispensed through commercial television. I saw leaf-blowers replacing rakes. I saw CNN holding hostage the travelers in airport lounges and the shoppers in supermarket checkout lines. I saw the 486 chip replacing the 386 and being replaced in turn by the Pentium so that, despite new economies of scale, the price of entry-level notebook computers never fell below a thousand dollars. I saw Penn State win the Blockbuster Bowl.

Even as I was sanctifying the reading of literature, however, I was becoming so depressed that I could do little after dinner but flop in front of the TV. We didn't have cable, but I could always find something delicious: Phillies and Padres, Eagles and Bengals, *M*A*S*H*, *Cheers*, *Homicide*. Naturally, the more TV I watched, the worse I felt. If you're a novelist and even *you* don't feel like reading, how can you expect anybody else to read your books? I believed I *ought* to be reading, as I believed I *ought* to be writing a third novel. And not just any third novel. It had long been a prejudice of mine that putting a novel's characters in a dynamic social setting enriched the story that was being told; that the glory of the genre consisted of its spanning of the expanse between private experience and public context. And what more vital context could there be than television's short-circuiting of that expanse?

But I was paralyzed with the third book. I was torturing the story, stretching it to accommodate ever more of those things-in-the-world that impinge on the enterprise of fiction writing. The work of transparency and beauty and obliqueness that I wanted to write was getting bloated with issues. I'd already worked in contemporary pharmacology and TV and race and prison life and a dozen other vocabularies; how was I going to satirize Internet boosterism and the Dow Jones as well, while leaving room for the complexities of character and locale? Panic grows in the gap between the increasing length of the project and the shrinking time increments of cultural change: How to design a craft that can float on history for as long as it takes to build it? The novelist has more and more to say to readers who have less and less time to read: Where to find the energy to engage with a culture in crisis when the crisis consists in the impossibility of engaging with the culture? These were unhappy days. I began to think that there was something wrong with the whole model of the novel as a form of "cultural engagement."

IN THE NINETEENTH CENTURY, when Dickens and Darwin and Disraeli all read one another's work, the novel was the preeminent medium of social instruction. A new book by Thackeray or William Dean Howells was anticipated with the kind of fever that a late-December film release inspires today.

The big, obvious reason for the decline of the social novel is that modern technologies do a much better job of social instruction. Television, radio, and photographs are vivid, instantaneous media. Print journalism, too, in the wake of *In Cold Blood*, has become a viable creative alternative to the novel. Because they command large audiences, TV and magazines can afford to gather vast quantities of information quickly. Few serious novelists can pay for a quick trip to Singapore, or for the mass of expert consulting that gives serial TV dramas like *E.R.* and *NYPD Blue* their veneer of authenticity. The writer of average talent who wants to report on, say, the plight of illegal aliens would be foolish to choose the novel as a vehicle. Ditto the writer who wants to offend prevailing sensibilities. *Portnoy's Complaint*, which even my mother once heard enough about to disapprove of, was probably the last American novel that could have appeared on Bob Dole's radar as a nightmare of depravity. Today's Baudelaires are hip-hop artists.

The essence of fiction is solitary work: the work of writing, the work of reading. I'm able to know Sophie Bentwood intimately, and to refer to her as casually as I would to a good friend, because I poured my own feelings of fear and estrangement into my construction of her. If I knew her only through a video of *Desperate Characters* (Shirley Mac-Laine made the movie in 1971, as a vehicle for herself), Sophie would remain an Other, divided from me by the screen on which I viewed her, by the surficiality of film, and by MacLaine's star presence. At most, I might feel I knew MacLaine a little better.

Knowing MacLaine a little better, however, is what the country mainly wants. We live in a tyranny of the literal. The daily unfolding stories of O. J. Simpson, Timothy McVeigh, and Bill Clinton have an intense, iconic presence that relegates to a subordinate shadow-world our own untelevised lives. In order to justify their claim on our attention, the organs of mass culture and information are compelled to offer something "new" on a daily, indeed hourly, basis. Although good novelists don't deliberately seek out trends, many of them feel a responsibility to pay attention to contemporary issues, and they now confront a culture in which almost all the issues are burned out almost all the time. The writer who wants to tell a story about society that's true not just in 1996 but in 1997 as well can find herself at a loss for solid cultural referents. What's topically relevant while she's planning the novel will almost certainly be passé by the time it's written, rewritten, published, distributed, and read.

None of this stops cultural commentators—notably Tom Wolfe—from blaming novelists for their retreat from social description. The most striking thing about Wolfe's 1989 manifesto for the "New Social Novel," even more than his uncanny ignorance of the many excellent socially engaged novels published between 1960 and 1989, was his failure to explain why his ideal New Social Novelist should not be writing scripts for Hollywood. And so it's worth saying one more time: Just as the camera drove a stake through the heart of serious portraiture, television has killed the novel of social reportage. Truly committed social novelists may still find cracks in the monolith to sink their pitons into. But they do so with the understanding that they can no longer depend on their material, as Howells and Sinclair and Stowe did, but only on their own sensibilities, and with the expectation that no one will be reading them for news.

THIS MUCH, at least, was visible to Philip Roth in 1961. Noting that "for a writer of fiction to feel that he does not really live in his own country—as represented by *Life* or by what he experiences when he steps out the front door—must seem a serious occupational impediment," he rather plaintively asked: "What will his subject be? His landscape?" In the intervening years, however, the screw has taken another turn. Our obsolescence now goes further than television's usurpation of the role as news-bringer, and deeper than its displacement of the imagined with the literal. Flannery O'Connor, writing around the time that Roth made his remarks, insisted that the "business of fiction" is "to embody mystery through manners." Like the poetics that Poe derived from his "Raven," O'Connor's formulation particularly flatters her own work, but there's little question that "mystery" (how human beings avoid or confront the meaning of existence) and "manners" (the nuts and bolts of how human beings behave) have always been primary concerns of fiction writers. What's frightening for a novelist today is how the technological consumerism that rules our world specifically aims to render both of these concerns moot.

O'Connor's response to the problem that Roth articulated, to the sense that there is little in the national mediascape that novelists can feel they *own*, was to insist that the best American fiction has always been regional. This was somewhat awkward, since her hero was the cosmopolitan Henry James. But what she meant was that fiction feeds on specificity, and that the manners of a particular region have always provided especially fertile ground for its practitioners.

Superficially, at least, regionalism is still thriving. In fact it's fashionable on college campuses nowadays to say that there is no America anymore, there are only Americas; that the only things a black lesbian New Yorker and a Southern

Baptist Georgian have in common are the English language and the federal income tax. The likelihood, however, is that both the New Yorker and the Georgian watch *Letterman* every night, both are struggling to find health insurance, both have jobs that are threatened by the migration of employment overseas, both go to discount superstores to purchase *Pocahontas* tie-in products for their children, both are being pummeled into cynicism by commercial advertising, both play Lotto, both dream of fifteen minutes of fame, both are taking a serotonin reuptake inhibitor, and both have a guilty crush on Uma Thurman. The world of the present is a world in which the rich lateral dramas of local manners have been replaced by a single vertical drama, the drama of regional specificity succumbing to a commercial generality. The American writer today faces a cultural totalitarianism analogous to the political totalitarianism with which two generations of Eastern bloc writers had to contend. To ignore it is to court nostalgia. To engage with it, however, is to risk writing fiction that makes the same point over and over: technological consumerism is an infernal machine, technological consumerism is an infernal machine . . .

Equally discouraging is the fate of "manners" in the word's more common sense. Rudeness, irresponsibility, duplicity, and stupidity are hallmarks of real human interaction: the stuff of conversation, the cause of sleepless nights. But in the world of consumer advertising and consumer purchasing, no evil is moral. The evils consist of high prices, inconvenience, lack of choice, lack of privacy, heartburn, hair loss, slippery roads. This is no surprise, since the only problems worth advertising solutions for are problems treatable through the spending of money. But money cannot solve the problem of bad manners—the chatterer in the darkened movie theater, the patronizing sister-in-law, the selfish sex partner—except by offering refuge in an atomized privacy. And such privacy is exactly what the American Century has tended toward. First there was mass suburbanization, then the perfection of at-home entertainment, and finally the creation of virtual communities whose most striking feature is that interaction within them is entirely optional—terminable the instant the experience ceases to gratify the user.

That all these trends are infantilizing has been widely noted. Less often remarked is the way in which they are changing both our expectations of entertainment (the book must bring something to us, rather than our bringing something to the book) and the very content of that entertainment. The problem for the novelist is not just that the average man or woman spends so little time F2F with his or her fellows; there is, after all, a rich tradition of epistolary novels, and Robinson Crusoe's condition approximates the solitude of today's suburban bachelor. The real problem is that the average man or woman's entire life is increasingly structured to avoid the kinds of conflicts on which fiction, preoccupied with manners, has always thrived.

Here, indeed, we are up against what truly seems like the obsolescence of serious art in general. Imagine that human existence is defined by an Ache: the Ache of our not being, each of us, the center of the universe; of our desires forever outnumbering our means of satisfying them. If we see religion and art as the historically preferred methods of coming to terms with this Ache, then what happens to art when our technological and economic systems and even our commercialized religions become sufficiently sophisticated to make each of us the center of our own universe of choices and gratifications? Fiction's response to the sting of poor manners, for example, is to render them comic. The reader laughs with the writer, feels less alone with the sting. This is a delicate transaction, and it takes some work. How can it compete with a system—screen your calls; go out by modem; acquire the money to deal exclusively with the privatized world, where workers must be courteous or lose their jobs—that spares you the sting in the first place?

In the long run, the breakdown of communitarianism is likely to have all sorts of nasty consequences. In the short run, however, in this century of amazing prosperity and health, the breakdown takes a heavy toll on the ancient methods of dealing with the Ache. As for the sense of loneliness and pointlessness and loss that social atomization may produce—stuff that can be lumped under O'Connor's general heading of mystery—it's already enough to label it a disease. A disease has causes: abnormal brain chemistry, childhood sexual abuse, welfare queens, the patriarchy, social dysfunction. It also has cures: Zoloft, recovered-memory therapy, the Contract with America, multiculturalism, the World Wide Web. A partial cure, or better yet, an endless succession of partial cures, but failing that, even just the consolation of knowing you have a disease—anything is better than mystery. Science attacked religious mystery a long time ago. But it was not until applied science, in the form of technology, changed both the demand for fiction and the social context in which fiction is written that we novelists fully felt its effects.

EVEN NOW, even when I carefully locate my despair in the past tense, it's difficult for me to confess to all these doubts. In publishing circles, confessions of doubt are widely referred to as "whining"—the idea being that cultural complaint is pathetic and self-serving in writers who don't sell, ungracious in writers who do. For people as protective of their privacy and as fiercely competitive as writers are, mute suffering would seem to be the safest course. However sick with foreboding you feel inside, it's best to radiate confidence and to hope that it's infectious. When a writer says publicly that the novel is doomed, it's a sure bet his new book isn't going well; in terms of his reputation, it's like bleeding in shark-infested waters.

Even harder to admit is how depressed I was. As the social stigma of depression dwindles, the aesthetic stigma increases. It's not just that depression has become fashionable to the point of banality. It's the sense that we live in a reductively binary culture: you're either healthy or you're sick, you either function or you don't. And if that flattening of the field of possibilities is precisely what's depressing you, you're inclined to resist participating in the flattening by calling yourself depressed. You decide that it's the world that's sick, and that the resistance of refusing to function in such a world is healthy. You embrace what clinicians call "depressive realism." It's what the chorus in *Oedipus Rex* sings: "Alas, ye generations of men, how mere a shadow do I count your life! Where, where is the mortal who wins more of happiness than just the seeming, and, after the semblance, a falling away?" You are, after all, just protoplasm, and some day you'll be dead. The invitation to leave your depression behind, whether through medication or therapy or effort of will, seems like an invitation to turn your back on all your dark insights into the corruption and infantilism and self-delusion of the brave new McWorld. And these insights are the sole legacy of the social novelist who desires to represent the world not simply in its detail but in its essence, to shine light on the morally blind eye of the virtual whirlwind, and who believes that human beings deserve better than the future of attractively priced electronic panderings that is even now being conspired for them. Instead of saying *I am depressed*, you want to say *I am right!*

But all the available evidence suggests that you have become a person who's impossible to live with and no fun to talk to. And as you increasingly feel, as a novelist, that you are one of the last remaining repositories of depressive realism and of the radical critique of the therapeutic society that it represents, the burden of news-bringing that is placed on your art becomes overwhelming. You ask yourself, why am I bothering to write these books? I can't pretend the mainstream will listen to the news I have to bring. I can't pretend I'm subverting anything, because any reader capable of decoding my subversive messages does not need to hear them (and the contemporary art scene is a constant reminder of how silly things get when artists start preaching to the choir). I can't stomach any kind of notion that serious fiction is *good for us*, because I don't believe that everything that's wrong with the world has a cure, and even if I did, what business would I, who feel like the sick one, have in offering it? It's hard to consider literature a medicine, in any case, when reading it serves mainly to deepen your depressing estrangement from the mainstream; sooner or later the therapeutically minded reader will end up fingering reading itself as the sickness. Sophie Bentwood, for instance, has "candidate for Prozac" written all over her. No matter how gorgeous and comic her torments are, and no matter how profoundly human she appears in light of those torments, a reader who loves her can't help wondering whether perhaps treatment by a mental-health-care provider wouldn't be the best course all around.

I resist, finally, the notion of literature as a noble higher calling, because elitism doesn't sit well with my American nature, and because even if my belief in mystery didn't incline me to distrust feelings of superiority, my belief in manners would make it difficult for me to explain to my brother, who is a fan of Michael Crichton, that the work I'm doing is simply *better* than Crichton's. Not even the French poststructuralists, with their philosophically unassailable celebration of the "pleasure of the text," can help me out here, because I know that no matter how metaphorically rich and linguistically sophisticated *Desperate Characters* is, what I experienced when I first read it was not some erotically joyous lateral slide of endless associations, but something coherent and deadly pertinent. I know there's a reason I loved reading and loved writing. But every apology and every defense seems to dissolve in the sugar water of contemporary culture, and before long it becomes difficult indeed to get out of bed in the morning.

TWO QUICK GENERALIZATIONS about novelists: we don't like to poke too deeply into the question of audience, and we don't like the social sciences. How awkward, then, that for me the beacon in the murk—the person who inadvertently did the most to get me back on track as a writer—should have been a social scientist who was studying the audience for serious fiction in America.

Shirley Brice Heath is a MacArthur Fellow, a linguistic anthropologist, and a professor of English and linguistics at Stanford; she's a stylish, twiggy, white-haired lady with no discernible tolerance for small talk. Throughout the eighties, Heath haunted what she calls "enforced transition zones"— places where people are held captive without recourse to television or other comforting pursuits. She rode public transportation in twenty-seven different cities. She lurked in airports (at least before the arrival of CNN). She took her notebook into bookstores and seaside resorts. Whenever she saw people reading or buying "substantive works of fiction" (meaning, roughly, trade-paperback fiction), she asked for a few minutes of their time. She visited summer writers' conferences and creative-writing programs to grill ephebes. She interviewed novelists. Three years ago she interviewed me, and last summer I had lunch with her in Palo Alto.

To the extent that novelists think about audience at all, we like to imagine a "general audience"—a large, eclectic pool of decently educated people who can be induced, by strong enough reviews or aggressive enough marketing, to treat themselves to a good, serious book. We do our best not to notice that, among adults with similar educations and similarly complicated lives, some read a lot of novels while others read few or none.

Heath has noticed this circumstance, and although she emphasized to me that she has not polled everybody in America, her research effectively demolishes the myth of the general audience. For a person to sustain an interest in literature, she told me, two things have to be in place. First, the habit of reading works of substance must have been "heavily modeled" when he or she was very young. In other words, one or both of the parents must have been reading serious books and must have encouraged the child to do the same. On the East Coast, Heath found a strong element of class in this. Parents in the privileged classes encourage reading out of a sense of what Louis Auchincloss calls "entitlement": just as the civilized person ought to be able to appreciate caviar and a good Burgundy, she ought to be able to enjoy Henry James. Class matters less in other parts of the country, especially in the Protestant Midwest, where literature is seen as a way to exercise the mind. As Heath put it, "Part of the exercise of being a good person is not using your free time frivolously. You have to be able to account for yourself through the work ethic *and* through the wise use of your leisure time." For a century after the Civil War, the Midwest was home to thousands of small-town literary societies in which, Heath found, the wife of a janitor was as likely to be active as the wife of a doctor.

Simply having a parent who reads is not enough, however, to produce a lifelong dedicated reader. According to Heath, young readers also need to find a person with whom they can share their interest. "A child who's got the habit will start reading under the covers with a flashlight," she said. "If the parents are smart, they'll forbid the child to do this, and thereby encourage her. Otherwise she'll find a peer who also has the habit, and the two of them will keep it a secret between them. Finding a peer can take place as late as college. In high school, especially, there's a social penalty to be paid for being a reader. Lots of kids who have been lone readers get to college and suddenly discover, 'Oh my God, there are other people here who read.'"

As Heath unpacked her findings for me, I was remembering the joy with which I'd discovered two friends in junior high with whom I could talk about J. R. R. Tolkien. I was also considering that for me, today, there is nothing sexier than a reader. But then it occurred to me that I didn't even meet Heath's first precondition. I told her I didn't remember either of my parents ever reading a book when I was a child, except aloud to me.

Without missing a beat Heath replied: "Yes, but there's a second kind of reader. There's the social isolate—the child who from an early age felt very different from everyone around him. This is very, very difficult to uncover in an interview. People don't like to admit that they were social isolates as children. What happens is you take that sense of being different into an imaginary world. But that world, then, is a world you can't share with the people around you—because it's imaginary. And so the important dialogue in your life is with the *authors* of the books you read. Though they aren't present, they become your community."

Pride compels me, here, to draw a distinction between young fiction readers and young nerds. The classic nerd, who finds a home in facts or technology or numbers, is marked not by a displaced sociability but by an *anti*sociability. Reading does resemble more nerdy pursuits in that it's a habit that both feeds on a sense of isolation and aggravates it. Simply being a "social isolate" as a child does not, however, doom you to bad breath and poor party skills as an adult. In fact, it can make you hypersocial. It's just that at some point you'll begin to feel a gnawing, almost remorseful need to be alone and do some reading—to reconnect to that community.

According to Heath, readers of the social-isolate variety (she also calls them "resistant" readers) are much more likely to become writers than those of the modeled-habit variety. If writing was the medium of communication within the community of childhood, it makes sense that when writers grow up they continue to find writing vital to their sense of connectedness. What's perceived as the antisocial nature of "substantive" authors, whether it's James Joyce's exile or

J. D. Salinger's reclusion, derives in large part from the social isolation that's necessary for inhabiting an imagined world. Looking me in the eye, Heath said: "You are a socially isolated individual who desperately wants to communicate with a substantive imaginary world."

I knew she was using the word "you" in its impersonal sense. Nevertheless, I felt as if she were looking straight into my soul. And the exhilaration I felt at her accidental description of me, in unpoetic polysyllables, was my confirmation of that description's truth. Simply to be recognized for what I was, simply not to be misunderstood: these had revealed themselves, suddenly, as reasons to write.

BY THE SPRING of 1994 I was a socially isolated individual whose desperate wish was mainly to make some money. After my wife and I separated for the last time, I took a job teaching undergraduate fiction-writing at a small liberal arts college, and although I spent way too much time on it, I loved the work. I was heartened by the skill and ambition of my students, who hadn't even been born when *Rowan & Martin's Laugh-In* first aired. I was depressed, though, to learn that several of my best writers had vowed never to take a literature class again. One evening a student reported that his contemporary fiction class had been encouraged to spend an entire hour debating whether the novelist Leslie Marmon Silko was a homophobe. Another evening, when I came to class, three women students were hooting with laughter at the utopian-feminist novel they were being forced to read for an honors seminar in Women and Fiction.

The therapeutic optimism now raging in English literature departments insists that novels be sorted into two boxes:

Symptoms of Disease (canonical work from the Dark Ages before 1950) and Medicine for a Happier and Healthier World (the work of women and of people from nonwhite or nonhetero cultures). But the contemporary fiction writers whose work is being put to such optimistic use in the Academy are seldom, themselves, to blame. To the extent that the American novel still has cultural authority—an appeal beyond the Academy, a presence in household conversations—it's largely the work of women. Knowledgeable booksellers estimate that seventy percent of all fiction is bought by women, and so perhaps it's no surprise that in recent years so many crossover novels, the good books that find an audience, have been written by women: fictional mothers turning a sober eye on their children in the work of Jane Smiley and Rosellen Brown; fictional daughters listening to their Chinese mothers (Amy Tan) or Chippewa grandmothers (Louise Erdrich); a fictional freedwoman conversing with the spirit of the daughter she killed to save her from slavery (Toni Morrison). The darkness of these novels is not a political darkness, banishable by the enlightenment of contemporary critical theory; it's the darkness of sorrows that have no easy cure.

The current flourishing of novels by women and cultural minorities shows the chauvinism of judging the vitality of American letters by the fortunes of the traditional social novel. Indeed, it can be argued that the country's literary culture is *healthier* for having disconnected from mainstream culture; that a universal "American" culture was little more than an instrument for the perpetuation of a white, male, heterosexual elite, and that its decline is the just desert of an exhausted tradition. (Joseph Heller's depiction of women in *Catch-22*, for example, is so embarrassing that I hesitated to recommend the book to my students.) It's possible that the American experience has become so sprawling and diffracted that no single "social novel," à la Dickens or Stendhal, can ever hope to mirror it; perhaps ten novels from ten different cultural perspectives are required now.

Unfortunately, there's also evidence that young writers today feel imprisoned by their ethnic or gender identities— discouraged from speaking across boundaries by a culture in which television has conditioned us to accept only the literal testimony of the Self. And the problem is aggravated when fiction writers take refuge in university creative-writing programs. Any given issue of the typical small literary magazine, edited by MFA candidates aware that the MFA candidates submitting manuscripts need to publish in order to obtain or hold on to teaching jobs, reliably contains variations on three generic short stories: "My Interesting Childhood," "My Interesting Life in a College Town," and "My Interesting Year Abroad." Fiction writers in the Academy do serve the important function of teaching literature for its own sake, and some of them also produce strong work while teaching, but as a reader I miss the days when more novelists lived and worked in big cities. I mourn the retreat into the Self and the decline of the broad-canvas novel for the same reason I mourn the rise of suburbs: I like maximum diversity and contrast packed into a single exciting experience. Even though social reportage is no longer so much a defining function of the novel as an accidental by-product—Shirley Heath's observations confirm that serious readers aren't reading for instruction—I still like a novel that's alive and multivalent like a city.

_____

THE VALUE of Heath's work, and the reason I'm citing her so liberally, is that she has bothered to study empirically what nobody else has, and that she has brought to bear on the problem of reading a vocabulary that is neutral enough to survive in our value-free cultural environment. Readers aren't "better" or "healthier" or, conversely, "sicker" than nonreaders. We just happen to belong to a rather strange kind of community.

For Heath, a defining feature of "substantive works of fiction" is *unpredictability*. She arrived at this definition after discovering that most of the hundreds of serious readers she interviewed have had to deal, one way or another, with personal unpredictability. Therapists and ministers who counsel troubled people tend to read the hard stuff. So do people whose lives haven't followed the course they were expected to: merchant-caste Koreans who don't become merchants, ghetto kids who go to college, openly gay men from conservative families, and women whose lives have turned out to be radically different from their mothers'. This last group is particularly large. There are, today, millions of American women whose lives do not resemble the lives they might have projected from their mothers', and all of them, in Heath's model, are potentially susceptible to substantive fiction.

In her interviews, Heath uncovered a "wide unanimity" among serious readers that literature "'makes me a better person.'" She hastened to assure me that, rather than straightening them out in a self-help way, "reading serious literature impinges on the embedded circumstances in people's lives in such a way that they have to deal with them. And, in so dealing, they come to see themselves as deeper and more capable of handling their inability to have a totally predictable life." Again and again, readers told Heath the same thing: "Reading enables me to maintain a sense of something *substantive*

—my ethical integrity, my intellectual integrity. 'Substance' is more than 'this weighty book.' Reading that book gives *me*

substance." This substance, Heath adds, is most often transmitted verbally, and is felt to have permanence. "Which is why," she said, "computers won't do it for readers."

With near-unanimity, Heath's respondents described substantive works of fiction as, she said, "the only places where there was some civic, public hope of coming to grips with the ethical, philosophical and sociopolitical dimensions of life that were elsewhere treated so simplistically. From Agamemnon forward, for example, we've been having to deal with the conflict between loyalty to one's family and loyalty to the state. And strong works of fiction are what refuse to give easy answers to the conflict, to paint things as black and white, good guys versus bad guys. They're everything that pop psychology is not."

"And religions themselves are substantive works of fiction," I said.

She nodded. "This is precisely what readers are saying: that reading good fiction is like reading a particularly rich section of a religious text. What religion and good fiction have in common is that the answers aren't there, there isn't closure. The language of literary works gives forth something different with each reading. But unpredictability doesn't mean total relativism. Instead it highlights the persistence with which writers keep coming back to fundamental problems. Your family versus your country, your wife versus your girlfriend."

"Being alive versus having to die," I said.

"Exactly," Heath said. "Of course, there is a certain predictability to literature's unpredictability. It's the one thing that all substantive works have in common. And *that* predictability is what readers tell me they hang on to—a sense of having company in this great human enterprise."

"A friend of mine keeps telling me that reading and writing are ultimately about loneliness. I'm starting to come around."

"It's about not being alone, yes," Heath said, "but it's also about not hearing that there's no way out—no point to existence. The point is in the continuity, in the persistence of the great conflicts."

Flying back from Palo Alto in an enforced transition zone crewed by the employee-owners of TWA, I declined the headphones for *The Brady Bunch Movie* and a special one-hour segment of *E!*, but I found myself watching anyway. Without sound, the segment of *E!* became an exposé of the hydraulics of insincere smiles. It brought me an epiphany of inauthenticity, made me hunger for the unforced emotion of a literature that isn't trying to sell me anything. I had open on my lap Janet Frame's novel of a mental hospital, *Faces in the Water*: uningratiating but strangely pertinent sentences on which my eyes would not stick until, after two and a half hours, the silent screen in front of me finally went blank.

Poor Noeline, who was waiting for Dr. Howell to propose to her although the only words he had ever spoken to her were How are you? Do you know where you are? Do you know why you are here?—phrases which ordinarily would be hard to interpret as evidence of affection. But when you are sick you find yourself in a new field of perception where you make a harvest of interpretations which then provides you with your daily bread, your only food. So that when Dr. Howell finally married the occupational therapist, Noeline was taken to the disturbed ward.

Expecting a novel to bear the weight of our whole disturbed society—to help solve our contemporary problems—seems to me a peculiarly American delusion. To write sentences of such authenticity that refuge can be taken in them: Isn't this enough? Isn't it a lot?

AS RECENTLY AS FORTY YEARS AGO, when the publication of Hemingway's *The Old Man and the Sea* was a national event, movies and radio were still considered "low" entertainments. In the fifties and sixties, when movies became "film" and demanded to be taken seriously, TV became the new low entertainment. Finally, in the seventies, with the Watergate hearings and *All in the Family*, television, too, made itself an essential part of cultural literacy. The educated single New Yorker who in 1945 read twenty-five serious novels in a year today has time for maybe five. As the modeled-habit layer of the novel's audience peels away, what's left is mainly the hard core of resistant readers, who read because they must.

That hard core is a very small prize to be divided among a very large number of working novelists. To make a sustainable living, a writer must also be on the five-book lists of a whole lot of modeled-habit readers. Every year, in expectation of this jackpot, a handful of good novelists get six- and even seven-figure advances (thus providing ammunition for cheery souls of the "American literature is booming!" variety), and a few of them actually hit the charts. E. Annie Proulx's *The Shipping News* has sold nearly a million copies in the last two years; the hardcover literary best-seller of 1994, Cormac McCarthy's *The Crossing*, came in at number fifty-one on *Publishers Weekly*'s annual best-seller list. (Number fifty was *Star Trek: All Good Things*.)

Anthony Lane, in a pair of recent essays in *The New Yorker*, has demonstrated that while most of the novels on the contemporary best-seller list are vapid, predictable, and badly written, the best-sellers of fifty years ago were also vapid, predictable, and badly written. Lane's essays usefully destroy the notion of a golden pre-television age when the American masses had their noses stuck in literary masterworks; he makes it clear that this country's popular tastes have become no worse in half a century. What *has* changed is the economics of book publishing. The number-one best-seller of 1955, *Marjorie Morningstar*, sold a hundred and ninety thousand copies in bookstores. In 1994, in a country less than twice as populous, John Grisham's *The Chamber* sold more than three million. Publishing is now a subsidiary of Hollywood, and the blockbuster novel is a mass-marketable commodity, a portable substitute for TV.

The persistence of a market for literary fiction exerts a useful discipline on writers, reminding us of our duty to entertain. But if the Academy is a rock to ambitious novelists, then the nature of the modern American market—its triage of artists into Superstars, Stars, and Nobodies; its clear-eyed recognition that nothing moves a product like a personality—is a hard place indeed. It's possible, if you have the right temperament, to market yourself successfully with irony, by making fun of marketing. Thus the subject of the young writer Mark Leyner's fiction is the self-promotion of Mark Leyner, the young writer; he's been on *Letterman* three times. But most novelists feel some level of discomfort with marketing the innately private experience of reading by means of a public persona—on book tours, on radio talk shows, on Barnes & Noble shopping bags and coffee mugs. The writer for whom the printed word is paramount is, ipso facto, an untelevisable personality, and it's instructive to recall how many of our critically esteemed older novelists have chosen, in a country where publicity is otherwise sought like the Grail, to guard their privacy. Salinger, Roth, McCarthy, Don DeLillo, William Gaddis, Anne Tyler, Thomas Pynchon, Cynthia Ozick, and Denis Johnson all give few or no interviews, do little if any teaching or touring, and in some cases decline even to be photographed. Various Heathian dramas of social isolation are no doubt being played out here. But, for some of these writers, reticence is integral to their artistic creed.

In Gaddis's first novel, *The Recognitions* (1955), a stand-in for the author cries: "What is it they want from the man that they didn't get from the work? What do they expect? What is there left when he's done with his work, what's any artist but the dregs of his work, the human shambles that follows it around?" Postwar novelists like Gaddis and Pynchon and postwar artists like Robert Frank answered these questions very differently than Norman Mailer and Andy Warhol did. In 1954, before television had even supplanted radio as the regnant medium, Gaddis recognized that no matter how attractively subversive self-promotion may seem in the short run, the artist who's really serious about resisting a culture of inauthentic mass-marketed image must resist becoming an image himself, even at the price of certain obscurity.

For a long time, trying to follow Gaddis's example, I took a hard line on letting my work speak for itself. Not that I was exactly bombarded with invitations; but I refused to teach, to review for the *Times*, to write about writing, to go to parties. To speak extranovelistically in an age of personalities seemed to me a betrayal; it implied a lack of faith in fiction's adequacy as communication and self-expression and so helped, I believed, to accelerate the public flight from the imagined to the literal. I had a cosmology of silent heroes and gregarious traitors.

Silence, however, is a useful statement only if someone, somewhere, expects your voice to be loud. Silence in the 1990s seemed only to guarantee that I would be alone. And eventually it dawned on me that the despair I felt about the novel was less the result of my obsolescence than of my isolation. Depression presents itself as a realism regarding the rottenness of the world in general and the rottenness of your life in particular. But the realism is merely a mask for depression's actual essence, which is an overwhelming estrangement from humanity. The more persuaded you are of your unique access to the rottenness, the more afraid you become of engaging with the world; and the less you engage with the world, the more perfidiously happy-faced the rest of humanity seems for continuing to engage with it.

Writers and readers have always been prone to this estrangement. Communion with the virtual community of print requires solitude, after all. But the estrangement becomes much more profound, urgent, and dangerous when that virtual community is no longer densely populated and heavily trafficked; when the saving continuity of literature itself is under electronic and academic assault; when your alienation becomes generic rather than individual, and the business pages seem to report on the world's conspiracy to grandfather not only you but all your kind, and the price of silence seems no longer to be obscurity but outright oblivion.

I recognize that a person writing confessionally for a national magazine may have less than triple-A credibility in asserting that genuine reclusiveness is simply not an option, either psychologically or financially, for writers born after *Sputnik*. It may be that I've become a gregarious traitor. But in belatedly following my books out of the house, doing some journalism and even hitting a few parties, I've felt less as if I'm introducing myself to the world than as if I'm introducing the world to myself. Once I stepped outside my bubble of despair I found that almost everyone I met shared many of my fears, and that other writers shared *all* of them.

In the past, when the life of letters was synonymous with culture, solitude was possible the way it was in cities where you could always, day and night, find the comfort of crowds outside your door. In a suburban age, when the rising waters of electronic culture have made each reader and each writer an island, it may be that we need to be more active in assuring ourselves that a community still exists. I used to distrust creative-writing departments for what seemed to me their artificial safety, just as I distrusted book clubs for treating literature like a cruciferous vegetable that could be choked down only with a spoonful of socializing. As I grope for my own sense of community, I distrust both a little less now. I see the authority of the novel in the nineteenth and early twentieth centuries as an accident of history—of having no competitors. Now the distance between author and reader is shrinking. Instead of Olympian figures speaking to the masses below, we have matching diasporas. Readers and writers are united in their need for solitude, in their pursuit of substance in a time of ever-increasing evanescence: in their reach inward, via print, for a way out of loneliness.

ONE OF THE CHERISHED NOTIONS of cybervisionaries is that literary culture is antidemocratic—that the reading of good books is primarily a pursuit of the leisured white male—and that our republic will therefore be healthier for abandoning itself to computers. As Shirley Heath's research (or even a casual visit to a bookstore) makes clear, the cybervisionaries are lying. Reading is an ethnically diverse, socially skeptical activity. The wealthy white men who today have powerful notebook computers are the ones who form this country's most salient elite. The word "elitist" is the club with which they bash those for whom purchasing technology fails to constitute a life.

That a distrust or an outright hatred of what we now call "literature" has always been a mark of social visionaries, whether Plato or Stalin or today's free-market technocrats, can lead us to think that literature has a function, beyond entertainment, as a form of social opposition. Novels, after all, do sometimes ignite political debates or become embroiled in them. And since the one modest favor that any writer asks of a society is freedom of expression, a country's poets and novelists are often the ones obliged to serve as voices of conscience in times of religious or political fanaticism. Literature's aura of oppositionality is especially intense in America, where the low status of art has a way of turning resistant child readers into supremely alienated grownup writers. What's more, since the making of money has always been of absolute centrality to the culture, and since the people who make a lot of it are seldom very interesting, the most memorable characters in U.S. fiction have tended to be socially marginal: Huck Finn and Janie Crawford, Hazel

Motes and Tyrone Slothrop. Finally, the feeling of oppositionality is compounded in an age when simply picking up a novel after dinner represents a kind of cultural *Je refuse!*

It's all too easy, therefore, to forget how frequently good artists through the ages have insisted, as Auden put it, that "art makes nothing happen." It's all too easy to jump from the knowledge that the novel *can* have agency to the conviction that it *must* have agency. Nabokov pretty well summed up the political platform that every novelist can endorse: no censorship, good universal education, no portraits of heads of state larger than a postage stamp. If we go any further than that, our agendas begin to diverge radically. What emerges as the belief that unifies us is not that a novel can change anything but that it can *preserve* something. The thing being preserved depends on the writer; it may be as private as "My Interesting Childhood." But as the country grows ever more distracted and mesmerized by mass culture, the stakes rise even for authors whose primary ambition is to land a teaching job. Whether they think about it or not, novelists are preserving a tradition of precise, expressive language; a habit of looking past surfaces into interiors; maybe an understanding of private experience and public context as distinct but interpenetrating; maybe mystery, maybe manners. Above all, they are preserving a community of readers and writers, and the way in which members of this community recognize each other is that nothing in the world seems simple to them.

Shirley Heath uses the bland word "unpredictability" to describe this conviction of complexity; Flannery O'Connor called it "mystery." In *Desperate Characters*, Fox captures it like this: "Ticking away inside the carapace of ordinary life and its sketchy agreements was anarchy." For me, the word that best describes the novelist's view of the world is *tragic*. In Nietzsche's account of the "birth of tragedy," which remains pretty much unbeatable as a theory of why people enjoy sad narratives, an anarchic "Dionysian" insight into the darkness and unpredictability of life is wedded to an "Apollonian" clarity and beauty of form to produce an experience that's religious in its intensity. Even for people who don't believe in anything that they can't see with their own two eyes, the formal aesthetic rendering of the human plight can be (though I'm afraid we novelists are rightly mocked for overusing the word) redemptive.

It's possible to locate various morals in *Oedipus Rex*—"Heed oracles," say, or "Expect the unexpected," or "Marry in haste, repent at leisure"—and their existence confirms in us a sense of the universe's underlying orderliness. But what makes Oedipus human is that of course he doesn't heed the oracle. And though Sophie Bentwood, twenty-five hundred years later, "shouldn't" try to insulate herself from the rabid society around her, of course she tries to anyway. But then, as Fox writes: "How quickly the husk of adult life, its *importance*, was shattered by the thrust of what was, all at once, real and imperative and absurd."

I hope it's clear that by "tragic" I mean just about any fiction that raises more questions than it answers: anything in which conflict doesn't resolve into cant. (Indeed, the most reliable indicator of a tragic perspective in a work of fiction is comedy.) The point of calling serious fiction tragic is to highlight its distance from the rhetoric of optimism that so pervades our culture. The necessary lie of every successful regime, including the upbeat techno-corporatism under which we now live, is that the regime has made the world a better place. Tragic realism preserves the recognition that improvement always comes at a cost; that nothing lasts forever; that if the good in the world outweighs the bad, it's by the slimmest of margins. I suspect that art has always had a particularly tenuous purchase on the American imagination because ours is a country to which so few terrible things have ever happened. The one genuine tragedy to befall us was slavery, and it's probably no accident that the tradition of Southern literature has been strikingly rich and productive of geniuses. (Compare the literature of the sunny, fertile, peaceful West Coast.) Superficially at least, for the great white majority, the history of this country has consisted of success and more success. Tragic realism preserves access to the dirt behind the dream of Chosenness—to the human difficulty beneath the technological ease, to the sorrow behind the pop-cultural narcosis: to all those portents on the margins of our existence.

> *People without hope not only don't write novels, but what is more to the point, they don't read them. They don't take long looks at anything, because they lack the courage. The way to despair is to refuse to have any kind of experience, and the novel, of course, is a way to have experience.*
>
> —*Flannery O'Connor*

DEPRESSION, when it's clinical, is not a metaphor. It runs in families, and it's known to respond to medication and to counseling. However truly you believe there's a sickness to existence that can never be cured, if you're depressed you will sooner or later surrender and say: I just don't want to feel so bad anymore. The shift from depressive realism to tragic realism—from being immobilized by darkness to being sustained by it—thus strangely seems to require believing in the possibility of a cure. But this "cure" is anything but straightforward.

I spent the early nineties trapped in a double singularity. Not only did I feel that I was different from everyone around me, but I felt that the age I lived in was utterly different from any age that had come before. For me the work of regaining a tragic perspective has therefore involved a dual kind of reaching out: both the reconnection with a community of readers and writers, and the reclamation of a sense of history.

It's possible to have a general sense of history's darkness, a mystical Dionysian conviction that the game ain't over till it's over, without having enough of an Apollonian grasp of the details to appreciate its consolations. Until a year ago, for example, it would never have occurred to me to assert that this country has "always" been dominated by commerce.* I saw only the ugliness of the commercial present, and naturally I raged at the betrayal of an earlier America that I presumed to have been truer, less venal, less hostile to the enterprise of fiction. But how ridiculous the self-pity of the writer in the late twentieth century can seem in light of, say, Herman Melville's life. How familiar his life is: the first novel that makes his reputation, the painful discovery of how little his vision appeals to prevailing popular tastes, the growing sense of having no place in a sentimental re-

---

* I realize that this is a dismal confession, and that my managing to slip through college without ever taking a course in either American history or American literature is hardly an excuse.

public, the horrible money troubles, the abandonment by his publisher, the disastrous commercial failure of his finest and most ambitious work, the reputed mental illness (his melancholy, his *depression*), and finally the retreat into writing purely for his own satisfaction.

Reading Melville's biography, I wish that he'd been granted the example of someone like himself, from an earlier century, to make him feel less singularly cursed. I wish, too, that he'd been able to say to himself, when he was struggling to support Lizzie and their kids: Hey, if worse comes to worst, I can always teach writing. In his lifetime, Melville made about $10,500 from his books. Even today, he can't catch a break. On its first printing, the title page of the second Library of America volume of Melville's collected works bore the name, in twenty-four-point display type, HERMAN MEVILLE.

Last summer, as I began to acquaint myself with American history, and as I talked to readers and writers and pondered the Heathian "social isolate," there was growing inside me a realization that my condition was not a disease but a nature. How could I *not* feel estranged? I was a *reader*. My nature had been waiting for me all along, and now it welcomed me. All of a sudden I became aware of how very hungry I was to construct and inhabit an imagined world. The hunger felt like a loneliness of which I'd been dying. How could I have thought that I needed to cure myself in order to fit into the "real" world? I didn't need curing, and the world didn't, either; the only thing that did need curing was my understanding of my place in it. Without that understanding— without a sense of *belonging* to the real world—it was impossible to thrive in an imagined one.

At the heart of my despair about the novel had been a conflict between a feeling that I should Address the Culture and Bring News to the Mainstream, and my desire to write about the things closest to me, to lose myself in the characters and locales I loved. Writing, and reading too, had become a grim duty, and considering the poor pay, there is seriously no point in doing either if you're not having fun. As soon as I jettisoned my perceived obligation to the chimerical mainstream, my third book began to move again. I'm amazed, now, that I'd trusted myself so little for so long, that I'd felt such a crushing imperative to engage explicitly with all the forces impinging on the pleasure of reading and writing: as if, in peopling and arranging my own little alternate world, I could ignore the bigger social picture even if I wanted to.

As I was figuring all this out, I got a letter from Don De-Lillo, to whom I'd written in distress. This, in part, is what he said:

> The novel is whatever novelists are doing at a given time. If we're not doing the big social novel fifteen years from now, it'll probably mean our sensibilities have changed in ways that make such work less compelling to us—we won't stop because the market dried up. The writer leads, he doesn't follow. The dynamic lives in the writer's mind, not in the size of the audience. And if the social novel lives, but only barely, surviving in the cracks and ruts of the culture, maybe it will be taken more seriously, as an endangered spectacle. A reduced context but a more intense one.
>
> Writing is a form of personal freedom. It frees us from the mass identity we see in the making all around us. In

the end, writers will write not to be outlaw heroes of some underculture but mainly to save themselves, to survive as individuals.

DeLillo added a postscript: "If serious reading dwindles to near nothingness, it will probably mean that the thing we're talking about when we use the word 'identity' has reached an end."

The strange thing about this postscript is that I can't read it without experiencing a surge of hope. Tragic realism has the perverse effect of making its adherents into qualified optimists. "I am very much afraid," O'Connor once wrote, "that to the fiction writer the fact that we shall always have the poor with us is a source of satisfaction, for it means, essentially, that he will always be able to find someone like himself. His concern with poverty is with a poverty fundamental to man." Even if Silicon Valley manages to plant a virtual-reality helmet in every American household, even if serious reading dwindles to near-nothingness, there remains a hungry world beyond our borders, a national debt that government-by-television can do little more than wring its hands over, and the good old apocalyptic horsemen of war, disease, and environmental degradation. If real wages keep falling, the suburbs of "My Interesting Childhood" won't offer much protection. And if multiculturalism succeeds in making us a nation of independently empowered tribes, each tribe will be deprived of the comfort of victimhood and be forced to confront human limitation for what it is: a fixture of life. History is the rabid thing from which we all, like Sophie Bentwood, would like to hide. But there's no bubble that can stay unburst. On whether this is a good thing or a bad thing, tragic realists offer no opinion. They simply represent it. A generation ago, by paying close attention, Paula Fox could discern in a broken ink bottle both perdition and salvation. The world was ending then, it's ending still, and I'm happy to belong to it again.

[1996]

LOST IN THE MAIL

THE FALL of the Chicago post office began before the public could see the portents: before the undead letters rose up in every corner of the city to haunt the guilty management—a hundred sacks of months-old mail in the back of a North Side letter carrier's truck, two hundred pounds of fresh mail burning underneath a South Side viaduct, more than fifteen hundred pieces of mail moldering in a shallow grave beneath a West Side porch, and a truckload of mail and parcels in the closets of a Chicago carrier's suburban condo. The fall began on Thursday, January 20, 1994, at about two in the afternoon, when a woman named Debra Doyle called the manager of her local station and told him that her family had not received mail since the previous Thursday.

Over the years, Doyle had come to expect poor service from the Uptown station, which served her neighborhood.

Two- and three-day hiatuses in delivery no longer surprised her. But an entire week without mail, even a very cold week in January, seemed extreme. On the telephone, the station manager, Thomas Nichols, explained to Doyle that his carriers could not deliver the mail because their trucks wouldn't start. He said that if Doyle wanted her mail she would have to get it from him at the station. Perhaps Nichols didn't think that Doyle would actually venture out in the subzero weather, but after speaking to him she went straight to her car.

The population served by Chicago's Uptown station is, in its diversity, practically an encyclopedia of contemporary American city dwellers. Professionals and retirees live in high-rises and large houses near Lake Michigan, transients and drug addicts come and go on Lawrence and Bryn Mawr Avenues, and on either side of the El tracks Asian and Eastern European immigrants share alleys with lifelong middle-class Chicagoans like Doyle. For years, the one thing all these people had in common was the 60640 zip code—that, and the unpleasant experience that was in store for them whenever they had to visit the Uptown station. The lobby smelled like a subway platform. The clerks seemed to have no pleasure in life but breaking for coffee at peak hours and hurling parcels marked "Fragile" at distant hampers. Customers budgeted an hour when they went to claim a package.

When she arrived at the station, Doyle asked to speak to Nichols. She was told that he was not in the building. Skeptical, she dialed the station's number from the pay phone in the lobby. Nichols answered. What ensued was an archetypical Chicago scene: an angry postal customer confronting an evasive, unhelpful postal manager. Scenes like this ended, at best, with a promise of better service in the future; at worst, with the manager shouting obscenities at the customer.

On this particular afternoon, however, as Doyle and Nichols locked horns on the telephone, a tall, energetic woman strode into the Uptown lobby and asked if she could help. She introduced herself as Gayle Campbell. Doyle explained her problem, and Campbell disappeared into the back of the station. A few minutes later she returned with a week's worth of Doyle's mail. She also gave Doyle the numbers of her beeper and her home telephone, and urged her to call her if she had any more trouble with her delivery. Then she disappeared into the back of the station again.

The United States Postal Service, the country's universal hard-copy delivery system, has a problem with big cities. Last winter, when Doyle met Campbell, eighty-eight percent of the nation's households found their mail service "good," "very good," or "excellent," but cities like New York and Washington had satisfaction indices in the mid-seventies, and Chicago, with a score of sixty-four percent, ranked dead last. More than a third of Chicagoans rated their service as "poor" or "fair," and the discontent was even greater in the city's crowded, affluent north-lakefront districts, where service had been execrable for a decade and consumer frustration had reached an intensity that seemed comic to those who didn't share it.

A representative Chicago horror story, unusual only in its protraction, is that of Marilyn Katz, a media and political consultant. In 1986, Katz and her husband bought a ninety-year-old house on Magnolia Avenue, a stable, uncrowded neighborhood in the Uptown district. When they had lived there for three years, their mail abruptly stopped coming. Katz called the Uptown station four times, over a period of two weeks, before the station manager provided an explanation. The explanation was that Katz's mail carrier had declared her house abandoned.

Service then resumed, but only fitfully. Katz's mail came late, if it came at all, and often it was heavily seasoned with mail for other houses in her neighborhood. She engaged in especially lively trade with the 5500 block of Lakewood. Her homeowner's insurance was canceled, and so was her health insurance; she had never received the bills. Before leaving on a ten-day vacation in August of 1990, she received notice that her phone service would be terminated for nonpayment. When she returned from vacation, her phone bills from May, June, July, and August were waiting for her. A few months later, she noticed that she had stopped getting *The New Yorker*. When she called the subscription service, she learned that the Uptown station had sent notification that she had moved away.

In the winter of 1992, Katz hand-delivered copies of a questionnaire on mail service to every household in a sixteen-block area of her neighborhood. The returns brought a litany of complaints similar to her own, plus fresh horrors. "Mailman drinks, erratic, hangs out with peculiar friends during delivery"; "Mailwoman delivers mail with her children and has children deliver the mail"; "Mailman harasses us at night, asks for money."

Katz sent her survey results to the Chicago postmaster. Six months later, having received no reply, she began to work with her alderman, Mary Ann Smith, whose office had been processing postal complaints since 1988. Smith extracted a promise from Jimmie Mason, the new postmaster, to respond to Katz's survey by October 2, but it was midwinter before Smith was able to arrange for Katz and her neighbors to meet with him. Mason asked them for their help in monitoring mail service. Katz said that she didn't want to monitor the mail, she just wanted to get it. Mason said improvement would take time. In the interim, he promised to repaint Uptown's corner mailboxes, which had been heavily tagged by local youth. He also offered to provide the community with its own blue paint to keep the boxes clean. To Katz, this seemed the ultimate in codependency: "Not only can we do delivery and monitoring for them. We can also paint."

Although Mary Ann Smith continued to arrange "town meetings," at which various postal officials made various promises, service in Uptown did not improve. Finally, last winter, after six years of steady agitation, Smith concluded that no force she could muster locally would compel the United States Postal Service to listen. She urged the City Council's Committee on Finance to hold hearings on the economic impact of poor postal service, and then she gave up. "We'd done our part," she says. "I'm not really supposed to spend my time on this."

Katz, meanwhile, had turned over her important outgoing mail to Federal Express and had arranged for direct deposit of her checks. She made sure that all valuable documents were sent to her office downtown. Just as she avoided other universal public services by driving a car to work and sending her children to private school, she now bypassed the Postal Service, as much as possible, with her telephone, fax machine, and computer. She, too, had given up. "There was no accountability," she says. "It was clear that the post office didn't care."

For Marilyn Katz and Mary Ann Smith and Debra Doyle—and for others as well, like U.S. Representative Sidney R. Yates of the Ninth District of Illinois, who had been criticizing Chicago postal operations for a decade—the most frustrating part of dealing with the post office was that nobody connected with it could explain why the mail was not being delivered. Katz occasionally heard excuses (for instance, the Uptown manager confided to her that postal workers' unions prevented him from disciplining his carriers), but she never received even a token explanation of the failures that her survey had uncovered. Officials were cordial at town meetings and silent afterward. It was as if they not only didn't care; they didn't even know they had a problem.

When Doyle met Gayle Campbell in the Uptown lobby, she found an administrator who plainly did care. Later in the evening, when she spoke to Campbell at home, she realized she had also found an administrator who knew the post office had a problem. Campbell was voluble and angry, and Doyle quickly recognized—so quickly that she called her alderman, Patrick O'Connor, the very next morning—that frustration inside the post office had finally reached the level of frustration on the outside. With this equalization, information began to flow.

THE POSTAL SERVICE, though forever maligned, is the most constant and best-loved presence of federal government in the nation's daily life. My sense of being an American devolves in some small part from knowing that we still have the best mail service and lowest postage rates and ugliest stamps of any industrialized nation. (How Italian the Italian post office is; how German the German.) For a bureaucracy, moreover, the Postal Service performs a difficult task creditably. I suspect that postal horrors would fade to insignificance if every household in the country had to deal with the Department of Labor or the Navy six times a week. Although the Postmaster General, Marvin Runyon, is fond of calling his fifty-billion-dollar-a-year operation the eighth-largest corporation in the country, he labors under constraints that no private-sector CEO has to deal with: responsibilities to congressional committees; maintenance of genuine diversity in hiring and promotion, with special attention to veterans and the handicapped; and, above all, the provision of universal flat-rate first-class service. The Postal Service embodies the dream of democracy. Any citizen, even a convict or a child, can communicate with any other for the same low price. This abiding ideal of universal service is what preserves an institution that for most of its existence has dwelled at the dangerous intersection of big government, big business, and local politics. Were it not for this ideal, Washington would have long ago sold off the whole operation.

The strain in the relations between Chicago and its post office is, to some extent, a consequence of universal service. I've noticed that whenever I talk to postal workers I feel uncomfortably transparent, epistemically disadvantaged. The workers don't have to know the particulars of my personal involvement with mail, like the fact that I religiously make carbon copies of my personal letters, or that I've changed my address sixteen times in the last five years (in the last year alone I've had four addresses in Philadelphia), or that as a boy I collected all three variations of the famously flawed 1962 Dag Hammarskjöld issue, or that I consider a postage scale the one really indispensable small appliance. What postal workers know about me is what they know about absolutely everybody: I'm a customer.

Like the Catholic clergy, the Postal Service is stranger to us than we are to it. Oprah Winfrey makes a koan of the question: Why do postal workers shoot each other? Despite its ubiquity, the post office remains among the most recondite of American work environments. It's a foreign country within the country. It has its own interactive satellite television network, via which workers receive news and exhortations from L'Enfant Plaza in Washington.

Many workers keep their postal lives strictly separate from their private lives. Chicago clerks and carriers who live in rough neighborhoods tell me they don't reveal their occupation to their neighbors, because working for the post office marks you as a person of means, a target for muggers. A high-level administrator tells me he's learned to say that he works for "the government," because otherwise people ask him why they didn't get their mail last Wednesday.

When postal workers hang out together, they talk about who slept with whom for a promotion, and which handler was found dead of natural causes on a sofa in the employee lounge. They speculate about the reason that Marvin Runyon's eyes weren't blinking during a television interview, about whether it was due to medication for his back pain. They revel in dog lore. I'm advised that if I'm ever set upon by a pack of strays I should Mace the one that barks first. I'm told the story of a suburban carrier who was forced to take refuge from an enraged German shepherd in a storage mailbox that he'd been throwing his banana peels and milk cartons into all summer.

On a hot June morning, I stand in the comfortably shabby work area of the Cragin station, on Chicago's West Side, while a carrier named Larry Johnson finishes tossing mail into his "case"—a console of pigeonholes with a slot for every pair of addresses on his route. Sorting a day's mail takes a carrier anywhere from an hour and a half to four hours; the workday starts as early as 5:30. "It doesn't take a hell of a lot of brains to do this job," Johnson tells me, "other than the fact that you've got to know how to read." He adds, with a laugh, that in the post office you can't always take literacy for granted. Johnson is a burly man whose blue postal slacks ride low on his hips; he's thirty-five, but his physical weariness makes him seem older. He gives me a canister of Mace (his own canister sees action two or three times a week), and I follow him outside to his car, a scarred burgundy Lincoln sedan, whose trunk he has to prop open with a tire iron while he fills it with bundles of mail and one shoebox-size parcel. In Chicago, not all carriers are provided with mail trucks.

Johnson spends more of his workday in the station than on the street, but the street is where he finds whatever meaning his job has to offer. As he loads his mailbag for the first leg of the route, he tells me that he doesn't socialize with his coworkers. "They talk too much," he says. "They tell each other their business." Like the majority of mailmen, Johnson moonlights; he's the minister of a Protestant church. Johnson's congregation doesn't know he carries mail, and his fellow carriers don't know he preaches. On the street, however, the old women waiting at their gates to exchange "good morning"s with him know exactly who he is. They give him letters to mail, money to buy them stamps, and news of the neighborhood. He points out to me a house whose owner died the previous Saturday.

It's a light mail day in a working-class neighborhood. Johnson has little but hospital bills and Walgreens flyers to feed the slots and boxes. His job is simply legwork and concentration. If he lets his mind wander—lets himself wonder whether the family at the end of the block remembered to lock up their crazy dog this morning—he forgets to deliver magazines or catalogues, which are pigeonholed separately, and he has to backtrack. His shirt darkens with sweat as we walk through the long morning shadows, through the vacancy of a residential neighborhood emptied by the morning rush hour. Children who stay home sick and writers who stay home working know this emptiness. It brings a sense of estrangement from the world, and for me that sense has always been sharpened and confirmed by the sound of a mailman's footsteps approaching and receding. To be a mailman is to inhabit this emptiness for hours, to disturb five hundred abandoned lawns, one after another. I ask Johnson to tell me the most interesting thing that has happened to him in his nine years of carrying mail. After a moment's thought, he says that nothing interesting has ever happened to him.

Perhaps the most important fact about postal work is that it's seen by those who do it as lucrative and secure; a letter carrier with six years' tenure makes better than thirty thousand dollars and can be fired only if he really messes up. Another important fact is that the work can be scary and unpleasant. The post office functions both as a springboard out of housing-project poverty and as a sanctuary for the downwardly mobile, for loners like Bartleby the Scrivener. (Melville ascribed Bartleby's emotional damage to employment at the Dead Letter Office.) Managers worry about disgruntled clerks and carriers, since many postal workers are veterans with weapons skills, and almost everybody worries about punitive assignments—to the midnight shift, to a high-crime route, to North Dakota. The organization relies heavily on top-down military-style discipline to enforce productivity, and the flip side of this discipline is deception and resentment. There are carriers who will stop at a gas station to watch a baseball game if they can get away with it. Dope is smoked and whiskey drunk on loading docks. Further up in the bureaucracy, the drugs are legal: managers tell me about their prescriptions for Valium, Klonopin, Zoloft, Prozac, Paxil. I spend an evening drinking double margaritas with three administrators who are profoundly frustrated by incompetent colleagues. They tell me that once you enter the world of postal salaries and benefits it's hard to leave, even if you hate it.

"Most people say we're overpaid and do nothing," one of them says.

"We couldn't get a job in Chicago," the second, a woman in her late forties, says. "We being with the Chicago post office? And *looking* for a job? I guess I could be a waitress somewhere. But they'd watch me very carefully."

"It's like testing positive for HIV," the third tells me.

GAYLE CAMPBELL, the person who played the central role in the fall of the Chicago post office, is a captive of both the postal world and her own perfectionism. She is a lanky, handsome woman with large eyes, a communicative brow, and thick auburn hair that she wears pinned up or in a pageboy. She has an obvious intelligence, an intensity of gesture and feeling, that can inspire devotion. The customers she has helped all characterize her as a ministering angel. Robert Pope, an interior designer, tells me, "I have not spoken to one straight shooter in the post office, except Gayle Campbell. She's a rare individual, a shining light." Other admirers of Campbell, while no less enthusiastic, admit to being unsettled by the extremity of her dedication to the Postal Service. She has turned a processing plant upside down looking for some misdirected airline tickets. She has taken packages home to her apartment, in the Uptown district, and has got out of bed to deliver them to a customer in her lobby. She routinely spends seventy hours a week on the job, while getting paid for forty. There's little boundary between her work and her identity. She calls herself a "mail freak." Her husband is a letter carrier.

Although Campbell's history is exceptional in its details, it fits the model of the career postal worker who, as an outsider in the larger world, finds a mission in service and a home in regimental authority. Campbell was born in Canada in 1950 and grew up in Edmonton and Moose Jaw. Culturally, she still considers herself Canadian, and she describes her ancestry as African, Irish, and Native American. In 1962, her family moved to Harvey, a small town south of Chicago, and Campbell, an excellent student, finished high school there before her sixteenth birthday. She immediately enlisted in the Army and served in Vietnam for two years. When she was home on leave, she took the civil-service exam and scored 99.6 out of a possible 100. Immediately upon her discharge from the Army, she reported to the postmaster in Harvey. "I was a child bride of the Postal Service," she says. "It's all I know."

Campbell worked as a letter carrier for fifteen years. In 1987 she was promoted into mail processing and began to rise rapidly. By 1991 she was a general supervisor of automation and mechanization in Chicago, with two hundred employees and thirteen supervisors working beneath her. Over the next year and a half she was shifted throughout the processing system as a troubleshooter, trainer, and auditor. In the fall of 1992, however, a reorganization of the postal bureaucracy eliminated several intermediate civil-service grades in mail processing; this appeared to preclude her further advancement. She decided to seek a slight demotion and move into delivery; her plan was to get training there, sit in an intermediate-level job for a year, and then try to jump back into processing at a high level. In January 1993 she became a delivery supervisor at the Hyde Park station, on Chicago's South Side.

That same winter, corporate customers of the Postal Service, including a consortium of regional banks known as the Chicago Clearing House, were lodging bitter complaints about their service. For fear of scaring customers away, the group never publicized the complaints, but they were in a state of acute distress about, among other things, the lockboxes, located in the Central Post Office, in which they received large checks from institutional and corporate investors. The Postal Service was officially committed to delivering ninety percent of lockbox mail in standard time. (For mail sent and delivered within the Chicago area, the standard is one day, i.e., overnight. For mail sent from Seattle, the standard for Chicago delivery is three days.) By the winter of 1993, the percentage of on-time delivery to the lockboxes was in the low sixties.

Facing heat on many fronts, Ormer Rogers, the Postal Service's Great Lakes Area manager, set up an eight-member Service Improvement Team to identify breakdowns in the processing and distribution system and work aggressively to repair them. Some of Rogers's appointments were political; others reflected professional accomplishment. The latter group included Gayle Campbell, who became the de facto leader of the team.

There was no end to the trouble she uncovered. She found carriers walking their routes with makeshift plastic tubs strapped to their carts because no one had requisitioned satchels for them. She found carriers putting undelivered mail in corner mailboxes to be collected and reprocessed. She overheard a station supervisor shouting at a customer whose post-office-box lock had been broken, "Get the fuck out of here!" She found carriers who sat in their trucks on cold days from noon to 7:30 p.m. and then returned to the station, with all their mail, to collect four hours of overtime. She went to the airmail facility at O'Hare Airport and found that jets were being allowed to depart without their contractually specified complement of mail. She went to the NBC Tower, downtown, and found that mail was delivered in sacks that were left out where anyone could open them. She dropped test letters randomly in corner mailboxes throughout the city and kept track of when they were picked up and canceled. Some of the letters ended up at a dead-letter office in Minneapolis.

Such findings, and the reports they generated, hardly endeared the Service Improvement Team to Chicago station managers. In October of 1993, Postmaster Jimmie Mason met with the team and urged it to tone down its reports. Instead of putting its criticisms in writing, he said, the team should endeavor to cooperate with the station managers; as outsiders, the team members didn't understand the pressures that a station manager had to contend with.

To Campbell, this sounded like a plea for business as usual. Her life was so bound up in the post office that she considered it an extension of herself. A "dirty" post office offended her like a dirty bathroom. Instead of toning down her reports, she made them even harsher. On November 15 and 16, during a follow-up visit to the Graceland Annex, a north-lakefront station, she listed the number of linear feet of mail that were "curtailed," or left behind, when carriers set out on their routes. Case No. 5706 had seventy-seven feet of curtailment. Other troubled cases had eighty-five, a hundred, and ninety-three feet. Under Case No. 5709 the team discovered two large sacks of collected but unprocessed mail with week-old postage meter dates. On November 17, at the Lakeview station, Campbell found mail that had been held for vacations in July still awaiting delivery. At Case No. 1342 she found Priority Mail dating from October and an Internal Revenue Service communication from September. At Case No. 1346 she turned up General Mills cereal samples from June.

Throughout 1993, Campbell had assured irate customers that Jimmie Mason was serious about cleaning up Chicago. Tenaciously optimistic, she still believed she would get a promotion for her long workdays and for the improvements her team had produced. But either she was wrong about Mason from the start or Chicago had changed him. In late November, according to Campbell, he promised a gathering of the city's station managers that the Service Improvement Team would be gone by year's end, and that they need not worry about further harassment.

That same week, however, a man named Jerry Stevens went to the Graceland station to inquire about his business mail, which had failed to materialize for four straight days. Venturing briefly into a work area, he saw a mountain of curtailment. Ninety minutes after phoning a postal-complaint line, he got a call from Graceland's station manager, who apologized for his poor service and then threatened him with arrest if he ever entered the work area again. Stevens immediately called the *Chicago Sun-Times*, and their reporter

Charles Nicodemus made the anecdote the nucleus of a blistering account of North Side postal complaints.

When the story appeared, on December 13, Rogers, the Great Lakes Area manager, ordered his staff to audit the north-lakefront stations, and requested that the Postal Inspection Service carry out a parallel study. The Inspection Service is a watchdog on a long leash: it investigates everything from employee pilferage and drug use to S&L fraud and Internet pornography. Having worked with the inspectors and found them trustworthy, Campbell had quietly begun to send them copies of her reports. Before Jimmie Mason could put the Service Improvement Team out of business, the chief postal inspector asked it to assist him in the audit.

When the new reports were completed, in early February of 1994, Mason met with each team member to discuss what he called their "upward mobility." Campbell told him she thought she would make a good station manager at Uptown, since it served her own neighborhood. Mason said she didn't have the proper background. He offered to make her a supervisor under the then Uptown manager, Thomas Nichols—who had been a frequent target of her criticisms. She said no thank you. A week later, Mason reassigned her to Hyde Park as a delivery supervisor.

THE CHICAGO POST OFFICE first became an emblem of an institution in crisis when, in October of 1966, it suffered a nasty seizure. A backlog of ten million pieces of mail overwhelmed the huge, obsolescent Central Post Office. Railroad cars and mail trucks were gridlocked on the building's approaches. For nearly three weeks, delivery was paralyzed in the city and millions of letters and parcels headed elsewhere were delayed.

Two years later, the President's Commission on Postal Organization, known as the Kappel Commission, placed the blame for the shutdown on outmoded, poorly maintained facilities and on a variety of management problems, including a vacancy in the office of city postmaster over the previous six months, the "retirement of an unusually large number of experienced supervisors at the end of 1965," low employee morale, "a sick leave ratio double the national average," and "the lowest postal productivity record in the nation." *Plus ça change*: the list is practically a point-by-point diagnosis of the Chicago postal crisis of 1994.

The Central Post Office at 433 West Van Buren Street, now sixty-one years old, is still the largest freestanding postal facility in the country, and is a monument to all the ways in which vital information is no longer transmitted. The green waters of the Chicago River lap against its underpinnings. Its subbasements give onto the platforms of Union Station, to which trains have all but ceased to carry mail, and the eight-lane Eisenhower Expressway punches straight through its flanks. In the quiet, cavernous lobby, brass bas-relief medallions depict five transport options that the post office had availed itself of by 1933: sailing ship, steamship, airplane, stagecoach, and railroad. A freestanding Philatelic Center sells hummingbirds and self-adhesive squirrels and, in every shape and color, love, **LOVE**, *Love*—the cheery abstraction that American postage commemorates like royalty.

The functions of the Central Post Office will soon be divided between a new plant being built across the street, at a cost of a quarter billion dollars, and a smaller plant in the northwest corner of the city, which is beginning to come on line. For now, the old plant still processes most of the Second City's mail. At six in the evening, workers of both sexes toil in the eternal diesely gloom of subterranean loading docks, taking plastic tubs of mail from collection trucks and sending them upstairs to the "waterfall"—a system of belts and chutes up which incoming letters must struggle like spawning salmon. A carpeted roller shunts everything unfit for automated processing (bent things, thick things, ragged things) into a hamper for special treatment. Automation and mechanization have vastly speeded mail processing since 1966, but over the same period the overall volume of mail has more than doubled. Four-foot shrink-wrapped blocks of *TV Guide*, brute cubes of commercial matter, sit idly on pallets. Supervisors wear buttons that say, "I am part of the solution." There's a backwater dustiness to the place. Sooty windows spread evening sunshine onto battered parquet floors and government-issue gray furniture. Clerks moving neither swiftly nor slowly carry trays from egress points to ingress points. The plant, in its antiquity, is appallingly vertical. The upper-floor loading ramps were designed to accommodate dray horses.

My official guide through the Chicago postal system is a sunny, petite, softspoken communications specialist named Debra Hawkins. Everywhere we go inside the Central Post Office, she meets former coworkers plangent with delight at seeing her, and Hawkins is eloquent on the theme of "the postal family." She speaks of postal bowling teams, postal golf teams, postal basketball teams. "The atmosphere is very close-knit," she says. "We have individuals here with fifty-plus years of service. This is their real family. They live to come to work at the post office."

If the family works so well together, then why are Chicago's customer satisfaction ratings consistently so low? Of the various explanations that Hawkins and other family members offer me, an impressive number implicate the public. (1) Customers don't understand that not everyone can be the first stop on a carrier's route. (2) Customers remember the one bad experience they ever had and forget the frequent good experiences. (3) Customers move a lot, and they misuse or fail to fill out Change of Address cards. (4) Customers don't believe in apartment numbers, and often they change apartments within the same building without correcting their address. (5) Customers refuse to put their names on their mailboxes. (6) Immigrants address their mail in a foreign style. (7) With gentrification, the population on the North Side has grown more rapidly than stations can be expanded. (8) More and more people are starting home-based businesses, which add to the postal burden. (9) Customers address mail in a scrawl that automated sorters can't decipher. (10) Press coverage accentuates the negative. And anyway (11) service is just as bad in many other big cities.

On the one hand, these explanations reflect the kind of denial, both literal and psychological, that has allowed service in Chicago to remain terrible despite the constant drumming of informed complaint. All manner of codependencies can flourish in the bosom of a family under stress. Rather than admit that someone in the family is doing a very bad job, some employees of the post office will argue (Explanation No. 12) that "the people who get the most mail"—in other words, the Postal Service's most valuable customers—"complain the most."

On the other hand, some of the family's impatience with the public is justified. When I use Federal Express, I accept as a condition of business that its standardized forms must be filled out in printed letters. An e-mail address off by a single character goes nowhere. Transposing two digits in a phone number gets me somebody speaking heatedly in Portuguese. Electronic media tell you instantly when you've made an error; with the post office, you have to wait. Haven't we all at some point tested its humanity? I send mail to friends in Upper Molar, New York (they live in Upper Nyack), and expect a stranger to laugh and deliver it in forty-eight hours. More often than not, the stranger does. With its mission of universal service, the Postal Service is like an urban emergency room contractually obligated to accept every sore throat, pregnancy, and demented parent that comes its way. You may have to wait for hours in a dimly lit corridor. The staff may be short-tempered and dilatory. But eventually you will get treated. In the Central Post Office's Nixie unit—where mail arrives that has been illegibly or incorrectly addressed—I see street numbers in the seventy thousands; impossible pairings of zip codes and streets; addresses without a name, without a street, without a city; addresses that consist of the description of a building; addresses written in water-based ink that rain has blurred. Skilled Nixie clerks study the orphans one at a time. Either they find a home for them or they apply that most expressive of postal markings, the vermilion finger of accusation that lays the blame squarely on you, the sender.

Not all of the postal family's explanations of Chicago's woes implicate the public. There's a great deal of talk about the harsh winter of 1994 (Explanation No. 13). There's also talk about management. Debra Hawkins notes that Chicago has had seven postmasters in the last seven years, each with a different plan, and that postal executives transferred from warmer, more suburban parts of the country often lack the heart to deal with the system's problems and take early retirement instead. Chicago real estate is a particular headache: modernization of the city's processing facilities was delayed for years when the post office set its heart on a piece of land for which the city planning commission had other ideas.

Finally, and most plausibly, the postal family blames Marvin Runyon's reorganization of the Postal Service. A longtime auto-company executive and a former head of the Tennessee Valley Authority, Runyon became Postmaster General in July 1992, and immediately launched an attack on the postal bureaucracy. He announced his intention to eliminate thirty thousand "overhead" personnel, and he offered a bonus of six months' pay to any eligible employee who took retirement by October 3, 1992. The buyout offer—part of the most radical reorganization of a federal agency since Eisenhower overhauled the Pentagon—proved immensely popular. By the time all the forms were in, forty-eight thousand postal employees had taken the early out. The trouble was that only fourteen thousand of them occupied "overhead" positions. The rest were senior carriers, clerks, mail handlers, and postmasters.

The buyout hit Chicago particularly hard. A system as antiquated as Chicago's runs on expertise, and in late 1992 it lost fifteen hundred of its most senior employees, or nearly ten percent of its workforce. Former processing and administrative personnel were sent to work in stations with few skilled people available to train them. Throughout 1993, there simply weren't enough bodies to do the job. Because management could not afford to suspend anyone, it instituted a program of "paper suspensions," under which workers could receive as many as three suspensions for misconduct and still not miss a day of pay.

All this had a predictable effect on discipline. More subtle was the damage to morale. Without good supervision, the only reward for letter carriers who work hard and complete their routes by early afternoon—and such carriers, it should be stressed, form the majority at most stations—is to be given the leftover work of lazy coworkers. The reward for bad carriers, however, the ones who drink away the afternoon and finish their routes at nightfall, is overtime pay. Poor supervision produces a system of inverted incentives, a system that executives in Washington like to call "the Culture." Those postal workers who are under the sway of the Culture do as little work as they can get away with, except on alternate Thursdays. Two Thursdays a month, carriers can pick up their paychecks as soon as they complete their route, and the entire city of Chicago has its mail by early afternoon.

Erich Walch, a lifelong Chicagoan who works in Evanston, is one of the many carriers for whom service is its own reward. Walch believes that Postal Service management fails to appreciate the intelligence and hard work of dedicated carriers. He says that's why the frustration level among them is so high. "A lot of people get to the point where they say, 'I have done everything I can, so I'm going to do less. I will take out only first- and second-class mail. I will take out maybe an extra one or two bulk-rate letters. And I'll walk real slow. And there's always tomorrow.'"

Station managers, for their part, complain that cumbersome labor agreements and obstructionist unions prevent them from enforcing discipline. This view is contested by union officials, including Walch (he's an assistant steward), who insist that managers are simply too lazy or uninformed or snowed under with paperwork to follow the rules. Indeed, the supposed adversarial relationship between supervisors and unions has the aspect of a convenient myth. The unions provide managers with an excuse for their failure to manage, which, in turn, enhances union power at a station; productivity falls through the cracks.

The Culture pervades the bureaucracy as well. Administrators in Chicago, an amazingly demoralized lot, still lament the incompetence of the managers who came to power under the 1992 reorganization. Most Postal Service employees believe career advancement to be tainted by favoritism; and although nepotism is seldom flagrant, the Chicago post office is quite literally a family, an extended family of aunts, uncles, brothers-in-law, and girlfriends. One upper-level administrator tells me, "The people who've been promoted above us, we've been asked by management to train."

This particular administrator, in despair over her boss's stupidity, recently bought a straw voodoo doll from a vendor in the Haitian community in Rogers Park. She paid ten dollars extra to have the doll cursed in her boss's name. The doll came with three pearl-headed hatpins, with which she pierced its head, heart, and stomach. The following morning, her office was abuzz with the news that her boss was being transferred out of Chicago. Not long after the transfer, he was struck by a serious illness of an undisclosed nature.

EARLY IN THE MORNING of February 4, 1994, in the parking lot of the Lakeview station on Irving Park Road, the postal family's dysfunction bore spectacular fruit. A letter carrier who couldn't start his truck opened the truck of a coworker, Carrier 1345, for a jump start. In the rear cargo area he found a hundred sacks of undelivered mail—what turned out to be 40,100 pieces in all, with 484 different addresses. The oldest envelopes bore postmarks from December.

Word of the discovery reached Gayle Campbell when the postal inspectors asked the Service Improvement Team to count the contents of the hundred sacks. (They did it mechanically, with optical character readers.) She was bitterly unsurprised by Carrier 1345's malfeasance. In a November report she had cited him as an ineffective worker who habitually curtailed his mail, and it was obvious that nothing had been done in the meantime to improve his performance. Now she decided to pass the information to a person who might actually use it.

The person she chose was Charles Nicodemus. Since his December *Sun-Times* article appeared, Chicagoans had been bombarding the newspaper's offices with postal anecdotes, but the newspaper didn't have enough hard news to pursue a follow-up. Then, on January 21, Nicodemus got a call from Alderman Patrick O'Connor. O'Connor said that one of his constituents—Debra Doyle—had been speaking to a postal worker who was willing to tell stories and name names. Nicodemus leaped at the chance to cultivate Gayle Campbell.

When Nicodemus tried to confirm the story of Carrier 1345, the post office lied to him repeatedly. Even after the *Sun-Times* ran the first of three stories on the incident, postal spokesmen continued to deny, for nearly a full day, that the sacks of mail had been discovered accidentally. These lies, along with the news that Chicago's postal-customer-satisfaction index had dropped to an all-time low of sixty-four percent, led the *Sun-Times*, on February 20, to run an editorial calling for the removal of Jimmie Mason.

By the time the editorial appeared, Campbell had returned to Hyde Park. But even as she began to work with Nicodemus, she'd kept hoping that Ormer Rogers, the regional manager, would be as appalled as she was by his staff's reports. Her final disillusionment occurred at the Ashburn station, in southwest Chicago, where she attended an all-city delivery-management meeting in late February. The main floor of the station was a chin-high sea of mail. "I opened the door and I said, '*God*, this is not a post office, it's a *warehouse*,'" she says. On their way to the second floor, Ormer Rogers and fifty station managers and more than two hundred supervisors waded through the mail without remark, as if it didn't exist. "I knew then that I was working for the wrong ones," Campbell says. "I knew then that they were not serious about improving anything." Despairing, she gave Nicodemus the final reports on the audits that Rogers had commissioned in December. The reports produced a *Sun-Times* cover on March 2 ("POSTAL PROBES FIND A MESS") and a string of rich follow-ups: eight hundred linear feet of mail going nowhere at the Lincoln Park station; supervisors tolerating drug and alcohol use by workers during working hours; the Service Improvement Team silenced and disbanded.

Campbell also faxed copies of the team's final report to the Washington office of Senator Paul Simon, who had heard about her from Patrick O'Connor. Simon and his fellow Illinois senator, Carol Moseley-Braun, sent a joint letter to Marvin Runyon urging him to visit Chicago personally. Runyon, afraid of walking into a hornet's nest, refused. Simon then called him at his home in Nashville (Runyon commutes by jet to Washington) and persuaded him to reconsider. Runyon dispatched his second-in-command, chief operating officer Joseph R. Caraveo, along with two other national vice-presidents, to prepare the way for his own visit.

On the Friday before Runyon's visit, in one of those "accidents" that fuel paranoid conspiracy theories, twenty thousand pieces of mail bearing dates between 1979 and 1992 turned up in garbage cans behind a house in southwest Chicago; the retired carrier who had owned the house confessed that because he was unable to finish his route on time he had habitually taken his work home with him. On that same Friday, the police found a two-hundred-pound pile of fresh mail burning in a walkway beneath a rail viaduct. The guilty carrier, Darnesia Bullock, later explained that, with Caraveo conducting random inspections throughout the city, carriers had been under intense pressure not to leave mail behind in stations. The walkway had presented itself to her as a logical repository. Bullock conjectured that homeless people had set fire to the mail.

The city was in a fractious mood when Runyon arrived. His visit culminated in a "town meeting" at the Broadway Armory, in the Uptown district. Officially the meeting was a City Council Finance Committee hearing on the economic impact of poor mail service. Runyon, Mason, and the Chicago mail-processing director, Celestine Green, sat at a table with the air of defendants at a war-crimes tribunal, facing an ocean of accusers and a sprinkling of defenders. While members of the Progressive Labor Party passed out flyers demanding eight hours' pay for six hours' work, Runyon offered his apologies to Chicago and promised to send in a task force to clean things up. Witnesses at the open mikes told caustic jokes and sang derisive songs. Marilyn Katz articulated her frustration, and Debra Doyle related a sound-bite-sized story of missing gas bills—one that was rebroadcast on TV for months afterward.

After Runyon left Chicago, a twenty-seven-member task force of skilled managers from around the country arrived to continue the work of the unthanked and largely unpromoted Service Improvement Team. Familiar promises were made as if for the first time, and media attention waned temporarily. But Jimmie Mason's days as postmaster were numbered.

On April 25, Van H. Seagraves, the publisher of the *Business Mailers Review*, broke the story that Celestine Green had spent two hundred thousand dollars of maintenance funds to refurbish her office suite with hardwood kitchen cabinets, a marble bathroom, and an air conditioner for each of the suite's seven windows. Rumor had it that word of the renovation quite literally leaked out when water from Green's whirlpool bath came through the ceiling of the express-mail unit, two floors down. What made things worse was that by the end of 1995 the entire Central Post Office was to be vacated. Green's misjudgment was so egregious that postal management in Washington had no choice but to remove her. While they were at it, on May 3 they removed Ormer Rogers and Jimmie Mason. This being the Postal Service, it was all done gently. Although Rogers received a demotion, none of the executives took a cut in pay or benefits. Rogers was sent to Kansas City, Mason to South Carolina, and Green to the southern suburbs of Chicago, where her husband manages the processing plant.

With Runyon's task force at work in Chicago and the top managers gone, the cloud of fallout drifted east toward Washington. At congressional hearings held in early June, members of the board of postal governors—the presidentially appointed overseers of the Postal Service—expressed contrition and anger. Marvin Runyon announced yet another reorganization of the postal hierarchy, reuniting Delivery with Processing, divisions that he'd divorced in 1992. The reorganization drew fire from U.S. Representative William L. Clay, who noted that only one of ten new regional vice-presidents was black, and it apparently exhausted the patience of one postal governor, Robert Setrakian, who privately called on his fellow governors to remove Runyon before the Postal Service fell apart altogether. The sense of crisis deepened in July, when the *Washington Post* reported that postal inspectors had found millions of pieces of mail in four trailers at a processing plant in suburban Maryland, which was unable or unwilling to do its daily job.

In each of these events, the fall of the Chicago post office resonated. When Debra Doyle met Gayle Campbell, the boundary between two worlds had been breached. Doyle brought Campbell to Nicodemus, who in turn opened the postal world to the Chicago public; with the arrival of Marvin Runyon from Washington and *Eye to Eye with Connie Chung* from New York, it became inevitable that heads would roll.

A coda to the fall was provided on Saturday, May 7, when firefighters responding to an electrical fire in a condominium in Palatine Township, a northwestern suburb of Chicago, found their access to the attic blocked by a wall of letters and parcels in the master-bedroom closet. A stray bundle of mail fell on a fireman's foot; it bore addresses on the North Side of Chicago. The haul consisted of 3,396 pieces of first-class mail (including one Visa card taken from its envelope but never signed or used), 1,138 pieces of second-class mail, 364 pounds of bulk business mail, and 1,136 compact discs.

The condominium belonged to Robert K. Beverly, a seven-year postal veteran letter carrier attached to Chicago's Irving Park station, who began taking mail home with him in his used Jaguar for fear of being disciplined for not completing his route. What's mystifying about this story is that no one on his route is known to have complained about missing mail. His arrest took the Irving Park station completely by surprise.

The postal family tells me that the incident was an anomaly. It calls Beverly a bad apple or a sicko, his actions an indication of nothing but the darkness in his own heart. The family says the clustering of bad apples in Chicago this spring was adventitious. Publicity from one discovery led to others. Many of the misdeeds that came to light were unfresh. Things are no different in any other city.

When I recite these excuses to Gayle Campbell, she shakes her head grimly, like the hanging judge she is. She says that in a Service Improvement Team report in 1993 she flagged Beverly's route as "a troubled case," littered with old mail. She believes that there are other, undiscovered Robert Beverlys in Chicago. Having interviewed Beverly's foreman ("the most lackadaisical, unconcerned gentleman I've ever met") and the Irving Park station manager, she is able to explain the mysterious lack of complaints. "There were complaints," she says. "But I know they didn't keep a complaint log, because I gigged them for that. They didn't have one complaint log for me. I addressed that issue. They had their feet up on the desk and they were talking about the ballgame. There were twenty people outside waiting to be serviced and two clerks at the window."

———

THAT SYSTEMIC FAILURES could persist for ten years in the primary communication network for one of the country's largest cities and financial centers, and that it took the combined impact of a maverick administrator, media attention, and a congressional delegation to force the system to address those failures, raises serious questions about the long-term viability of both the United States Postal Service and United States cities.

Five years after the Chicago crisis of 1966, the old Post Office Department was reorganized as the United States Postal Service, a federally owned "corporation" over which Congress and the President had oversight but no direct control. The Kappel Commission had concluded that only by operating as a self-supporting business could the Post Office become flexible enough to survive in the modern world. Congress and the President lost the power of political patronage at the post office, but they also shed the burden of running it and covering its deficits. Instead of taking the heat when the public complained about rates or service, they could join in the criticism.

The Chicago postal crisis of 1994 shows the results of this policy. The inhabitants of large cities are now, more than ever, second-class citizens. It's poignant to see an old Congressman like Sidney Yates, who worked in Washington with Truman, shake his head with nostalgia for the days of patronage. The Postmaster Generalship used to be the plum awarded to the national chairman of the President's party, and until 1971 all big-city postmasters were political appointees. If your mail service was bad, you could phone your ward boss and get action. By the early nineties, as Yates discovered, you could phone the Postmaster General himself and get nothing. With fifteen thousand employees, the Chicago post office was still a political power base, handing out applications for jobs the way precinct captains once handed out pounds of bacon; but it served no master except itself. The same reorganization that protected postmasters from political harassment, and allowed craft employees to aspire to high postal office, now effectively isolated a city post office from its constituents.

In Chicago, machine politics has given way to racial politics. It escapes public comment but not private observation that unrest among white North Side postal customers began not long after Chicago got its first black postmaster, and that black postmasters have presided over increasingly strident complaints ever since. Earlier in the century, postal work was one of the few respectable careers open to educated African-Americans (Cross Damon, the main character in Richard Wright's *The Outsider*, has Sartrean dialogues with three coworkers from 433 West Van Buren Street), and it remains a primary way out for poor inner-city blacks. By the late seventies, when much of the white middle class had withdrawn to the suburbs, the Chicago post office was predominantly black. The figure today is nearly ninety percent.

Many of the problems at a station like Uptown—rampant absenteeism, rapid turnover of employees, poor morale—are aggravated by its distance from the black South Side neighborhoods where most postal workers live. Workers with tenure quickly transfer to more convenient neighborhoods. The same is true of supervisors and managers, who have been known to refer to Uptown as Siberia. The result is a perpetually inexperienced North Side workforce.

Race shaped the crisis in more fundamental ways as well. The north-lakefront stations were perceived as "troubled" because the volume of complaints was so high. In fact, other stations in Chicago were equally badly managed, but residents in poor neighborhoods either worked all day or received little in the mail besides welfare or Social Security checks. On the North Side, there were self-employed people and people of leisure who noticed when the mail came late and when they missed a week of *Wall Street Journals*. The North Side had expectations. It had learned, in the decades of the Daley machine, how to organize and how to complain. But now the rules had changed. The post office, though it looked like a city service and had once behaved like a city service, was not accountable.

In May, after the transfer of Mason, Rogers, and Green—all of them African-American—the Chicago chapter of the NAACP, noting that two of the three replacements were white and that Thomas Ranft, Green's white boss, had survived the shakeup, denounced the moves as racist. The denunciation was specious in its implication that the thousands of dedicated black postal workers in Chicago owed their jobs to skin color rather than to competence. But it illuminated, behind the post office's long reluctance to admit its shortcomings, the fear of losing black control. Gayle Campbell says that what made her a "traitor" was less her public betrayal of the postal family than the fact that she had, in the words of one manager, "brought the white man in." The white men she brought in were not only William Good and David Fields, who replaced Rogers and Green, and white politicians like Simon and Smith and Yates, but the white media establishment, which many American blacks and almost all Chicago postal workers believe to be biased against them.

In his first months in office, Rufus F. Porter, the new postmaster, has eschewed the rhetoric of family, preferring the corporate vocabulary of "initiative" and "communication" and "the entrepreneurial spirit." Porter, forty-six, is a native Californian, a onetime mail handler who earned a master's degree at night school. Visiting him on the fourth floor of the Central Post Office, I see why Celestine Green, whose bureaucratic rank was equivalent to Jimmie Mason's, had felt the need to redecorate. The Chicago postmaster's office is a sprawling plain of deep-pile carpeting with scattered settlements of heavy, carved furniture. Porter, a stocky man with strikingly erect posture, sits on the edge of a chair with his hands folded on an enormous boardroom table. He answers my questions in the clipped, forceful cadences of a cadet being drilled. "You can't teach initiative," he says. "But what you can do is create an atmosphere, an environment, where people can feel empowered. And that's what we're attempting to do. We're trying to create that atmosphere."

By most accounts, Porter is succeeding. He has removed precisely the faulty managers whom Campbell targeted in her reports, reinstituted disciplinary suspensions, and shown a willingness to spend whatever it takes to improve service in Chicago. Postal executives frustrated by their superiors may stick pins in straw dolls; but the transfer of a nonperforming administrator probably owes less to the power of voodoo than to Porter's determination as a reformer. Even the uncompromising Campbell is a convert. "He's the one that Chicago's been waiting for," she says. "We won't be the last for long."

SIMPLY NOT to be the worst anymore: it's an aspiration whose modesty must temper the optimism that Porter's efforts inspire. When I ask Frank Brennan, a national Postal Service spokesman, why cities like Chicago have been neglected for so long, he speaks of his organization's historical association with "small-town America," where a community's identity and connection to the republic were wrapped up in its little post office. Big cities, Brennan says, are part of an "evolving America," where the daily personal connections that define the postal mission are far less workable. Viewed in this way, the neglect of the Chicago post office shows itself to be part of a larger pattern of federal frustration with cities. William Henderson, the Postal Service's new chief operating officer, says, "There's no subject in a major American city that's not difficult to tackle, and the post office is one of them." Henderson believes that high population densities, in the form of traffic jams and high-rises, inevitably impede the flow of surface mail. "It's just a fact we face. Everybody is annoyed with cities, and we're annoyed, too."

The urban impediments aren't only logistical. In the early eighties, when a long-repressed urban minority gained control of the post office, many of its members were understandably less interested in attacking the deep structural problems they had inherited than in acquiring (like Celestine Green) the trappings of power long enjoyed by the old ruling faction. At the root of the troubles of the Chicago post office is the gap between the two tiers of American society, which is nowhere more visible than in big cities and which is bridged, nowadays, by little but the universal Postal Service. Maximal wealth and cutting-edge technology exist side by side with a second- and third-generation urban underclass for which employment at the post office may seem less a responsibility than an extension of its federally funded entitlements. Angry as Campbell was at postal management's betrayal of the public, she was no less angry at the betrayal of the city's entry-level workers. "They *want* instruction," she says. "They *want* guidance. But if you've got somebody who's back there in the office sucking on a cup of coffee and talking on the phone to Janie in the next station, you're not going to get that production."

However much big cities vex the Postal Service, they still generate the high volume of mail that pays for universal service. If they are structurally doomed to slower service, as Henderson suggests, then something has to suffer—either the cities or the Postal Service. And it's clear that the cities are suffering already. By subtracting from the quality of life and adding to the cost of doing business, poor mail service helps drive corporations and affluent individuals to the suburbs. It's a process that dismays committed city dwellers, like Marilyn Katz. "To me," Katz says, "cities are the lifeblood of culture, the lifeblood of democracy, because they're one of the few places where you have a real integration of different kinds of people. One of the things that's happened, as society has become more stratified, is that in almost every realm of public service cities have become second-class citizens. The Postal Service works in Wilmette. It doesn't work in Chicago."

The Postal Service, for its part, is not harmed by the flight to Wilmette. What does pose a threat is virtual flight, the flight to alternative information-delivery systems. Business-to-business correspondence, which the Postal Service estimates has diminished by a third in the last five years, is where the impact of faxes and e-mail is most visible. So far, this loss has been offset by a robust flow of first- and third-class advertising mail. And boosters of the Postal Service, like William Henderson, sound confident that its usefulness will survive the development of the national information superstructure that Vice-President Gore so warmly heralds. "Mail is the most interactive product in the United States today," Henderson says. "You can put a letter in your pocket, read it anywhere. It's the ultimate in interactivity."

The problem is that the Postal Service need not lose much business to run into serious trouble. In his first appearance before Congress, in 1992, Marvin Runyon described how rising postal rates had already driven third-class advertisers to alternative forms of delivery, like television, or flyers hung from doorknobs. "As we increase our rates," Runyon said, "the Postal Service will be privatized by outside sources. Not by us but by outside sources."

Because of its commitment to universal service, the Postal Service has large fixed infrastructure costs. It can't shrink and grow like most ordinary companies. For this reason, the Internet won't have to render it obsolete in order to throw it into crisis. The information superhighway need merely exist as an increasingly attractive alternative. If enough mailers, private and corporate, begin to use it, an economic thunderstorm of upward-spiraling rates and downward-spiraling service and mail volume will ensue. When this happens, Congress will have two choices: either subsidize or privatize. Returning to federal subsidy of postal rates would require an honest admission that universal flat-rate service is an expensive ideal; it would cost taxpayers money. The possibility exists, therefore, that the Postal Service will be privatized, with lucrative markets like Wilmette and the Chicago Loop being sold off to the highest bidder, and the post office remaining as an underfunded rump, a carrier of last resort, serving the rural and urban poor.

AT 2:30 on a humid summer afternoon, I drive west from the Loop on a superhighway. While staying in the city I haven't spent more than twenty-five minutes traveling to an appointment, on the El or on foot. On the national transportation infrastructure, by maneuvering aggressively, I reach the city limits in just under an hour. Traffic in the suburbs is no better. Cars stretch bumper to bumper into the western distance on roads that are being widened, or widened further, even as we drive on them. Only at my destination, a new mail-processing plant in Carol Stream, have the industrial parks and condos paused in their advance across the cornfields.

The Postal Service's hopes of survival are pinned on growth. To avoid an upward rate spiral, losses in the volume of personal communication must be offset by gains in business-to-household mailings. Already, in the United States one in five advertising dollars is spent on direct mailing, and William Henderson believes that the figure will increase as companies realize the potential of sending out advertisements in envelopes that contain bills or that masquerade as bills. He's particularly excited about the recent proliferation of credit cards.

To keep pace with rising volumes, the Postal Service of the future will also have to be further automated, and at Carol Stream full automation is close to being a reality. The plant is a technological showcase, with conveyor belts and hoppers and pathways all painted in gum-ball colors, and a control room on whose friendly CRT screens you need only touch an interesting or troubled node with your finger and it interacts with you. There are machines that shuffle and reshuffle envelopes into the order in which a carrier delivers them. There's a machine that sprays a phosphorescent bar code on the back of each hand-addressed letter and transmits a video image of the address to Knoxville, Tennessee, where workers read and key in the zip code, which is then beamed back to Carol Stream and applied to the front of the envelope in the form of a black bar code. There's a din from facer-cancelers, from optical character readers, from letter-sorting machines, from passing motorized mule trains, from hook belts and flat-sorters and delivery bar-code sorters; but it's a level din, a supportive din. The only product of this plant is order. The fluid to which order is brought is predominantly white. It conforms agreeably to friction belts and robotic claspers. It floats, it whispers. It's called the mail stream, and, unlike the mail at Chicago's Central Post Office, it has no discernible personality. I'm absurdly pleased when I discover, in a small-parcel sack labeled "Nixie," a solitary padded mailer, somewhat torn, that is addressed to a pouch number in Prudhoe Bay, Alaska, and bears a return address of Uncertain, Texas.

Leaving Carol Stream, I drive past soybean fields and a plant that bottles Zima. At the end of a strip mall thirty-seven hundred feet long and one store thick, I happen on K's Mail Center, a bright, clean outfit that offers not only mailboxes and United States stamps but also a notary service, plain-paper faxing, desktop publishing, key duplication, wrapping paper, and humorous greeting cards. The proprietor, a personable Nigerian immigrant named Chris Kator, keeps long business hours and provides every imaginable shipping service. Kator tells me he acquired his franchise because of the synergy among the services he offers, the opportunities for growth. He says he has no complaints with the Postal Service, although few of his customers choose it for sending packages.

In the air-conditioned cool of Kator's store, amid unhumming beige equipment in its Powr-Savr mode, the march to-ward privatization—toward a fragmented republic of terrific bargains and unconscionable gougings—seems to me irre-sistible. So does the idea that the place to which Americans should go to participate directly in the system that governs them is not a small-town post office with Old Glory in its lobby but an exurban retail outlet with Day-Glo banners (WE SELL BEEPERS) in its plate-glass window.

Back in the city, however, after another unpleasant super-highway experience, I succumb to nostalgia. I think of the delight with which Mary Ann Smith describes the Christmas card, "with a gold-foil envelope and a gold-stamped return address," that a former alderman sent her from prison. I think of my own delight when I discover that before Debra Hawkins became a communications specialist she was a clerk in the Central Post Office who sorted mail for the neigh-borhood of Pilsen, and so may have personally handled the letters I sent to my brother in his apartment there. I think of the Evanston carrier, Erich Walch, who says that the customers on his new route all hated their ex-mailman and therefore hated him. "It took over a year for some of these people to look at me as a human being, to not grunt when I said good morning to them, but I've changed their percep-tions," he says. I think of the old Polish-American women who stand on their porches and break into smiles as they take envelopes from the hand of the African-American car-rier who is also, in his other life, a minister. I think of the mail piling up for me at home in Philadelphia, and I feel a keen anticipation.

What makes the sight of a person in postal uniform a welcome one is not simply the possibility that he is bring-ing us a billet-doux or a sweepstakes check. It's the hope and faith that the Postal Service *serves* us. Ever since it came by stage rider to remote Appalachian settlements, the U.S. Mail has offered to a lonely people a universal laying on of human hands. It's as sacred as anything gets in this country. The burning of mail in a viaduct deals the same blow to our innocence as the pederasty of priests; and as soon as a sacrament is administered virtually, in the manner of televised evangelism, it reduces worshippers to consumers. Of all the Chicagoans I've spoken with, not even the most despairing has suggested that the Postal Service be dismantled.

On August 1, Rufus Porter granted Gayle Campbell's long-standing request to be transferred from the Hyde Park station. She is now coordinator of the External First-Class Measurement Team. When Campbell told her doctor what her new job entailed—monitoring the pick-up and delivery of first-class mail without being able to affect what she monitors—he said, "They're trying to kill you." She recently paid $278 of her own money to a Kelly girl who entered measurement data for a day, and when even this didn't satisfy her she got up at two in the morning to enter data herself in a notebook computer. "If I don't do it," she says, "who will?"

Campbell and I differ on what's killing her. As the actual victim, she looks for agents. She sees an evil alliance of deceptive managers and arrogant unions who are trashing her ideal of customer service. I, on the other hand, am afflicted with a double vision of the personal and the structural. I see a woman whose work is her life. I also see an economic system killing the city that Campbell lives in—the very city that invented the modern commodities market. Chicago's post office is a relic of an older system of responsibilities, from which its own management in Washington is scrambling to distance itself. To survive in the corporatized world, the

Postal Service now aspires to be just another medium—to be the same efficient collector of consumer dollars and transmitter of products that the Internet, for all its champions' pious talk of "nonlinearity" and "pluralism," is going to be. Technological capitalism is an infernal machine. It always has its way with us. If it doesn't dismantle the Postal Service from without, it will steal its soul from within. The attachment of Americans to their post office is pure nostalgia. It's the double vision of a people whose hearts don't like what their desires have created.

When I finally get back home to Philadelphia, two inches of mail are waiting for me. William Henderson will be pleased to know that I've received four separate credit-card solicitations, each forwarded promptly and at no extra cost from one of my previous addresses. There are also bulk mailings from representatives whom I personally did not elect, bills for the credit cards I already have, four issues of the *Los Angeles Times Book Review*, whose yellow forwarding stickers urge me to Notify Sender of New Address, a large envelope with Ed McMahon's face on it, three meaty Val-Paks which I'm certain hold interesting offers of discount carpet shampooing and bonus pizzas at Little Caesars, and a solitary first-class letter from a friend of mine in England. Although he must have sent it weeks ago, I tear it open urgently. He asks me why I haven't written.

[1994]

ERIKA IMPORTS

FOR THREE YEARS, when I was in high school, I was the packing boy for a German émigré couple, Erika and Armin Geyer, who operated a small business, Erika Imports, in the basement of their gloomy house in suburban St. Louis. Several afternoons a week I left behind a pleasant-smelling world of liberty and sanity and climbed the stairs to the Geyers' dark front porch and peered into a living room where Erika and Armin and their overfed schnauzer were typically sprawled, snoring, on old wooden-ankled German chairs and sofas. The air inside was heavy with schnitzel grease and combusted cigarette. On the dining-room table were ruins of *Mittagessen*: plates flecked with butter and parsley, a partially trashed whipped-cream cake, an empty Moselle bottle. Erika, in a quilted housecoat that gaped to reveal an Old World bra or girdle, continued to snore while

Armin roused himself and led me to my work station in the basement.

Erika Imports had exclusive contracts with workshops in Communist East Germany that produced handmade giftwares—enameled Easter Bunny and Santa figurines, cunningly painted wooden eggs, deluxe carved crèche sets, hardwood tangram puzzles, candle-propelled Christmas carousels in sizes up to three feet tall—that gift shops throughout the central tier of states were forever mad to buy. Erika could therefore be high-handed with her customers. She sent out broken merchandise or merchandise reglued, by Armin, with insulting carelessness. She wrote her invoices in a German cursive illegible to Americans. She slashed the orders of customers who'd fallen out of favor; she said, "They want twenty—ach! I send them three."

My job in the basement consisted of assembling cardboard cartons, filling them with smaller boxes and excelsior, checking the invoices to be sure the orders were complete, and sealing the cartons with paper tape that I wetted with a sea sponge. Since I was paid better than the minimum wage, and since I enjoyed topological packing puzzles, and since the Geyers liked me and praised my German-language skills and gave me lots of cake, it was remarkable how fiercely I hated the job—how I envied even those friends of mine who manned the deep-fry station at Long John Silver's or cleaned the oil traps at Kentucky Fried Chicken.

I hated, in part, the arbitrary infringements of autonomy: the Saturday afternoons torpedoed by Erika's sudden barking, on the telephone, "Ja, komm immediately!" I hated the extravagant molds that grew on the sea sponge in its pan of scummy water. There was also the schnauzer and everything relating to the schnauzer. There was Armin's disinclination to perform any manual task without first licking his fingers; there was his stertorous breathing while he pecked out UPS slips on a manual Olivetti. There was Erika's powerful body odor and the powerful perfumes with which she failed to mask it. And there was the kitschy, high-volume side of her business, the seasonal flood of Styrofoam bells and sentimental snowmen and cheap plastic toys that caused me to imagine all too vividly the aesthetic wasteland of heartland hospital gift shops.

The main reason I envied my friends in the fast-food kitchens, though, was that their work seemed to me so wonderfully *impersonal*. They never had to see their supervisor's blue-veined stomach falling out of her housecoat, a toppled glass of cheap champagne soaking into the rug by her feet. Hamburger fragments and parsleyed potatoes weren't decaying in a dog's bowl at their job sites. Most important, their mothers did not feel sorry for their bosses.

My own mother was always after me, in the years following high school, to stop in at the Geyers' and "visit" with them when I came home from college, or to greet them after a church service and ease their social isolation for a moment, or to send them postcards when I went to Europe. My mother herself, in a spirit of Christian charity and masochism, sometimes invited the Geyers to dinner and a game of bridge during which Erika, at escalating volumes and with a diminishing ratio of English to German, abused Armin for his sins of bidding and his crimes of cardplay, and Armin went crimson in the face and began to bray in self-defense. Although my mother fervently believed in personal responsibility, she resorted to the most transparent ruses if I was in the house when Erika called. She handed me the phone ("Jonathan wants to say hello to you!") and then, when I tried to return the phone, she made me tell Erika that she would call her back "next week." Poor Erika and Armin, with their blood clots, their broken bones, their abrupt hospitalizations! Each step of their downward progress was faithfully reported by my mother in her letters to me. Now everyone is dead, and I wonder: Is there no escaping the personal? In twenty-five years I have yet to find a work situation that isn't somehow about family, or loyalty, or sex, or guilt, or all four. I'm beginning to think I never will.

[2001]

SIFTING THE ASHES

CIGARETTES are the last thing in the world I want to think about. I don't consider myself a smoker, don't identify with the forty-six million Americans who have the habit. I dislike the smell of smoke and the invasion of nasal privacy it represents. Bars and restaurants with a stylish profile—with a clientele whose exclusivity depends in part on the toxic clouds with which it shields itself—have started to disgust me. I've been gassed in hotel rooms where smokers stayed the night before and gassed in public bathrooms where men use the nasty, body-odorish Winston as a laxative. ("Winston tastes bad / Like the one I just had" runs the grammatically unimpeachable parody from my childhood.) Some days in New York it seems as if two-thirds of the people on the sidewalk, in the swirls of car exhaust, are carrying lighted cigarettes; I maneuver constantly to stay upwind. To stem the emissions of downstairs neighbors, I've used a caulking gun to seal gaps between the floorboards and baseboards in my apartment. The first casino I ever went to, in Nevada, was a vision of damnation: row upon row of middle-aged women with foot-long faces puffing on foot-long Kents and compulsively feeding silver dollars to the slots. When someone tells me that cigarettes are sexy, I think of Nevada. When I see an actress or actor drag deeply in a movie, I imagine the pyrenes and phenols ravaging the tender epithelial cells and hardworking cilia of their bronchi, the monoxide and cyanide binding to their hemoglobin, the heaving and straining of their chemically panicked hearts. Cigarettes are a distillation of a more general paranoia that besets our culture, the awful knowledge of our bodies' fragility in a world of molecular hazards. They scare the hell out of me.

Because I'm capable of hating almost every attribute of cigarettes (let's not even talk about cigars), and because I smoked what I believed was my last cigarette five years ago and have never owned an ashtray, it's easy for me to think of myself as nicotine-free. But if the man who bears my name is not a smoker, then why is there again a box fan for exhaust purposes in his living-room window? Why, at the end of every workday, is there a small collection of cigarette butts in the saucer on the table by this fan?

Cigarettes were the ultimate taboo in the culturally conservative household I grew up in—more fraught, even, than sex or drugs. The year before I was born, my mother's father died of lung cancer. He'd taken up cigarettes as a soldier in the First World War and smoked heavily all his life. Everyone who met my grandfather seems to have loved him, and however much I may sneer at our country's obsession with health—at the elevation of fitness to godliness and of sheer longevity to a mark of divine favor—the fact remains that if my grandfather hadn't smoked I might have had the chance to know him.

My mother still speaks of cigarettes with loathing. I secretly started smoking them myself in college, perhaps in part because she hated them, and as the years went by I developed a fear of exposure very similar, I'm convinced, to a gay man's fear of coming out to his parents. My mother had created my body out of hers, after all. What rejection of parentage could be more extreme than deliberately poisoning that body? To come out is to announce: this is who I am, this is my identity. The curious thing about "smoker" as a label of identity, though, is its mutability. I could decide tomorrow not to be one anymore. So why not pretend not to be one today? To take control of their lives, people tell themselves stories about the person they want to be. It's the special privilege of the smoker, who at times feels so strongly the resolve to quit that it's as if he'd quit already, to be given irrefutable evidence that these stories aren't necessarily true: here are the butts in the ashtray, here is the smell in the hair.

As a smoker, then, I've come to distrust not only my stories about myself but *all* narratives that pretend to unambiguous moral significance. And it happens that in recent months Americans have been subjected to just such a narrative in the daily press, as "secret" documents shed light on the machinations of Big Tobacco, industry scientists step forward to indict their former employers, nine states and a consortium of sixty law firms launch massive liability suits, and the Food and Drug Administration undertakes to regulate cigarettes as nicotine-delivery devices. The prevailing liberal view that Big Tobacco is Evil with a capital *E* is summed up in the *Times*'s review of Richard Kluger's excellent new history of the tobacco industry, *Ashes to Ashes*. Chiding Kluger for (of all things) his "objectivity" and "impartiality," Christopher Lehmann-Haupt suggests that the cigarette business is on a moral par with slavery and the Holocaust. Kluger himself, impartial or not, repeatedly links the word "angels" with antismoking activists. In the introduction to his book he offers a stark pair of options: either cigarette manufacturers are "businessmen basically like any other" or they're "moral lepers preying on the ignorant, the miserable, the emotionally vulnerable, and the genetically susceptible."

My discomfort with these dichotomies may reflect the fact that, unlike Lehmann-Haupt, I have yet to kick the habit. But in no national debate do I feel more out of synch with the mainstream. For all that I distrust American industry, and especially an industry that's vigorously engaged in buying congressmen, some part of me insists on rooting for tobacco. I flinch as I force myself to read the latest health news: SMOKERS MORE LIKELY TO BEAR RETARDED BABIES, STUDY SAYS. I pounce on particularly choice collisions of metaphor and melodrama, such as this one from the *Times*: "The affidavits are the latest in a string of blows that have undermined the air of invincibility that once cloaked the $45 billion tobacco industry, which faces a deluge of lawsuits." My sympathy with cohorts who smoke disproportionately— blue-collar workers, African-Americans, writers and artists, alienated teens, the mentally ill—expands to include the companies that supply them with cigarettes. I think: We're all underdogs now. Wartime is a time of lies, I tell myself, and the biggest lie of the cigarette wars is that the moral equation can be reduced to ones and zeroes. Or have I, too, been corrupted by the weed?

_____

I TOOK UP SMOKING as a student in Germany in the dark years of the early eighties. Ronald Reagan had recently made his "evil empire" speech, and Jonathan Schell was publishing *The Fate of the Earth*. The word in Berlin was that if you woke up to an undestroyed world on Saturday morning you were safe for another week; the assumption was that NATO was at its sleepiest late on Friday nights, that Warsaw Pact forces would choose those hours to come pouring through the Fulda Gap, and that NATO would have to go ballistic to repel them. Since I rated my chances of surviving the decade at fifty-fifty, the additional risk posed by smoking seemed negligible. Indeed, there was something invitingly apocalyptic about cigarettes. The nightmare of nuclear proliferation had a counterpart in the way cigarettes—anonymous, death-bearing, missilelike cylinders—proliferated in my life. Cigarettes are a fixture of modern warfare, the soldier's best friend, and, at a time when a likely theater of war was my own living room, smoking became a symbol of my helpless civilian participation in the Cold War.

Among the anxieties best suited to containment by cigarettes is, paradoxically, the fear of dying. What serious smoker hasn't felt the surge of panic at the thought of lung cancer and immediately lighted up to beat the panic down? (It's a Cold War logic: we're afraid of nuclear weapons, so let's build even more of them.) Death is a severing of the connection between self and world, and, since the self can't imagine not existing, perhaps what's really scary about the prospect of dying is not the extinguishment of my consciousness but the extinguishment of the world. The fear of a global nuclear holocaust was thus functionally identical to my private fear of death. And the potential deadliness of cigarettes was comforting because it allowed me, in effect, to become familiar with apocalypse, to acquaint myself with the contours of its terrors, to make the world's potential death less strange and so a little less threatening. Time stops for the duration of a cigarette: when you're smoking, you're acutely present to yourself; you step outside the unconscious forward rush of life. This is why the condemned are allowed a final cigarette, this is why (or so the story goes) gentlemen in evening dress stood puffing at the rail as the *Titanic* went down: it's a lot easier to leave the world if you're certain you've really been in it. As Goethe writes in *Faust*, "Presence is our duty, be it only a moment."

The cigarette is famously the herald of the modern, the boon companion of industrial capitalism and high-density urbanism. Crowds, hyperkinesis, mass production, numbingly boring labor, and social upheaval all have correlatives in the cigarette. The sheer number of individual units consumed surely dwarfs that of any other manufactured consumer product. "Short, snappy, easily attempted, easily completed or just as easily discarded before completion," the *Times* wrote in a 1925 editorial that Richard Kluger quotes, "the cigarette is the symbol of a machine age in which the ultimate cogs and wheels and levers are human nerves." Itself the product of a mechanical roller called the Bonsack machine, the cigarette served as an opiate for assembly-line workers, breaking up into manageable units long days of grinding sameness. For women, the *Atlantic Monthly* noted in 1916, the cigarette was "the symbol of emancipation, the temporary substitute for the ballot." Altogether, it's impossible to imagine the twentieth century without cigarettes. They show up with Zeliglike ubiquity in old photographs and newsreels, so devoid of individuality as hardly to be noticeable and yet, once noticed, utterly strange.

Kluger's history of the cigarette business reads like a history of American business in general. An industry that in 1880 was splintered into hundreds of small, family-owned concerns had by 1900 come under the control of one man, James Buchanan Duke, who by pioneering the use of the Bonsack roller and reinvesting a huge portion of his revenues in advertising, and then by alternately employing the stick of price wars and the carrot of attractive buyout offers, built his American Tobacco Company into the equivalent of Standard Oil or Carnegie Steel. Like his fellow monopolists, Duke eventually ran afoul of the trustbusters, and in 1911 the Supreme Court ordered the breakup of American. The resulting oligopoly immediately brought out new brands—Camel, Lucky Strike, and Chesterfield and Marlborough—that have vied for market share ever since. To American retailers, the cigarette was the perfect commodity, a staple that generated large profits on a small investment in shelf space and inventory; cigarettes, Kluger notes, "were lightweight and durably packed, rarely spoiled, were hard to steal since they were usually sold from behind the counter, underwent few price changes, and required almost no selling effort."

Since every brand tasted pretty much the same, tobacco companies learned early to situate themselves at the cutting edge of advertising. In the twenties, American Tobacco offered five free cartons of Lucky Strike ("it's toasted") to any doctor who would endorse it, and then launched a campaign that claimed "20,679 Physicians Say Luckies Are Less Irritating"; American was also the first company to target weight-conscious women ("When tempted to over-indulge, reach for a Lucky instead"). The industry pioneered the celebrity endorsement (tennis star Bill Tilden: "I've smoked Camels for years, and I never tire of their smooth, rich taste"), radio sponsorship (Arthur Godfrey: "I smoked two or three packs of these things [Chesterfields] every day—I feel pretty good"), assaultive outdoor advertising (the most famous was the "I'd Walk a Mile for a Camel" billboard in Times Square, which for twenty-five years blew giant smoke rings), and, finally, the sponsorship of television shows like *Candid Camera* and *I Love Lucy*. The brilliant TV commercials made for Philip Morris—Benson & Hedges smokers whose hundred-millimeter cigarettes were crushed by elevator doors; faux-hand-cranked footage of chambermaids sneaking smokes to the tune of "You've got your own cigarette now, baby"—were vital entertainments of my childhood. I remember, too, the chanted words "Silva Thins, Silva Thins," the mantra for a short-lived American Tobacco product that wooed the female demographic with such appalling copy as "Cigarettes are like girls, the best ones are thin and rich."

The most successful campaign of all, of course, was for the Marlboro, an upscale cigarette for ladies that Philip Morris reintroduced in 1954 in a filtered version for the mainstream. Like all modern products, the new Marlboro was intensively designed. The tobacco blend was strengthened so as to survive the muting of a filter, the "flip-top" box was introduced to the national vocabulary, the color red was chosen to signal strong flavor, and the graphics underwent endless tinkering before the final look, including a fake heraldic crest with the motto *Veni, vidi, vici*, was settled on; there was even market-testing in four cities to decide the color of the filter. It was in Leo Burnett's ad campaign for Marlboro, however, that the real genius lay. The key to its success was its transparency. Place a lone ranch hand against a backdrop of buttes at sunset, and just about every positive association a cigarette can carry is in the picture: rugged individualism, masculine sexuality, escape from an urban modernity, strong flavors, the living of life intensely. The Marlboro marks our commercial culture's passage from an age of promises to an age of pleasant, empty dreams.

It's no great surprise that a company smart enough to advertise as well as this ascended, in just three decades, to a position of hegemony in the industry. Kluger's account of the triumph of Philip Morris is the kind of thing that business schools have their students read for edification and inspiration: to succeed as an American corporation, the lesson might be, do exactly what Philip Morris did. Concentrate on products with the highest profit margin. Design new products carefully, then get behind them and push *hard*. Use your excess cash to diversify into businesses structurally similar to your own. Be a meritocracy. Bid preemptively. Avoid crippling debt. Patiently build your overseas markets. Never scruple to gouge your customers when you see the opportunity. Let your lawyers attack your critics. Be classy—sponsor *The Mahabarata*. Defy conventional morality. Never forget that your primary fealty is to your stockholders.

While its chief competitor, R. J. Reynolds, was growing logy and inbred down in Winston-Salem—sinking into the low-margin discount-cigarette business, diversifying disastrously, and nearly drowning in debt after its leveraged buyout by Kohlberg Kravis Roberts & Company—Philip Morris was becoming the global leader in the cigarette industry and one of the most profitable corporations in the world. By the early nineties, its share of the domestic non-discount-cigarette market was eighty percent. The value of a share of Philip Morris stock increased by a factor of 192 between 1966 and 1989. Healthy, wealthy, and wise the man who quit smoking in '64 and put his cigarette money into Philip Morris common.

The company's spectacular success is all the more remarkable for having occurred in the decades when the scientific case against cigarettes was becoming overwhelming. With the possible exception of the hydrogen bomb, nothing in modernity is more generative of paradox than cigarettes. Thus, in 1955, when the Federal Trade Commission sought to curb misleading advertising by banning the publication of tar and nicotine levels, the ruling proved to be a boon to the industry, enabling it to advertise filter cigarettes for their implicit safety even as it raised the toxic yields to compensate for the filters. So it went with the 1965 law requiring warning labels on cigarette packs, which preempted potentially more stringent state and local regulation and provided a priceless shield against future liability suits. So it went, too, with the 1971 congressional ban on broadcast cigarette advertising, which saved the industry millions of dollars, effectively froze out potential new competitors by denying them the broadcast platform, and put an end to the devastating antismoking ads then being broadcast under the fairness doctrine. Even such left-handed regulation as the 1982 increase in the federal excise tax benefited the industry, which used the tax as a screen for a series of price increases, doubling the price per pack in a decade, and invested the windfall in diversification. Every forward step taken by government to regulate smoking—the broadcast ban, the ban on in-flight smoking, the welter of local bans on smoking in public places—moved cigarettes a step further back from the consciousness of nonsmoking voters. The result, given the political power of tobacco-growing states, has been the specific exemption of cigarettes from the

Fair Labeling and Packaging Act of 1966, the Controlled Substances Act of 1970, the Consumer Product Safety Act of 1972, and the Toxic Substances Act of 1976. In the industry's defense in liability suits, the paradox can be seen in its purest form: because no plaintiff can claim ignorance of tobacco's hazards—i.e., precisely *because* the cigarette is the most notoriously lethal product in America—its manufacturers cannot be held negligent for selling it. Small wonder that until Liggett broke ranks this spring no cigarette maker had ever paid a penny in civil damages.

Now, however, the age of paradox may be coming to an end. As the nation dismantles its missiles, its attention turns to cigarettes. The wall of secrecy that protected the industry is coming down as surely as the Berlin Wall did. The Third Wave is upon us, threatening to extinguish all that is quintessentially modern. It hardly seems an accident that the United States, which is leading the way into the information age, is also in the forefront of the war on cigarettes. Unlike the nations of Europe, which have taken a more pragmatic approach to the smoking problem, taxing cigarettes at rates as high as five dollars a pack, the antismoking forces in this country bring to the battle a puritanical zeal. We need a new Evil Empire, and Big Tobacco fills the bill.

THE ARGUMENT for equating the tobacco industry with slave traders and the Third Reich goes like this: because nearly half a million Americans a year die prematurely as a direct consequence of smoking, the makers of cigarettes are guilty of mass murder. The obvious difficulty with the argument is that the tobacco industry has never physically forced anyone to smoke a cigarette. To speak of "killing" people, therefore, one has to posit more subtle forms of coercion. These fall into three categories. First, by publicly denying a truth well known to its scientists, which was that smokers were in mortal peril, the industry conspired to perpetrate a vast and deadly fraud. Second, by luring impressionable children into a habit very difficult to break, the industry effectively "forced" its products on people before they had developed full adult powers of resistance. Finally, by making available and attractive a product that it knew to be addictive, and by manipulating nicotine levels, the industry willfully exposed the public to a force (addiction) with the power to kill.

A "shocking" collection of "secret" industry documents, which was released by a disgruntled employee of Brown & Williamson and has now been published as *The Cigarette Papers*, makes it clear that Big Tobacco has known for decades that cigarettes are lethal and addictive and has done everything in its power to suppress and deny that knowledge. *The Cigarette Papers* and other recent disclosures have prompted the Justice Department to pursue perjury charges against various industry executives, and they may provide the plaintiffs now suing the industry with positive proof of tortious fraud. In no way, though, are the disclosures shocking. How could anyone who noticed that different brands have different (but consistent) nicotine levels fail to conclude that the industry can and does control the dosage? What reasonable person could have believed that the industry's public avowals of "doubt" about the deadliness of its products were anything but obligatory, ceremonial lies? If researchers unearthed a secret document proving that Bill Clinton inhaled, would we be shocked? When industry spokesmen impugn the integrity of the Surgeon General and persist in denying the undeniable, they're guilty not so much of fraud as of sounding (to borrow the word of one executive quoted by Kluger) "Neanderthal."

"The simple truth," Kluger writes, "was that the cigarette makers were getting richer and richer as the scientific findings against them piled higher and higher, and before anyone fully grasped the situation, the choice seemed to have narrowed to abject confession and surrender to the health advocates or steadfast denial and rationalization." In the early fifties, when epidemiological studies first demonstrated the link between smoking and lung cancer, cigarette executives did indeed have the option of simply liquidating their businesses and finding other work. But many of these executives came from families that had been respectably trading in tobacco for decades, and most of them appear to have been heavy smokers themselves; unlike the typical heroin wholesaler, they willingly ran the same risks they imposed on their customers. Because they were corporate officers, moreover, their ultimate allegiance was to their stockholders. If simply having stayed in business constitutes guilt, then the circle of those who share this guilt must be expanded to include every individual who held stock in a tobacco company after 1964, either directly or through a pension fund, a mutual fund, or a university endowment. We might also toss in every drugstore and supermarket that sold cigarettes and every publication that carried ads for them; the Surgeon General's warning, after all, was there for everyone to see.

Once the companies made the decision to stay in business, it was only a matter of time before the lawyers took over. Nothing emerges from *Ashes to Ashes* more clearly than the deforming influence of legal counsel on the actions of the industry. Many industry scientists and some executives appear to have genuinely wished both to produce a safer cigarette and to acknowledge frankly the known risks of smoking. But the industry's attempts to do good were no less paradoxically self-defeating than the government's attempts at regulation. When executives in R&D proposed that filtered cigarettes and reduced tar and nicotine yields be marketed as a potential benefit to public health, in-house lawyers objected that calling one brand "safe" or "safer" constituted an admission that other brands were hazardous and thus exposed the maker to liability claims. Likewise, after Liggett had spent millions of dollars developing a substantially less carcinogenic "palladium cigarette" in the seventies, it was treated like contagion by the company's lawyers. Marketing it was bad from a liability standpoint, and developing it and then *not* marketing it was even worse, because the company could then be sued for negligently failing to introduce it. Epic, as the new cigarette was called, was ultimately smothered in legal paper.

Kluger describes an industry in which lawyerly paranoia quickly metastasized into every vital organ. Lawyers coached the executives appearing before congressional committees, oversaw the woefully self-serving "independent" research the industry sponsored, and made sure that all paperwork connected with studies of addiction or cancer was funneled through outside counsel so that it could be protected under the attorney-client privilege. The result was a weird replication of the dual contradictory narratives with which I, as a smoker, explain my life: a true story submerged beneath a utilitarian fiction. One longtime Philip Morris executive quoted by Kluger sums it up like this:

There was a conflict in the company between science and the law that's never been resolved . . . and so we go through this ritual dance—what's "proven" and what isn't, what's causal and what's just an association—and the lawyers' answer is, "Let's stonewall." . . . If Helmut Wakeham [head of R&D] had run things, I think there would have been some admissions. But he was outflanked by the lawyers . . . who . . . were saying, in effect, "My God, you can't make that admission" without risking liability actions against the company. So there was no cohesive plan—when critics of the industry speak of a "conspiracy," they give the companies far too much credit.

In the inverted moral universe of a tobacco liability trial, every honest or anguished statement by an executive is used to prove the defendants' guilt, while every calculated dodge is used to support their innocence. There's something very wrong here; but absent a demonstration that Americans actually swallowed the industry's lies it's far from clear that this something qualifies as murder.

More damning are recent reports of the industry's recruitment of underage smokers. Lorrilard representatives have been observed handing out free Newports to kids in Washington, D.C.; Philip J. Hilts, in his book *Smoke Screen*, presents evidence that R. J. Reynolds deliberately placed special promotional displays in stores and kiosks known to be high-school hangouts; and the cuddly, penis-faced Joe Camel must rank as one of the most disgusting apparitions ever to appear on our cultural landscape. Tobacco companies claim that they are merely vying for market share in the vital eighteen-to-twenty-four age group, but internal industry documents described by Hilts suggest that at least one Canadian company has in fact studied how to target entry-level smokers as young as twelve. (According to Hilts, studies have shown that eighty-nine percent of today's adult smokers picked up the habit before the age of nineteen.) In the opinion of antitobacco activists, cigarette advertising hooks young customers by proffering images of carefree, attractive adult smokers while failing to hint at the havoc that smoking wreaks. By the time young smokers are old enough to appreciate the fact of mortality, they're hopelessly addicted.

Although the idea that a manufacturer might willingly stress the downside of its products is absurd—imagine McDonald's airing images of obesity or clogged arteries—I have no doubt that the tobacco industry aims its ads at young Americans. I do doubt, though, whether these ads cause an appreciable number of children to start smoking. The insecure or alienated teen who lights up for the first time is responding to peer pressure or to the example of grownup role models—movie villains, rock stars, supermodels. At most, the industry's ads function as an assurance that smoking is a socially acceptable grownup activity. For that reason alone, they should probably be banned or more tightly controlled, just as cigarette-vending machines should be outlawed. Most people who start smoking end up regretting it, and so any policy that reduces the number of starters is laudable.

That cigarettes innately appeal to teenagers, however, is hardly the fault of the manufacturers. In recent weeks I've noticed several antitobacco newspaper ads that offer, for its shock value, the image of a preadolescent girl holding a cigarette. The models are obviously not real smokers, yet despite their phoniness they're utterly sexualized by their cigarettes. The horror of underage smoking veils a horror of teen and preteen sexuality, and one of the biggest pleasant empty dreams being pushed these days by Madison Avenue is that a child is innocent until his or her eighteenth birthday. The truth is that without firm parental guidance teenagers make all sorts of irrevocable decisions before they're old enough to appreciate the consequences—they drop out of school, they get pregnant, they major in sociology. What they want most of all is to sample the pleasures of adulthood, like sex or booze or cigarettes. To impute to cigarette advertising a "predatory" power is to admit that parents now have less control over the moral education of their children than the commercial culture has. Here again I suspect that the tobacco industry is being scapegoated—made to bear the brunt of a more general societal rage at the displacement of the family by the corporation.

The final argument for the moral culpability of Big Tobacco is that addiction is a form of coercion. Nicotine is a toxin whose ingestion causes the smoker's brain to change its chemistry in defense. Once those changes have occurred, the smoker must continue to consume nicotine on a regular schedule in order to maintain the new chemical balance. Tobacco companies are well aware of all this, and an attorney cited by Kluger summarizes the legal case for coercion as follows: "You addicted me, and you knew it was addicting, and now you say it's my fault." As Kluger goes on to point out, though, the argument has many flaws. Older even than the common knowledge that smoking causes cancer, for example, is the knowledge that smoking is a tough habit to break. Human tolerance of nicotine varies widely, moreover, and the industry has long offered an array of brands with ultra-low doses. Finally, no addiction is unconquerable: millions of Americans quit every year. When a smoker says he wants to quit but can't, what he's really saying is, "I want to quit but I want even more not to suffer the agony of withdrawal." To argue otherwise is to jettison any lingering notion of personal responsibility.

If nicotine addiction were purely physical, quitting would be relatively easy, because the acute withdrawal symptoms, the physical cravings, rarely last more than a few weeks. At the time I myself quit, six years ago, I was able to stay nicotine-free for weeks at a time, and even when I was working I seldom smoked more than a few ultra-lights a day. But on the day I decided that the cigarette I'd had the day before was my last, I was absolutely flattened. A month passed in which I was too agitated to read a book, too fuzzy-headed even to focus on a newspaper. Another month went by before I could summon the concentration to write so much as a casual letter to a friend. If I'd had a job at the time, or a family to take care of, I might have hardly noticed the psychological withdrawal. But as it happened nothing much was going on in my life. "Do you smoke?" Lady Bracknell asks Jack Worthing in *The Importance of Being Earnest*, and when he admits that he does she replies, "I am glad to hear it. A man should always have an occupation of some kind."

There's no simple, universal reason why people smoke, but there's one thing I'm sure of: they don't do it because they're slaves to nicotine. My best guess about my own attraction to the habit is that I belong to a class of people whose lives are insufficiently structured. The mentally ill and the indigent are also members of this class. We embrace a toxin as deadly as nicotine, suspended in an aerosol of hydrocarbons and nitrosamines, because we have not yet found pleasures or routines that can replace the comforting, structure-bringing rhythm of need and gratification that the cigarette habit offers. One word for this structuring might be "self-medication"; another might be "coping." But there are very few serious smokers over thirty, perhaps none at all, who don't feel guilty for the harm they inflict on themselves. Even Rose Cipollone, the New Jersey woman whose heirs in the early eighties nearly sustained a liability judgment against the industry, had to be recruited by an activist. The sixty law firms that have pooled their assets for a class-action suit on behalf of all American smokers do not seem to me substantially less predatory than the suit's corporate defendants. I've never met a smoker who blamed the habit on someone else.

The United States as a whole resembles an addicted individual, with the corporate id going about its dirty business while the conflicted political ego frets and dithers. What's clear is that the tobacco industry would not still be flourishing, thirty years after the first Surgeon General's report, if our legislatures weren't purchasable, if the concepts of honor and personal responsibility hadn't largely given way to the power of litigation and the dollar, and if the country didn't generally endorse the idea of corporations whose ultimate responsibility is not to society but to the bottom line. There's no doubt that some tobacco executives have behaved despicably, and for public-health advocates to hate these executives, as the nicotine addict comes eventually to hate his cigarettes, is natural. But to cast them as moral monsters—a point source of evil—is just another form of prime-time entertainment.

BY SELLING ITS SOUL to its legal advisers, Big Tobacco long ago made clear its expectation that the country's smoking problem would eventually be resolved in court. The industry may soon suffer such a devastating loss in a liability suit that thereafter only foreign cigarette makers will be able to afford to do business here. Or perhaps a federal court will undertake to legislate a solution to a problem that the political process has clearly proved itself unequal to, and the Supreme Court will issue an opinion that does for the smoking issue what *Brown v. The Board of Education* did for racial segregation and *Roe v. Wade* for abortion.

Liggett's recent defection notwithstanding, the Medicare suits filed by five states seem unlikely to change the industry's ways. Kluger notes that these cases arguably amount to "personal injury claims in disguise," and that the Supreme Court has ruled that federal cigarette-labeling laws are an effective shield against such claims. Logically, in other words, the states ought to be suing smokers, not cigarette makers. And perhaps smokers, in turn, ought to be suing Social Security and private pension funds for all the money they'll save by dying early. The best estimates of the nationwide dollar "cost" of smoking, including savings from premature death and income from excise taxes, are negative numbers. If the country's health is to be measured fiscally, an economist quoted by Kluger jokes, "cigarette smoking should be subsidized rather than taxed."

Ultimately, the belief that the country's century-long love affair with the cigarette can be ended rationally and amicably seems as fond as the belief that there's a painless way to kick nicotine. The first time I quit, I stayed clean for nearly three years. I found I was able to work *more* productively without the distraction and cumulative unpleasantness of cigarettes, and I was happy finally to be the nonsmoker that my family had always taken me to be. Eventually, though, in a season of great personal loss, I came to resent having quit for other people rather than for myself. I was hanging out with smokers, and I drifted back into the habit. Smoking may not look sexy to me anymore, but it still *feels* sexy. The pleasure of carrying the drug, of surrendering to its imperatives and relaxing behind a veil of smoke, is thoroughly licentious. If longevity were the highest good that I could imagine, I might succeed right now in scaring myself into quitting. But to the fatalist who values the present more than the future, the nagging voice of conscience—of society, of family—becomes just another factor in the mental equilibrium that sustains the habit.

"Perhaps," Richard Klein writes in *Cigarettes Are Sublime*, "one stops smoking only when one starts to love cigarettes, becoming so enamored of their charms and so grateful for their benefits that one at last begins to grasp how much is lost by giving them up, how urgent it is to find substitutes for some of the seductions and powers that cigarettes so magnificently combine." To live with uncontaminated lungs and an unracing heart is a pleasure that I hope someday soon to prefer to the pleasure of a cigarette. For myself, then, I'm cautiously optimistic. For the body politic, rhetorically torn between shrill condemnation and Neanderthal denial, and habituated to the poison of tobacco money in its legal system, its legislatures, its financial markets, and its balance of foreign trade, I'm considerably less so.

A few weeks ago in Tribeca, in a Magritte-like twilight, I saw a woman in a lighted window on a high floor of a loft apartment building. She was standing on a chair and lowering the window's upper sash. She tossed her hair and did something complicated with her arms which I recognized as the lighting of a cigarette. Then she leaned her elbow and her chin on the sash and blew smoke into the humid air outside. I fell in love at first sight as she stood there, both inside and outside, inhaling contradiction and breathing out ambivalence.

[1996]

THE READER IN EXILE

A FEW MONTHS AGO, I gave away my television set. It was a massive old Sony Trinitron, the gift of a friend whose girlfriend couldn't stand the penetrating whistle the picture tube emitted. Its wood-look veneer recalled an era when TV sets were trying, however feebly, to pass as furniture—an era when their designers could still imagine them in a state of not being turned on. I kept it in inaccessible places, like the floor of a closet, and I could get a good picture only by sitting crosslegged directly in front of it and touching the antenna. It's hard to make TV viewing more unpleasant than I did. Still, I felt the Trinitron had to go, because as long as it was in the house, reachable by some combination of extension cords, I wasn't reading books.

I was born in 1959, on the cusp of a great generational divide, and for me it's a toss-up which is scarier: living without electronic access to my country's culture, or trying to survive in that culture without the self-definition I get from regular immersion in literature. I understand my life in the context of Raskolnikov and Quentin Compson, not David Letterman or Jerry Seinfeld. But the life I understand by way of books feels increasingly lonely. It has little to do with the mediascape that constitutes so many other people's present.

For every reader who dies today, a viewer is born, and we seem to be witnessing, here in the anxious mid-nineties, the final tipping of a balance. For critics inclined to alarmism, the shift from a culture based on the printed word to a culture based on virtual images—a shift that began with television and is now being completed with computers—feels apocalyptic. In much the same way that Silicon Valley dreams of the "killer application" that will make PCs indispensable to every American, alarmists seek a killer argument that will make the imminence of apocalypse self-evident.

One recent attempt at a such an argument is a book called *A Is for Ox*, by the literary scholar Barry Sanders, who takes as his starting point two dismal trends: rising violence among youth and falling verbal SAT scores. In answer to the well-documented fact that children don't read and write the way they used to, Sanders refreshingly declines to give the explanation that Barney has murdered Mother Goose. TV still plays the villain in his cosmology, but it works its evil less by displacing reading than by replacing verbal interaction with parents and peers. No matter how high the quality of the programming, an excess of passive reception stunts a child's oral development and prepares her or him to be frustrated by the seemingly arbitrary rules of standard English. Computers and video in the classroom only compound the estrangement from spoken language. Frustration turns to resentment: kids drop out of school and, in the worst case, join violent gangs of what Sanders calls "post-illiterates." It's his thesis that without a literacy rooted in orality there can be neither a self, as we understand it, nor self-consciousness. Interpreting the past, entertaining choices in the present, projecting a future, experiencing guilt or remorse—these are all, according to Sanders, activities foreclosed to the soulless young gangsters of today and to the fully computerized society, neither oral nor literate, of tomorrow.

The problem with Sanders's argument, as a killer, is that he has to finger too many culprits. He lays the blame for the national crisis in literacy as much on the decline in the quality time parents spend with their children as on the video input that has filled the vacuum. Young gangsters, he notes, not only are addicted to images but also come from impoverished, unstable homes. So are we facing a techno-apocalypse, or is it plain old-fashioned social dysfunction? Every mother I know restricts her children's TV intake and sows resistance to it by encouraging reading. Like the readers of this essay, my friends and I belong to that class of well-educated "symbolic analysts" which Labor Secretary Robert Reich believes is inheriting the earth. Sanders's generalizations about "young people today" apply only to the segment of the population (admittedly a large one) that lacks the money or the leisure to inoculate its children against the worst ravages of electronic media. What he describes as the self-immolation of civilization is in fact only a partitioning; and the irony of this partitioning is that those with the greatest access to information are the ones least tethered by the wires that bring it.

ANYONE WITH A TASTE for such ironies will enjoy Nicholas Negroponte's *Being Digital*, a guide to Tomorrowland for those who believe that technology has created no problems that better technology can't fix. Negroponte is the director of the Media Lab at M.I.T., and *Being Digital* is a compilation of his monthly columns in *Wired* magazine, the graphically adventurous "bible" (as I've seen it called) of the cyberworld. *Wired* attempts to celebrate the in-ness of the in crowd while leaving the door open for newcomers, and it manages the trick by selling both vision and inside dope. Negroponte's specialty is vision. He's the in-house oracle.

Leaders of government and industry flock to Negroponte for advice, and as a consequence, much of *Being Digital* is about (how else to put it?) resource allocation. Should developers of virtual-reality equipment spend their finite computing power on heightening video resolution, or on improving the equipment's reaction time to a user's head and neck movements? Go with the speed, says Negroponte. Should Wall Street invest in high-volume electronic pipelines or in TV technology that uses existing pipelines more efficiently? Go with the smart, small machine, says Negroponte.

Perhaps because the title *Being Digital* seems to promise the articulation of a new way of being human, it took me a while to realize that the book is not about the transformation of a culture but about money. The first question Negroponte asks of a development like virtual reality is whether there's a market for it. If a market exists, someone will inevitably exploit it, and so it's pointless to ask "Do we need this?" or "How might it harm us?" "The consumer" is a cheerful omnipresence in Negroponte's book, a most-favored arbiter.

Being Digital is awash in references to a world of moneyed internationalism—to the luxury hotels the author stays in, to his lunches with prime ministers, to transpacific flights, Burgundian vintners, Swiss boarding schools, Bavarian nannies. The ease with which jobs and capital and digital signals now cross national boundaries is matched by the mobility of the new informational elite, those lucky symbolic analysts who, like many a ruling class before them, are finding that they have more in common with the elect of other countries than with the preterite of their own. It's a revelation, when you notice it, how free of nationalism *Being Digital* is, how interchangeable the locales. In a brief aside, Negroponte complains that people lecture him about life in the real world—"as if," he says, "I live in an unreal world." He's right to complain. His world is as real as the ganglands that Barry Sanders evokes. But the two worlds are growing ever more unreal to each other.

High above the clouds, the sun always shines. Negroponte paints a tomorrow of talking toasters, smart refrigerators, and flavorized computers ("You will be able to buy a Larry King personality for your newspaper interface") that is *Jetsons*-like in its retention of today's suburban values. To find clues to a deeper transformation, you have to read between the lines. Negroponte has a habit, for example, of reducing human functions to machinery: the human eye is "the client for the image," an ear is a "channel," faces are "display devices," and "Disney's guaranteed audience is refueled at a rate that exceeds 12,500 births each hour." In the future, "CD-ROMs may be edible, and parallel processors may be applied like sun tan lotion." The new, digital human being will dine not only on storage devices but on narcissism. "Newspapers will be printed in an edition of one . . . Call it *The Daily Me*." Authors, meanwhile, as they move from text to multimedia, will assume the role of "stage-set or theme-park designer."

When Barry Sanders looks at young people, he sees lost, affectless faces. Negroponte sees a "mathematically able and more visually literate" generation happily competing in a cyberspace where "the pursuit of intellectual achievement will not be tilted so much in favor of the bookworm." He espouses a kind of therapeutic corporatism, defending video games as teachers of "strategies" and "planning skills," and recalling how his son had trouble learning to add and subtract until his teacher put dollar signs in front of the figures. The closest Negroponte comes to recognizing the existence of social dysfunction is in his description of the robots that in the near future will bring us our drinks and dust our empty bookshelves: "For security reasons, a household robot must also be able to bark like a ferocious dog."

IT'S EASY TO FAULT Negroponte's resolute ahistoricism; harder, however, to dislike an author who begins his book by confessing, "Being dyslexic, I don't like to read." Negroponte is nothing more and nothing less than a man who has profited by speculating on the future and is willing, like a successful stockbroker, to share his secrets. Apart from offering a few misty assurances ("Digital technology can be a natural force drawing people into greater world harmony"), he doesn't pretend his revolution will solve problems more serious than the annoyance of having to visit Blockbuster in the flesh to rent a movie.

In a culture of false perspective, where Johnny Cochran can appear taller than Boris Yeltsin, it's difficult to tell if the Internet is legitimately big news. Russell Baker has compared the hyping of the Net to the hyping of atomic energy in the fifties, when industry pitchmen promised that we would soon be paying "pennies" for our monthly utilities. Today's technology boosters can't offer ordinary consumers as measurable a benefit as cheap electricity. Instead, the selling points are intangible—conveyed through the language of health and hipness.

Digital technology, the argument goes, is good medicine for an ailing society. TV has given us government by image; interactivity will return power to the people. TV has produced millions of uneducable children; computers will teach them. Top-down programming has isolated us; bottom-up networks will reunite us. As a bonus, being digital is medicine that tastes good. It's a pop-cultural pleasure we're invited to indulge. Indeed, some of the best television these days is funded by IBM: nuns in an Italian convent whisper about the Net, Moroccan businessmen sip mint tea and talk interfacing. This is both advertising and luscious postmodern art. Of course, the aim of such art is simply to make the giving of our dollars to IBM seem inevitable. But popularity has become its own justification.

If I were fashioning my own killer argument against the digital revolution, I'd begin with the observation that both Newt Gingrich and Timothy Leary are crazy about it. Somewhere, something isn't adding up. Douglas Rushkoff, in *Media Virus!*—his book-length exploration of the media counterculture—quotes a skeptical New Age thinker as offering this bright side to the revolution: "There's no longer a private space. The idea of literate culture is basically a middle-class notion—it's the gentleman in his book-lined study with the privacy for reflection. That's a very elitist notion." Robert Coover, writing in a similar vein in a pair of essays for the *Times Book Review*, promises that hypertext will replace "the predetermined one-way route" of the conventional novel with works that can be read in any number of ways, and thus liberate readers from "domination by the author." At the same time, Speaker Gingrich's own clutch of New Age authors advertise the electronic town meeting as the perfect antidote to tired Second Wave liberalism. Where Wall Street sees a profit for investors, visionaries of every political persuasion see empowerment for the masses.

That news of this better future continues to arrive by way of print—in "the entombing, distancing oppression of paper," as a *Wired* columnist put it—may simply be a paradox of obsolescence, like the necessity of riding your horse to the dealer who sells you your first car. But Negroponte, in explaining his decision to publish an actual book, offers a surprising reason for his choice: interactive multimedia leave too little to the imagination. "By contrast," he says, "the written word sparks images and evokes metaphors that get much of their meaning from the reader's imagination and experiences. When you read a novel, much of the color, sound, and motion come from you."

If Negroponte took the health of the body politic seriously, he would need to explore what this argument implies about the muscle tone of our imaginations in a fully digital age. But you can trust him, and the hard-core corporate interests he advises, not to engage in sentimentality. The truth is simple, if unpretty. The novel is dying because the consumer doesn't want it anymore.

NOVELS are by no means dead, of course—just ask Annie Proulx or Cormac McCarthy. But the Novel, as a seat of cultural authority, is teetering on the brink, and in *The Gutenberg Elegies*, a collection of essays subtitled *The Fate of Reading in an Electronic Age*, Sven Birkerts registers his surprise and dismay that its decline has not been more widely mourned. Not even professional book critics, who ought to be the front line of the novel's defenders, have raised the alarm, and Birkerts, who is a critic himself, sounds like a loyal soldier deserted by his regiment. The tone of his elegies is brave but plaintive.

Birkerts begins his defense of the novel by recounting how, while growing up in an immigrant household, he came to understand himself by reading Jack Kerouac, J. D. Salinger, and Hermann Hesse. The authors as well as the alienated, romantic heroes of their books became models for emulation and comparison. Later, on the desolate emotional beach on which the wave of sixties idealism seems to have deposited so many people, Birkerts weathered years of depression by reading, by working in bookstores, and, finally, by becoming a reviewer. "Basically," he says, "I was rescued by books."

Books as catalysts of self-realization and books as sanctuary: the notions are paired because Birkerts believes that "inwardness, the more reflective component of self," requires a "space" where a person can reflect on the meaning of things. Compared with the state of a person watching a movie or clicking through hypertext, he says, absorption in a novel is closer to a state of meditation, and he is at his best when tracing the subtleties of this state. Here is his description of his initial engagement with a novel: "I feel a tug. The chain has settled over the sprockets; there is the feel of meshing, then the forward glide." And here is his neat reply to hypertext's promise of liberation from the author: "This 'domination by the author' has been, at least until now, the *point* of reading and writing. The author masters the resources of language to create a vision that will engage and in some way overpower the reader; the reader goes to the work to be subjected to the creative will of another." Birkerts on reading fiction is like M. F. K. Fisher on eating or Norman Maclean on fly-casting. He makes you want to go do it.

Counterposed to his idyll of the book-lined study, however, is a raging alarmism. In the decline of the novel, Birkerts sees more than a shift in our habits of entertainment. He sees a transformation of the very nature of humanity. His nightmare, to be sure, "is not one of neotroglodytes grunting and wielding clubs, but of efficient and prosperous information managers living in the shallows of what it means to be human and not knowing the difference." He grants that technology has made our perspectives more global and tolerant, our access to information easier, our self-definitions less confining. But, as he repeatedly stresses, "the more complex and sophisticated our systems of lateral access, the more we sacrifice in the way of depth." Instead of Augie March, Arnold Schwarzenegger. Instead of Manassas battlefield, a historical theme park. Instead of organizing narratives, a map of the world as complex as the world itself. Instead of a soul, membership in a crowd. Instead of wisdom, data.

In a coda to *The Gutenberg Elegies*, Birkerts conjures up, out of the pages of *Wired* magazine, the Devil himself, "sleek and confident," a "sorcerer of the binary order" who offers to replace the struggle of earthly existence with "a vivid, pleasant dream." All he wants in return is mankind's soul. Birkerts confesses to an envy for the Devil: "I wonder, as I did in high school when confronted with the smooth and athletic ones, the team captains and class presidents, whether I would not, deep down, trade in all this doubting and wondering and just be him." Yet, tempted as he is by the sexiness of the Devil's technology, a voice in his heart says, "Refuse it."

Technology as the Devil incarnate, being digital as perdition: considering that contemporary authors like Toni Morrison have vastly larger audiences than Jane Austen had in her day, something other than sober analysis would seem to be motivating Birkerts's hyperbole. The clue, I think, is in the glimpses he gives of his own life beneath the shallows of what it means to be human. He refers to his smoking, his quarts of beer, his morbid premonitions of disaster, his insomnia, his brooding. He names as the primary audience for his book his many friends who refuse to grant him the darkness of our cultural moment, who shrug off electronic developments as enhancements of the written word. "I sometimes wonder if my thoughtful friends and I are living in the same world . . . Naturally I prefer to think that the problem lies with them."

These lines are redolent with depression and the sense of estrangement from humanity that depression fosters. Nothing aggravates this estrangement more than a juggernaut of hipness such as television has created and the digital revolution's marketers are exploiting. It's no accident that Birkerts locates apocalypse in the arch-hip pages of *Wired*. He's still the high-school loner, excluded from the in crowd and driven, therefore, to the alternative and more "genuine" satisfactions of reading. But what, we might ask him, is so wrong with being an efficient and prosperous information manager? Do the team captains and class presidents really not have souls?

Elitism is the Achilles' heel of every serious defense of art, an invitation to the poisoned arrows of populist rhetoric. The elitism of modern literature is, undeniably, a peculiar one—an aristocracy of alienation, a fraternity of the doubting and wondering. Still, after voicing a suspicion that nonreaders view reading "as a kind of value judgment upon themselves, as an elitist and exclusionary act," Birkerts is brave enough to confirm their worst fears: "Reading *is* a judgment. It brands as insufficient the understandings and priorities that govern ordinary life." If he had stopped here, with the hard fact of literature's selective appeal, *The Gutenberg Elegies* would be an unassailable, if unheeded, paean. But because books saved his life and he can't abide the thought of a world without them, he falls under the spell of another, more popular defense of art. This is the grant-proposal defense, the defense that avoids elitism. Crudely put, it's that while technology is merely palliative, art is therapeutic.

I admit to being swayable by this argument. It's why I banished my Trinitron and gave myself back to books. But I try to keep this to myself. Unhappy families may be aesthetically superior to happy families, whose happiness is all alike, but "dysfunctional" families are not. It was easy to defend a novel about unhappiness; everybody knows unhappiness; it's part of the human condition. A novel about emotional dysfunction, however, is reduced to a Manichaeanism of utility. Either it's a sinister enabler, obstructing health by celebrating pathology, or it's an object lesson, helping readers to understand and overcome their own dysfunction. Obsession with social health produces a similar vulgarity: if a novel isn't part of a political solution, it must be part of the problem. The doctoral candidate who "exposes" Joseph Conrad as a colonialist is akin to the school board that exiles Holden Caulfield as a poor role model—akin as well, unfortunately, to Birkerts, whose urgency in defending reading devolves from the assumption that books must somehow "serve" us.

I love novels as much as Birkerts does, and I, too, have felt rescued by them. I'm moved by his pleading, as a lobbyist in the cause of literature, for the intellectual subsidy of his client. But novelists want their work to be enjoyed, not taken as medicine. Blaming the novel's eclipse on infernal technologies and treasonous literary critics, as Birkerts does, will not undo the damage. Neither will the argument that reading enriches us. Ultimately, if novelists want their work to be read, the responsibility for making it attractive and imperative is solely their own.

THERE REMAINS, however, the bitter circumstance that, as Birkerts puts it, "the daily life of the average American has become Teflon for the novelist." Once upon a time, characters inhabited charged fields of status and geography. Now, increasingly, the world is binary. You either have or you don't have. You're functional or you're dysfunctional, you're wired or you're tired. Unhappy families, perhaps even more than happy ones, are all identically patched in to CNN, *The Lion King*, and America Online. It's more than a matter of cultural references; it's the very texture of their lives. And if a novel depends on the realization of complex characters against a background of a larger society, how do you write one when the background is indistinguishable from the foreground?

"Fiction," according to Birkerts, "only retains its cultural vitality so long as it can bring readers meaningful news about what it means to live in the world of the present." He has in mind the broad-canvased, big-audience novels of Tolstoy and Dickens, of Bellow and Steinbeck, and indeed, there seems little doubt that the form is going the way of Shakespearean tragedy and Verdian opera. But the news of its passing is perhaps less meaningful than Birkerts makes it out to be. The audience may have collapsed in the last few decades, but cultural vitality has had to reconcile itself with silence, cunning, and exile throughout our technological century. Kafka told Max Brod he wanted his novels burned, Henry Green and Christina Stead fell into obscurity in their own lifetimes, Faulkner and O'Connor hid themselves away in the rural South. The most original and farseeing novelists of our own day not only accept the shadows but actively seek them. "Everything in the culture argues against the novel," Don DeLillo said in a *Paris Review* interview. "This is why we need the writer in opposition, the novelist who writes against power, who writes against the corporation or the state or the whole apparatus of assimilation."

The modern idea of the oppositional writer is a long-established tradition, and its modern variants have been around since at least the First World War, when the Austrian satirist Karl Kraus described himself as the "hopeless contrary" of the nexus of technology, media, and capital. Something that has taken longer to emerge, but is implicit in a work like *The Gutenberg Elegies*, is the idea of the oppositional *reader*. The paradox of literature's elitism is that it's purely self-selecting. Anyone who can read is free to be a part of it. And, as the informational elite continues to inoculate itself with literacy, a certain percentage of readers will inevitably, like the fabled marijuana smoker, get hooked on harder stuff. Likewise, as the ranks of the preterite swell with the downwardly mobile, restless souls will have ever greater reason to seek out methods of opposition—"to posit an elsewhere," as Birkerts describes reading, "and to set off toward it." The apparent democracy of today's digital networks is an artifact of their infancy. Sooner or later, all social organisms move from anarchy toward hierarchy, and whatever order emerges from the primordial chaos of the Net seems as likely to be dystopian as utopian. The possibility of terminal boringness looms particularly large. But even if the digital revolution evolves into a free-market version of the Stalinist totality to which the Bolshevik revolution gave rise, the perverse effect may be the elevation of reading's status. The world of samizdat, the flowering of a readership that memorized wholesale the poetry of Osip Mandelstam and Anna Akhmatova, ought to remind us that reading can survive, and even flourish, in exile.

Not just Negroponte, who doesn't like to read, but even Birkerts, who thinks that history is ending, underestimates the instability of society and the unruly diversity of its members. The electronic apotheosis of mass culture has merely reconfirmed the elitism of literary reading, which was briefly obscured in the novel's heyday. I mourn the eclipse of the cultural authority that literature once possessed, and I rue the onset of an age so anxious that the pleasure of a text becomes difficult to sustain. I don't suppose that many other people will give away their TVs. I'm not sure I'll last long myself without buying a new one. But the first lesson reading teaches is how to be alone.

[1995]

FIRST CITY

TWO THINGS that happened this year got me wondering why American cities in general and New York City in particular still bother to exist. The first was a plane ride back east from St. Louis. I sat next to a smart, pleasant woman from Springfield, Missouri, who was taking her eleven-year-old son to see relatives in Boston. The son had already scored points with me by removing a book, rather than a Game Boy, from his backpack, and when his mother told me that they were stopping in New York for two nights and that it was her son's first visit there, I asked what sights they planned to see. "We want to go to the Fashion Cafe," she said, "and we want to try to get on the *Today* show. There's that window you can stand in front of? My son wants to do that." I said I hadn't heard about this window, and it certainly did sound interesting, but what about the Statue of Liberty and the Empire State Building? The woman gave me a funny look. "We'd love to see *Letterman* too," she said. "Do you think there's any chance of getting tickets?" I told her she could always hope.

The second thing that happened, after this reminder that for the rest of the country New York is now largely a city of the mind—at best, a site for the voodoo transformation of image into flesh—was a walk I took down Silicon Alley, in lower Manhattan. Silicon Alley is a district where the romance between downtown hipsters and the digital revolution has emerged from upper-floor bedrooms and set up house behind plate glass; I could see girls with fashion-model looks who wouldn't be caught dead at the Fashion Cafe clustering around monitors while gurus with shaved heads helped them to configure. The Cyber Cafe, at 273 Lafayette Street, is a strange phenomenon. According to Web dogma, it ought not to exist. "Click, click through cyberspace," William J. Mitchell writes in his recent manifesto, *City of Bits*. "This is the new architectural promenade . . . a city unrooted to any definite spot on the surface of the earth, shaped by connectivity and bandwidth constraints rather than by accessibility and land values, largely asynchronous in its operation, and inhabited by disembodied and fragmented subjects who exist as collections of aliases and agents." Yet the Cyber Cafe—to say nothing of the thousands of clubs and galleries and bookstores and noncyber cafes doing business within a mile of it—resembles nothing so much as an old-fashioned see-and-be-seen promenade.

Two New Yorks, then: one a virtual province of Planet Hollywood; the other a definite spot on the surface of the earth, populated by young people who even as they disembody and fragment themselves cannot resist the urge to Be There. Between the New York of Springfield's imaginings and the New York of Lafayette Street is a disjunction that I feel well equipped to appreciate. I grew up in Missouri, and in the last fifteen years I've moved to New York six times. At no point was a job or a ready-made community waiting for me. As a self-employed writer, I can live anywhere I want, and it would make sense for me to choose an inexpensive place. Yet whenever I'm in one of those inexpensive places I feel drawn to reinflict New York on myself—this despite my fear of neighbors with televisions and pianos, my aversion to Gothamite provinciality, and my immunity to the city's "cultural vitality." When I'm here, I spend a lot of time at home; as a rule, I hit the museums and theaters only in a last-minute panic, before moving somewhere else. And, fond though I am of Central Park and the subways, I have no overpowering ♥ for the Apple as a whole. The city has little of the soul-stirring desolation of Philadelphia, say, and none of the deep familiarity of Chicago, where I was born. What draws me back, again and again, is safety. Nowhere else am I safe from the question: Why *here*?

Manhattan, in particular, offers the reassurance of high rents, which means that this is a city that people want to live in, not escape from. It's no accident that Parisians adore New York. Its orthogonal street grid notwithstanding, they feel right at home here, since one of the things that makes Europe Europe is that its urban centers are still attractors, rather than repellers, of public life. Conversely, for an American Midwesterner like me, hungry for a feeling of cultural placement, New York is the next best thing to Europe.

Most North American metropolises are wildly centrifugal, however, and the contrast between our lifeless inner grids and Europe's thriving centers has prompted the architect and essayist Witold Rybczynski to ask, "Why aren't our cities like that?" In his recent book, *City Life*, he sets out to examine "urban expectations" in the New World. Although he devotes much of the book to explaining the different *look* of our cities, Rybczynski understands that "like that" means something deeper: an urban vitality, an at-homeness with the idea of living in cities. Washington, D.C., has Parisian-style diagonal boulevards, height uniformity, and monumental architecture, and yet no one would mistake the feel of a residential D.C. street at ten in the evening for the Fourteenth Arrondissement. Nor is there any mistaking our country's current mood of hostility toward cities. Upstate New York has taken revenge on Gotham in the person of George Pataki; planned cuts in Medicare, welfare, and other federal programs target city centers like ICBMs; and the groups that the Western and suburban Republicans now ascendant in Congress have identified as flies in the ointment—poor people, gay people, liberal elites, rap musicians, NEA-sponsored performance artists, government bureaucrats—all happen to be concentrated in big cities.

City Life traces the provenance of this hostility. Paying a visit to Williamsburg, Virginia, Rybczynski reports being struck not "by its strenuous 'historical' character . . . but rather by how familiar it seemed." Williamsburg is the prototype of the American small town, distinctive not only in its "spatial liberality" but in its relation to nature. European towns were traditionally enclosed by walls of stone and walls of class; membership in the bourgeoisie (literally, "town dwellers") brought various jealously guarded privileges. American towns were open from the start. Surrounded by wilderness, Rybczynski says, "town builders reacted not by emphasizing the contrast between the natural and the man-made, but by incorporating natural elements in the town as much as possible, whether as green squares, tree-lined streets, or ample gardens." That the colonial town became specifically "a celebration of the house," however, resulted from the accident of North America's being settled by the English and Dutch, whose wealthier citizens, unlike their counterparts in other European countries, had a marked preference for individual home ownership. In America, even people of modest means could afford private ownership, and land was so plentiful that each house could have a private yard. Nor was the deconcentration of society simply spatial. Rybczynski discerns in our earliest history "a startling tendency toward a far-flung homogeneity," and he relates how Alexis de Tocqueville, scouring the backwoods for an American peasantry in the 1830s, instead found a settler who had books and newspapers and spoke "the language of towns." With the rule-proving exception of African slaves and Native Americans, there was no peasantry above the Rio Grande, and the result of this disjunction between the rural and the rustic was distinctively American: urbanity without urbanness.

In Rybczynski's telling of it, the first century and a half of postcolonial American history was essentially a detour in the inevitable fulfillment of these proto-suburban ideals. Quaker practicality and a profusion of immigrants ensured that Philadelphia, for example, which William Penn had laid out as a "green country town," quickly saw its spacious grid parceled up by speculators and bricked up with row houses. It was Penn's grid, not his green vision, that became the norm for big American cities. In the absence of a belief in cities as unique repositories of culture, moreover, there was little to prevent American cities from becoming purely commercial enterprises. However much the country's urban gentry came to hunger for European refinements, attempts at making cities more "like Paris"—Daniel Burnham's plan for a horizontal Chicago of parks and boulevards is perhaps the most famous—soon foundered on the economics of skyscrapers or sank beneath waves of immigration. As Rybczynski puts it, "the city profitable replaced the city beautiful."

Yet the city profitable worked. The first decades of this century were the heyday of urban life in America. I generally resist wishing I'd lived in an earlier era (I always imagine myself dying of some disease whose cure was just around the corner), but I make an exception for those years when the country's heart was in its cities, the years of Lou Gehrig and Harold Ross, Automats and skyscrapers, trolley cars, fedoras, and crowded train stations. I make this exception precisely because the era seems so anomalous, so extraneous to the continuum connecting Williamsburg colonials and Tocqueville's urbane woodsmen to the far-flung tract-housing dwellers of today. It seems like a time when the country could have turned in a less wasteful, more public-spirited, more *European* direction.

Ironically, these decades were a time, perhaps the only time, when European cities were looking westward for inspiration. If there's a villain in *City Life*, it's Le Corbusier, who, with what Rybczynski calls "a Warholian gift for self-promotion," toured the world publicizing his vision of the Radiant City of the future. *City Life* offers a nice contrast between the heroic descriptive work of the nineteenth-century Tocqueville and the malignant fatuity of the twentieth-century Le Corbusier, whose vision was prescriptive: superskyscrapers surrounded by grass and superhighways; a Cartesian separation of work from play, of housing from commerce. When Le Corbusier proposed razing six hundred acres of central

Paris, he was ignored by everyone but his fellow French intellectuals. In America, however, his ideas influenced a generation of city planners and eventually inspired hundreds of urban "renewal" projects. In Manhattan we still live with the radiance of NYU's dorms and East Harlem's projects.

Radiant City planning, whose wrongheadedness is old news now, by no means killed the American inner city singlehanded. Kenneth T. Jackson concluded his study of American suburbanization, *Crabgrass Frontier*, with an excellent analysis of the "residential deconcentration" of America. Jackson pinned the unique degree of American suburbanization on two fundamental causes: racial prejudice and inexpensive housing. Suburbs provide uneasy whites with a safe haven, and a variety of factors—high per capita wealth, cheap land and transportation, government subsidies and tax breaks—have made flight affordable to the great middle class.

The most salient contemporary American urban expectations, therefore, are that core cities will be poor and nonwhite, and that the suburbs will be soothingly homogeneous. Rybczynski is strangely oblivious to these particular expectations. In *City Life*'s final chapter, "The Best of Both Worlds," he celebrates the Philadelphia community of Chestnut Hill, which became a middle-class haven in the first decades of this century, when a local millionaire named George Woodward and his father-in-law built several hundred beautiful rental houses of Wissahickon schist. With medium population density, a parklike ambience, and carefully planned architecture, the Woodward development showed the influence of the Hampstead Garden Suburb, a model development begun outside London in 1906. In *The Death and Life of Great American Cities*, Jane Jacobs observed that garden suburbs, since they have neither the street life of real cities nor the privacy of real suburbs, succeed only if their residents are homogeneous and relatively affluent. Rybczynski, who now owns a house in Chestnut Hill, contradicts Jacobs by asserting that the community "has become more socially and economically heterogeneous." He extols it as "a small town and a city both," "an only slightly urbanized Arcadia" whose central shopping street, Germantown Avenue, is "precisely the sort of old-fashioned pedestrian district people find so attractive." He speaks of the "long" waiting list for Woodward house rentals.

For a check on the reality of American cities, it's worth taking a closer look at the neighborhood Rybczynski calls home. The last time I moved to New York, it was from Philadelphia. My wife and I had heard about the waiting list for Woodward houses, and we were surprised when, at the interview required of all applicants, we were told that several houses were immediately available. Only later did we learn that every one of the dozens of families in Woodward houses on our block, in the predominantly black city of Philadelphia, was white. At the closest good supermarket and the closest mall, both of which are in mixed neighborhoods, you will rarely see a white shopper from Chestnut Hill. When I shopped at these places I was struck by the exemplary warmth and courtesy with which I was treated. Knowing that a black male shopper at a predominantly white mall or supermarket would probably have had quite a different experience, I couldn't help wondering whether the courtesy wasn't meant to be *literally* exemplary. As in: We would like to be treated the way we are treating you.

THE FIRST CITIES of European countries have tended to be capitals in every way—commercially, culturally, governmentally, and demographically. Early America, however, was so far-flung and so distrustful of concentrated authority that it was not until 1900 or so, when Wall Street and the big media had established themselves as the country's shadow government, that the four functions fully converged in New York. One measure of New York's enduring primacy is that it continues to act as a lightning rod for national resentment. When Americans rail against "Washington," they mean the abstraction of federal government, not the District of Columbia. New York is resented as an actual place—for its rudeness, its arrogance, its crowds and dirt, its moral turpitude, and so forth. Global resentment is the highest compliment a city can receive, and by nurturing the notion of the Apple as the national Forbidden Fruit such resentment guarantees not only that ambitious souls of the "If I can make it there, I'd make it anywhere" variety will gravitate toward New York but that the heartland's most culturally rebellious young people will follow. There's no better way of rejecting where you came from, no plainer declaration of an intention to reinvent yourself, than moving to New York; I speak from personal experience.

It worries me a little, therefore, that the city has now been paid the additional compliment of a million-and-a-half-word encyclopedia. There's something decidedly valedictory about *The Encyclopedia of New York City*, edited by the same Kenneth Jackson who wrote *Crabgrass Frontier*. The *Encyclopedia* has the heft and ambition of a monument. It's a grand list for an age in love with lists. As soon as I got the book, I paged to the entry for "Sewers," a topic of perennial fascination. I found a good historical overview of the subject but no hint of the daily drama of contemporary sewers. Indeed, a numbing sameness afflicts nearly all the longer articles in the *Encyclopedia*. Each entry begins with vaguely colorful arcana from the city's earliest history (reading about "Intellectuals," for example, we learn that "the leading intellectual circle of the late eighteenth century was the Friendly Club"), goes on to pursue the subject doggedly decade by decade, often achieving a full head of steam around 1930 (thus, under "Intellectuals," *The New Republic* and *Partisan Review* are treated at some length), and finally peters out rather sadly in the present ("In the mid 1990s . . . major magazines of opinion continued to be published in the city but lacked the urgency and influence that they had enjoyed in earlier times"). It's an odd thing to experience the present, which is, after all, so *present*, again and again as the dusty terminus of historical spurs. Reviewers of the *Encyclopedia* have dwelled on what's missing from it, and their quibbles reinforce the notion of the city as a work completed, rather than a work in progress.

The chief pleasure of the *Encyclopedia* lies in a kind of Derridean lateral slide of association. I move from "Terrorism" to read about "Anarchism," across the page to "Amphibians and Reptiles," on to "Birds," and (after a side trip to "Birdland" and a courtesy call on "Parker, Charlie") to "Cockroaches," which "are known to be attracted to toothpaste," which brings me to "Colgate-Palmolive" and its founder "Colgate, William," who fled England in 1795 "to escape public hostility toward his father, who had supported the French Revolution." It's like a game of Telephone: "Anarchism" connecting with the sansculottes not by way of history but, rather, via "Cockroaches."

Yet there's something empty about this pleasure. A city lives in the eye, ear, and nose of the solitary beholder. You turn to literature to find the interior point of intersection between subject and city, and as a living connection to New York's history a few lines of Herman Melville or Don DeLillo outweigh whole pages of an encyclopedia. This is Ishmael downtown:

> There now is your insular city of the Manhattoes, belted round by wharves as Indian isles by coral reefs—commerce surrounds it with her surf. Right and left, the streets take you waterward.

This is DeLillo's Bucky Wunderlick, walking the same streets more than a century later:

> It was early afternoon and soon to rain, nondeliverance in the air, a chemical smell from the river. The bridges were cruelly beautiful in this weather, gray ladies nearly dead to all the poetry written in their names.

DeLillo, an essential New York artist, is unmentioned in the *Encyclopedia*, whose lengthy "Literature" article has little more to say about the post–Norman Mailer scene than this: "Many of the writers who had become well known in the 1960s left the city during the 1970s and 1980s."

DURING those 1970s and 1980s, Rybczynski says, a new shopping center opened in the United States every seven hours. In *City Life* he asserts that as malls increasingly come to have hotels attached to them and museums and skating rinks and public libraries housed within them, they are entitled to be considered "the new downtown." He marvels at the "variety" at a shopping-center food court ("Tex-Mex, Chinese, Italian,

Middle Eastern") and compares the scene to a sidewalk cafe. What ultimately attracts people to malls, he believes, is that they supply "a reasonable (in most eyes) level of public order; the right not to be subjected to outlandish conduct, not to be assaulted and intimidated by boorish adolescents, noisy drunks, and aggressive panhandlers." He adds, "It does not seem too much to ask." To "academic colleagues" who might object to the "hyperconsumerism" and "artificial reality" of malls, Rybczynski replies that "commercial forces have always formed the center of the American city" and that "it is unclear to me why sitting on a bench in the mall should be considered any more artificial than a bench in the park."

For my part, I'm willing to admit to an almost physical craving for the comforts of the suburban mall. Natural opiates flood my neural receptors when I step from the parking lot into the airlock. Inside, the lighting is subdued, and every voice sounds far away. Never mind that Waldenbooks doesn't stock Denis Johnson and that Sam Goody has no Myra Melford; I have cash in my wallet, my skin is white, and I feel utterly, utterly welcome. Is this a community? Is the reality artificial, or am I part of a genuine promenade? I don't know. When I'm not being actively repelled by the purple and teal that are this year's favored suburban leisure-wear colors, I'm too busy enjoying the rush of purchase to pay much attention.

My craving for city life feels entirely different. It's often tinged with anxiety; I'm never entirely relaxed until I'm back at home; there's a world of difference between inside and outside. How is it possible that life in New York, whose buildings are like ossified upwellings of pure molten capital, can be so much *less* beholden to the world of consumerism than life in the suburbs, which ostensibly offer more freedom and privacy? The answer is, narrowly, that cities represent an older, less advanced stage in the development of buying and selling, in which producers work cheek by jowl with consumers and the whole economic mechanism is open to inspection and so is less susceptible to the seamless enchantment of modern sales pitches; and, more generally, that there's something in the very nature of cities which enforces adult responsibility. I don't mean to suggest that we city dwellers are any less mad for products than suburb dwellers are, or that the cleansing and police actions of various Business Improvement Districts are not, even now, transforming large swaths of Manhattan into outdoor malls—only that it's far easier on the streets of New York to have experiences that have nothing to do with the spending of money than it is in the typical galleria.

Rybczynski is correct, nevertheless, in stressing that "civic" and "commercial" have always been near-synonyms in America. Although European cities, too, historically functioned as trading and manufacturing centers, they had more ancient functions as well: as fortification, as the sites of cathedrals and universities, as the residences of princes, and, most important, as the embodiment of regional or national identities. Barcelona *is* Catalonia, and every new building erected there serves to make Catalonia's identity that much more glorious and concrete. It's impossible to imagine an American city being cherished in the same way, if only because we have no regional identities as coherent and enduring—as *tribal*—as the Catalonian. This country was populated largely by immigrants in search of freedom or economic opportunity, or both, and I suspect it's no accident that the heyday of American cities directly followed the decades of peak immigration. These immigrants were similar only in their rejection of the Old World and so could never develop urban fealties that extended beyond a given ethnic neighborhood. It was only a matter of time before they adopted the New World ideal of house-as-kingdom, with its implications that what you earn and what you buy matters far more than where you do it.

The real mystery, therefore, is not that we have so few cities "like Paris" but that we have any at all. However many Americans prefer the suburbs, there are still millions who expressly choose cities. "Yuppie" is not a kind appellation, but the people who put the *u* in the word remain impressive in their sheer numbers. Even the most woebegone urban centers—Syracuse in the Rust Belt, Colorado Springs in the midst of neo-Californian sprawl—manage a few blocks of mixed-use vitality. And many larger cities—New York, Boston, San Francisco, Chicago, Los Angeles, Seattle—have a clearly sustained critical mass. For better or worse, the most reliable measure of a city's vitality is whether rich people are willing to live in the center of it. Once upon a time, the middle class was the bellwether of urban vitality; in Mayor Giuliani's speeches, it still is. But, as Labor Secretary Robert Reich has observed, the term "middle class" today has a definition more sociological than economic. And the best definition might be "suburban."

However reliable the presence of the rich may be as an indicator, it's merely the final effect in a chain of causes which begins with a city's ability to attract young people. How long would the upper crust persevere on Park Avenue without the horde of young singles who fill Yorkville? How long would downtown remain a capital of culture without constant infusions of young artists, students, and musicians? We hear a lot about the dependence of poor people on cities, but young people, especially creative young people, need them just as much. The suburbs may be an ideal place to spend a child-hood, but people in the years between leaving the nest and building a nest of their own need a place to congregate. So cities will continue to see, at a minimum, heavy nighttime and weekend use—unless, of course, Internet-brokered mar-riages become common; and the only thing more dismal to imagine than virtual courtship is daily life in the marriage of two people who would court that way.

HIKING is what I do for fun in Manhattan on windy days or after sundown, when the diesel fumes lift. I'm a recreational walker, and in the last few years I've noticed something odd when I've hit the sidewalks of suburban St. Louis and subur-ban Colorado: a not negligible percentage of the men speed-ing by me in their cars or sport-utility vehicles (it's always men) feel moved to yell obscenities at me. It's hard to know why they do this. The only things unusual about me are that I'm not driving and that I'm not wearing teal and purple or a backward baseball cap. My guess is that they yell at me simply because I'm a stranger, and from the perspective of their glassed-in vehicles I have no more human reality than the coach on their TV screens who has elected to punt on fourth and short.

I've been yelled at in New York, too, but only by deinsti-tutionalized psychotics, and then only in the midst of fellow subway riders who sympathized with me. Jane Jacobs identi-fied as a hallmark of city life the existence of privacy in heavy crowds—a privacy whose maintenance depends not on the pseudoparental expedients of isolated houses and controlled shopping environments but on modes of adult behavior best learned in public spaces like the sidewalk. That the country's widely decried "breakdown of civility" began at home, rather than in so-called urban jungles, can be confirmed at any movie theater, where audiences accustomed to watching videos in the bedroom have forgotten how to shut up.

In *Death and Life* Jacobs also quoted Paul Tillich, who believed that the city, by its very nature, "provides what otherwise could be given only by traveling; namely, the strange." Familiarity, whether of chain stores or of cookie-cutter subdivisions, erodes the autonomous intelligence and, in a weird way, undermines privacy. In the suburbs, *I'm* the stranger; I feel exposed. Only in a crowded, diverse place like New York, surrounded by strangeness, do I come home to myself.

I'm not so innocently enamored of cities, of course, as not to see that the plate-glass windows of Silicon Alley serve purposes of display similar to those of the CRT screens behind them: that the hidden link between Fashion Cafe and Cyber Cafe is a culture of Being Seen. It's possible to worry, too, that young people who come to Manhattan seeking what I seek—centrality, the privacy of crowds, the satisfaction of being a fly in the ointment—will eventually be repelled by the miasma of Disneyfication that is hanging over SoHo and Fifty-seventh Street and creeping into the East Village and Times Square. For now, though, I work and sleep in a building that houses two dressmakers, a realtor, an antiques dealer, a caterer, and a fish seller. When I lie on the floor and relax by listening to my breathing, I can hear the slower respirations of the city itself, a sound like the rumble of a surf: subway trains crowded with people who are teaching themselves how to be here.

[1995]

SCAVENGING

(N)OT MANY WAREHOUSES masquerade as châteaux, and of those that do, the Mercer Museum in Doylestown, Pennsylvania, is surely one of the largest. The museum is a hundred feet tall, has the flat face and square turrets of a reform school or a sandcastle, and is made entirely of poured concrete. A wealthy eccentric named Henry Mercer built it in the first decade of the century, in part as an advertisement for concrete and in part as housing for his unparalleled collection of the tools that American industrialization was rendering useless. Mercer had cruised the barns and auctions of his changing world and had brought back to Bucks County every imaginable style of cobbler's last, cider press and blacksmith's bellows, also a whaling launch complete with harpoons. In the museum's highest turret you'll find a trapdoor gallows and a horse-drawn hearse. Dozens of hand-carved sleds and cradles are stuck, as by poltergeist, to the vaulted concrete ceiling of the seven-story atrium.

The Mercer can be a very frosty place. Toward the end of a visit on a recent December afternoon, I was devoting my most serious attention to the displays on the ground floor, where the heaters are. It was here that I encountered my own telephone, lodged in a glass case labeled OBSOLETE TECHNOLOGY.

My telephone is a basic black AT&T rotary, first leased from New England Bell in 1982, then acquired outright in the chaos of Ma Bell's breakup two years later. (I seem to recall not paying for it.) The Mercer's identical copy was perched uneasily on a heap of eight-track tapes—a pairing that I right away found hurtful. Eight-track tapes are one of the great clichés of obsolescence. A rotary phone, on the other hand, still served proudly in my living room. Not long ago I'd used it to order computer peripherals from the 408 area code, if you want to talk about modern.

The display at the Mercer was an obvious provocation. And yet the harder I tried to dismiss it, the more deeply I felt accused. I became aware, for example, of the repressive energy it was costing me to ignore my visits to the Touch-Tone in my bedroom, which I now relied on for account balances and flight information and train schedules. I became aware of additional energy spent on hating the voice-mail systems that relegate a rotary to second-class ("please hold for an operator") status. I became aware, in a word, of codependency. My rotary was losing its ability to cope with the modern world, but I continued to cover for it and to keep it on display downstairs, because I loved it and was afraid of change. Nor was it the only thing I protected in this way. I was suddenly aware of having a whole dysfunctional family of obsolete machines.

My TV set was a hulking old thing that showed only

snow unless the extension-cord wire that served as an antenna was in direct contact with my skin. I wonder, is it possible to imagine a grimmer vision of codependency than the hundreds of hours I logged with sharp strands of copper wire squeezed between my thumb and forefinger, helping my TV with its picture? As for a VCR, it happened that the friend with whom I was visiting the Mercer had stepped off a plane from Los Angeles, the night before, with a VCR in a plastic shopping bag. He was giving it to me to make me stop talking about not having one.

I do still talk about not owning a CD player, and I pretend not to own any CDs. But for more than a year I've been finding myself in the houses of friends, in borrowed apartments, even in an artists-colony library, furtively making tapes of CD-only releases. Afterward I play the tapes on my tape deck and forget where they came from—until, in one of those squalid repetitions that codependency fosters, I need to convert another CD.

The display at the Mercer, on that cold December afternoon, was like a slap in the face from the modern world: *It was time to grow up.* Time to retire the rotary. Time to recall: Change is healthy. Accepting the inevitable is healthy. If you don't watch out, you'll be an old, old man at thirty-five.

As I write this, however, months later, my rotary phone is still in service. I've portrayed my appliances' obsolescence as a character defect of theirs for which I, like an addict's spouse, am trying to compensate. The truth is that the defect, the disease, inheres in me. The obsolescence is my own. It stems directly from what I do and don't do for a living. At the root of both of my reasons for keeping the rotary is a fiction-writer's life.

One reason, the obvious one, is that while phones may be

cheap, they're not free. As a fiction writer, pulling down a four-figure income, I'm the de facto inheritor of two hopelessly obsolete value systems: the Depression-era thrift of my parents' generation and the sixties radicalism of my older brothers' generation. People in the sixties were innocent enough to wonder: "Why should I work a job all week to pump more consumer dollars into a corrupt and dehumanizing system?" This is not a question you often hear asked anymore.

In his novel, *The Notebooks of Malte Laurids Brigge*, Rilke draws a parallel between the development of a poet and the history of Venice. He describes Venice as a city that has made something out of a nothing, as a city "willed in the midst of the void on sunken forests," a "hardened body, stripped to necessities," a "resourceful state, which bartered the salt and glass of its poverty for the treasures of the nations." Rilke himself was a paragon of mooching, the nonpareil of total avoidance of gainful employment, and he helped as much as anyone to shape my idea of what literature ought to be and of how a young writer might best achieve it. Fiction, I believed, was the transmutation of experiential dross into linguistic gold. Fiction meant taking up whatever the world had abandoned by the road and making something beautiful out of it.

Like one of those New Guineans who allegedly are unable to distinguish between a photograph and what is photographed, I spent my twenties literally combing weeds and Dumpsters and incinerator rooms for material, trying to make my life a more perfect metaphor for my art. The triumphant return home with scavenged loot—snow shovels, the business end of a broken rake, floor lamps, still-viable poinsettias, aluminum cookware—was as much a part of writing fiction as the typing up of final drafts. An old phone was as much a character in a narrative as an appliance in a home.

Thrift, then, literal and metaphoric, is one reason the rotary is still around. The other reason is that Touch-Tones repel me. I don't like their sterile rings, their plethora of features, their belatedness of design, the whole complacency of their hegemony. I prefer the reproachful heaviness of my rotary, just as I prefer the seventies clunkiness of my stereo components for the insult it delivers to the regiments of tasteful black boxes billeted in every house across the land.

For a long time, aesthetic resistance like this seemed valuable, or at least innocuous. But one day I wake up and find I've been left behind by *everyone*. One day the beauty of thrift and the ideal of simplicity end up petrified into barren, time-devouring obsessions. One day the victim of the market turns out to be not a trivial thing, like a rotary phone or a vinyl disc, but a thing of life-and-death importance to me, like the literary novel. One day at the Mercer it's not my telephone but my copies of Singer and Gaddis and O'Connor that are piled on top of eight-tracks with inflammatory carelessness ("OBSOLETE TECHNOLOGY, OR: THE JUDGMENT OF THE MARKET"), as on the ash-heap of history. One day I visit the Mercer, and the next day I wake up depressed.

> *For six years the antidepressant drug Prozac has been lifting the spirits of millions of Americans and thousands of Eli Lilly shareholders.*
> —*lead sentence of a* New York Times *story, January 9, 1994*

IT'S HEALTHY to adjust to reality. It's healthy, recognizing that fiction such as Proust and Faulkner wrote is doomed, to interest yourself in the victorious technology, to fashion a niche for yourself in the new information order, to discard and then forget the values and methods of literary modernism which older readers are too distracted and demoralized to appreciate in your work and which younger readers, bred on television and educated in the new orthodoxy of identity politics and the reader's superiority to the text, are almost entirely deaf and blind to. It's healthy to stop giving yourself ulcers and migraines doing demanding work that may please a few harried peers but otherwise instills unease or outright resentment in would-be readers. It's healthy to cry uncle when your bone's about to break. Likewise healthy, almost by definition, to forget about death in order to live your life: healthy to settle for (and thereby participate in) your own marginalization as a writer, to accept as inevitable a shrinking audience, an ever-deteriorating relationship with the publishing conglomerates, a retreat into the special Protective Isolation Units that universities now provide for writers. Healthy to slacken your standards, to call "great" what five years ago you might have called "decent but nothing special." Healthy, when you discover that your graduate writing students can't distinguish between "lie" and "lay" and have never read Jane Austen, not to rage or agitate but simply bite the bullet and do the necessary time-consuming teaching. Healthier yet not to worry about it—to nod and smile in your workshops and let sleeping dogs lay, let the students discover Austen when Merchant and Ivory film her.

In describing as "healthy" these responses to the death sentence obsolescence represents, I'm being no more than halfway ironic. Health really is the issue here. The pain of consciousness, the pain of knowing, grows apace with the information we have about the degradation of our planet and the insufficiency of our political system and the incivility of our society and the insolvency of our treasury and the injustice in the one-fifth of our country and four-fifths of our world that isn't rich like us. Given this increasing pain, it's understandable that a large and growing segment of the population should take comfort in the powerful narcotics that technology offers. The more popular these narcotics become, the more socially acceptable their use—and the lonelier the tiny core of people who are temperamentally incapable of deluding themselves that the "culture" of technology is anything but a malignant drug. It becomes a torture each time you see a friend stop reading books, and each time you read of another cheerful young writer doing TV in book form. You become depressed. And then you see what technology can do for those who become depressed. It can make them undepressed. *It can bring them health*. And this is the moment at which I find myself: I look around and see absolutely everyone (or so it seems) finding health. They enjoy their television and their children and they don't worry inordinately. They take their Prozac and are undepressed. They are all civil with each other and smile undepressed smiles, and they look at me with eyes of such pure opacity that I begin to doubt myself. I seem to myself a person who shrilly hates health. I'm only a phone call away from asking for a prescription of my own . . .)

SO ENDS THE FRAGMENT of essay that I've scavenged in assembling this one. I wrote the fragment two years ago when I was alone and unable to write fiction—unable, almost, to read a newspaper, the stories depressed me so much. The world hasn't changed much in the last two years, but I feel as if I have. Who knows if I can generalize from my own experience. All I know is that, soon after I wrote that fragment, I gave up. Just plain gave up. No matter what it cost me, I didn't want to be unhappy anymore. And so I stopped trying to be a writer-with-a-capital-W. Just to desire to get up in the morning was all I asked.

And then it was as if I began to remember. I remembered that as a boy I had spent long Saturday hours extracting rusty nails from the piles of paneling my father had torn out in the basement. I remembered hammering them straight on the piece of scrap iron my father had scavenged for an anvil, and then watching my father reuse these nails as he built himself a workshop and repaneled the basement. I remembered my adolescent adoration of my older brother Tom, who for a while in the seventies was an avant-garde filmmaker in Chicago, and who rehabbed an apartment in Pilsen with tools and materials largely scrounged from the now-defunct Maxwell Street market. Tom had two old Karmann Ghias, a bad yellow one handed down from our other brother, Bob, and an even worse pale blue one that had cost Tom one hundred fifty dollars. He alternately cannibalized each to feed the other; it was very time-consuming. I was riding with him the day the yellow one threw a rod and died and also the day the hood of the blue one blew open on the Dan Ryan Expressway and blocked the windshield. I clearly remember wishing to be nowhere in the world but standing next to Tom on the muffler- and tailpipe-strewn shoulder as he wired the Ghia's hood back into place.

When I began to write seriously in college, I used a hulking black Remington that rose nearly a foot off my desk, weighed as much as a small airconditioner, and took all my carpal strength to operate. Later, I wrote my first novel and half of my second on two portable Silver-Reed typewriters (fifty dollars in 1980, still only sixty-nine dollars in 1985). When they broke, I fixed them. A triumph, in a week when various journals returned five short stories with rejection letters, was my substitution of dental floss for the nylon cord that supplied carriage-advancing tension.

For typing up clean drafts, my wife and I shared a forty-pound electric Smith-Corona. Our old Chevy Nova was strictly a fair-weather friend, and it always seemed to be snowing when the Smith-Corona broke down. In the early eighties, in Boston, snow would pile up in drifts that my wife and I would struggle over, bundled like peasants as we half-dragged and half-carried the Smith-Corona to the Harvard Coop. Somewhere in the Coop's bowels dwelt a man named Mr. Palumbo. I never met Mr. Palumbo face to face, but we spoke on the telephone often. He had a raspy voice and you knew he was up to his elbows in machine oil. Mr. Palumbo loved the inexpensive fix, and I loved him for loving it. Once, on one of those prematurely indigo late afternoons that descend on Boston, he called to tell me that the main shaft had broken off the Smith-Corona's motor and that the motor would have to be replaced, at a cost of fifty dollars. It was obvious that he hated to have to tell me this. An hour or two later, well after nightfall, he called me again. "I fixed it!" he shouted. "I *glued* it. I *epoxy-glued* the shaft back on the motor!" As I recall, he charged us eighteen dollars for this service.

I bought my first computer in 1989. It was a noisy metal box made by Amdek. In good codependent form, I came to appreciate the noise of the Amdek's fan's hum. I told myself I liked the way it cut out the noise from the street and other apartments. But after about two years of heavy use the Amdek developed a new, frictive squeal whose appearance and disappearance seemed to follow the rise and fall of the air's relative humidity. My first solution was to wear earplugs on muggy days. After six months of earplugs, however, with the squeal becoming more persistent, I removed the computer's sheet-metal casing. Then the squeal stopped for no reason, and for several days I wrote fiction on a topless machine, its motherboard exposed. When the squeal returned, I discovered that I could make it stop by applying pressure to the printed-circuit board that controlled the hard disk. There was a space that I could wedge a pencil into, and if I torqued the pencil with a rubber band, the corrective pressure held. The cover of the computer didn't fit right when I put it back on; I stripped the threads off a screw and had to leave one corner of the cover sort of flapping.

To some extent, of course, everyone who is less than wealthy learns to cope with ailing equipment. Some of us are simply more vain about our coping. But it's not simply for their affirmation of my nature that I value my memories of writing prose on half-broken machines. The image of my decrepit but still-functional Amdek is also, for me, an image of America's enduring *raggedness*. Obsolescence is the leading product of our national infatuation with technology, and I now believe that obsolescence is not a darkness but a beauty: not perdition but salvation. The more headlong the progress of technological development, the greater the volume of obsolete detritus. And the detritus isn't simply material. It's angry religion, resurgent countercultural ideologies, the newly unemployed, the eternally unemployable. These are the fiction writer's guarantee that he or she will never be alone. Obsolescence is our legacy.

Because imaginative writing is fundamentally amateur. It's the lone person scouring the trash heap, not the skilled team assembling an entertainment, and we Americans are lucky enough to live in the most wonderful world of junk. Once, when I lived in Munich, I stole two cobblestones from a sidewalk construction site. I intended to wrap them in newspaper and make bookends. It was a Saturday afternoon, the streets were empty, and yet my theft seemed so terribly, terribly transgressive that I ran for blocks, a stone in each hand, before I was sure I was safe. And still I felt the stern eye of the State on me. Whereas in New York, where I now live, the Dumpsters practically *invite* me to relieve them of their useful bricks and lumber. Street people share lore with me over curbside dumps at midnight, under streetlamps. In the wee hours they spread their finds on soiled quilts at the corner of Lexington and 86th Street and barter dubious clock-radios for chipped glass doorknobs. Use and abandonment are the aquifer through which consumer objects percolate, shedding the taint of mass production and emerging as historied individuals.

It's tempting to imagine the American writer's resistance to technoconsumerism—a resistance which unfortunately in most cases takes the form of enforced economic hardship—as some kind of fungible political resistance. Not long ago, one of my former undergraduate workshop students came to visit, and I took him on a walk in my neighborhood. Jeff is a skilled, ambitious young person, gaga over Pynchon's critique of technology and capitalism, and teetering between pursuing a Ph.D. in English and trying his hand at fiction. On our walk, as I was ranting at him, telling him that fiction is about refuge, not about social change, we passed a delicious trash pile. There was a paint- and plaster-spattered wooden chair with a broken seat, and I found a scrap of two-by-four to knock the bigger clumps of plaster off. It was grubby work. Jeff said: "This is what my life will be like if I write fiction?"

After years of depression, I didn't care how forgiving of myself I sounded. I said that what mattered to me was the rescue. I could probably afford a new chair; that I prefer to live among the scavenged and reborn is my own private choice.

A sponge bath, a scrap of sturdy ash plywood from a dresser drawer abandoned at curbside, eight scavenged brass screws to attach the plywood to the underside of the seat, and a black magic marker to mask the spatters of white paint: this is how the chair was rescued.

[1996]

CONTROL UNITS

FROM COLORADO Route 67, the gatehouse of the Federal Correctional Complex looks like a pavilion from an upscale park. It has jade-colored accents and is bordered with pink gravel. As I approach it in my car, I can make out two black men in neckties behind the smoked glass windows. One of them emerges to check my ID and ask if I have weapons. I tell him I'm supposed to meet Mr. Louis Winn at one o'clock.

The guard says, "Who?"

I tell him again. With a puzzled look he returns to the pavilion, and the other man comes out. He has an ebbing hairline and a vaguely Langston Hughesish air. He's wearing a beautiful gray pin-striped suit. "Louis Winn," he says without a smile, shaking my hand through the open window.

"Oh, you're Mr. Winn," I reply with smile big enough for both of us. I'm convinced he thinks that I'm surprised because he isn't white. He tells me to follow his car up the hill. Feeling ill-served by the guard, I dig my hole deeper by persisting: "The guard didn't seem to know who you were."

Mr. Winn gives me a look of withering disappointment and, without a word, proceeds to his car.

Here in Florence, Colorado, the business of American law and order is booming. The Federal Correctional Complex is the showy new product of a war on drugs which, however much or little it has curbed the nation's illicit appetites, has helped double the federal prison population in less than a decade. The people of Florence were so keen to have its business that they bought land for the complex and presented it as a gift to the Bureau of Prisons. I've come to look at how the business works, inside and outside the fences.

The centerpiece of FCC Florence is the Administrative Maximum Facility, a sixty-million-dollar state-of-the-art warehouse for what the popular press likes to call the "worst of the worst" federal prisoners. ADX Florence, Alcatraz of the Rockies, and Admax are some of its aliases. John Gotti may eventually be shipped here, but Manuel Noriega won't. (He's a Panamanian national, and ADX's protocols violate the Geneva Convention.) ADX currently houses about 250 prisoners—just over half its capacity—and they are locked in their cells for as many as twenty-three hours a day, deprived almost entirely of human contact. Unless capital punishment should happen to become routine, the logic and technology of American corrections are unlikely to advance any further than the systems of control at ADX.

According to Bureau of Prisons (BOP) literature, the mission of ADX "is to impact inmate behavior such that inmates who demonstrate non-dangerous behavior and participate in required programs progress to another, more open Bureau

of Prisons facility." Most of ADX's inmates have been transferred from less secure prisons for misbehavior. Eighteen
percent have murdered a fellow inmate, sixteen percent have
assaulted a fellow inmate with a weapon, fifteen percent have
escaped or attempted escape, and ten percent have assaulted
prison staff members with a weapon. There is also a handful of inmates whom, because of their subversive political
views, the Fed considers terrorists. I've requested interviews
with two political prisoners: Mutulu Shakur and Ray Luc
Levasseur.

FCC Florence has four facilities. From the gatehouse, the
road winds uphill past a fenceless minimum-security prison
camp ("Club Fed"), an inviting medium-security Federal
Correctional Institution, a stern maximum-security penitentiary, and the triangular brick bunker that is ADX. Arid
high prairie has, with federal correction, become a sprinkled,
landscaped campus. When I lived in Colorado Springs, I
often passed the construction site of this complex on my way
to hiking trails in the Sangre de Cristos. The architecture is
stripy and angular, full of teal and salmon. Until the razor
wire went up I thought some real-estate cowboy was building a strangely isolated office park with energy-conserving
windows.

At the check-in counter, a blond receptionist named
Donna signs me in, backs me against a red brick wall, and
shoots me three times with a Polaroid. All the while, she's
casually communicating with someone deep in the bowels of
ADX, telling them to "bring Shakur up." The volume and
signal strength of ADX's radios are calibrated so that voices
commence speaking at conversational strength, without
crackle or distortion; the speaker seems almost to be physically present. Word comes back to Donna that Shakur is be-

ing fetched. She stamps my forearm with invisible ink and holds it under a black light. The word TAMP fluoresces.

"It's supposed to say STAMP," Donna says, stamping me again. We check under the black light, and the second word is also TAMP. She stamps me a third time and makes a complete mess. Mr. Winn intercedes with an impatient mutter, and already I'm grateful that someone besides me has incurred his disappointment.

Although ADX is the first federal prison designed specifically for round-the-clock isolation of prisoners, the institution of solitary confinement is nearly as old as the republic. In 1823 the Commonwealth of Pennsylvania opened the Eastern State Penitentiary in Philadelphia, and what became known as the "Pennsylvania system" was copied by jail builders around the world. The Quakers who designed Eastern State believed that jails in which prisoners were housed in common rooms bred depravity, and so at Eastern State each prisoner had a cell and private exercise yard which he never left. If the prisoner had to be moved, a black hood was placed over his head to bar the ingress of free-floating depravity. That prisoners in perpetual solitary confinement often hanged themselves or battered themselves to death was attributed to insanity induced by masturbation.

Over the decades, as American jail space became more precious and penological thinking evolved, routine solitary confinement fell out of favor. By the middle of this century, court rulings had placed strict limits on the use of isolation for discipline. Beginning in the seventies, however, the idea of perpetual lockdown was resurrected as "segregation" for "administrative" purposes. Isolation as a means of controlling prisoners, rather than of punishing them, was considered "administrative" and therefore OK.

Supermaxes represent a hardening of the battle lines between society and its criminal products, and more than twenty-five states now have them. The most notorious is in California, where the confluence of a vengeful public's know-nothingism and rising intramural gang violence led to the construction of a huge high-tech "control unit" facility at Pelican Bay, just south of the Oregon border. In January of 1995, five years after Pelican Bay opened, several aspects of its brand of punishment were deemed cruel and unusual by a federal district judge, Thelton Henderson, who said, in effect, that Californians' wish to "lock 'em up and throw away the key" had created a nightmare. Prisoners at Pelican Bay were routinely denied access to medical and mental-health care, suffered gratuitous violence from guards, and showed signs of psychological damage—sleeplessness, inability to concentrate, suicidal thoughts, an aggravated rage against society—almost certainly caused by prolonged isolation. Because Judge Henderson did not go so far as to shut the facility down, however, state prison officials considered his ruling a victory.

The first thing I notice at ADX Florence are the floors. They are mostly linoleum, in checkerboard patterns and custom colors like adobe red and poppy-seed gray, and they're waxed and buffed to a remarkable sheen. They seem to beg notice and comment. Ditto the cleanliness of ADX, the solidness of its steel fittings, the dapper white shirts and garnet ties and outstanding grooming of its guards, its disorienting nonrectilinear layout, and its unobtrusive but effective protocols: these are all on display. Indeed, it's possible to read into the place's high gloss a conscious effort to buff away the tarnish that the "control unit" concept received from Pelican Bay and from ADX's own predecessor in Marion, Illinois—a supermax whose reputation Amnesty International has blackened periodically.

Even as I admire the sheen at ADX, however, there are things that I won't notice until after I leave. Not until I get back in my baking car and nearly scald my mouth by drinking from the water bottle I left in it, for example, will I realize that the temperature in ADX has been perfect. Same deal with ADX's smell, of which there is a complete absence except in one corridor where I catch a whiff of something pleasant, something on the cusp between organic and inorganic—fresh spackle, maybe. ADX's lighting is ideal: never harsh, easy to read by. The sounds: no clanking, no distant shouts, no barking intercom. The automatic doors hum when they open and click shut without echo. Mr. Winn speaks in a low voice—

MR. WINN: (to a lieutenant passing by) How's it going?
LIEUTENANT: (worried, bending closer) *What did you say?*
MR. WINN: (wearily, disappointed) I said, How's it going?
LIEUTENANT: (obviously relieved) Oh, fine, fine.

—but I can hear him without straining. I'm tempted to say that the ambience of ADX is one of sensory deprivation. But the impression that ADX leaves on visitors is one of peace, not deprivation. Indeed, more than once on my tour, I find myself thinking that this would be *an excellent place to read and write.* However, I'm suspicious enough of large systems of control to believe that this is exactly what Mr. Winn would like me to feel.

Each time we encounter a checkpoint, he passes one of the Polaroids that Donna took of me through a metal drawer to a guard behind heavy glass, and the guard slides back a carrot-size portable black light to check my stamp. It's apparently enough that something on my forearm glow.

Here is how a prisoner enters a "contact" visit room at ADX. Mr. Winn and I are standing on the free-world side of the cast-concrete table that divides the room, and the door behind us has been locked from outside. Through the tiny window on the opposite door I hear rattling and clinking and glimpse some heads and shoulders. The door opens, and Mutulu Shakur steps in, hands cuffed behind his back. The door closes behind him. With a complex expression of nonchalance, anger, and dignity on his face, he places his back against the door, crouches, and lets the guard outside open a shoebox-sized slot and reach through to uncuff him. The cuffs disappear, the slot is closed and locked.

Mr. Winn props himself against the wall behind me. During the interview I don't look back at him, not once, but the vibe I get is that he's glancing at his watch a lot.

Shakur is wearing a knit watch cap and generic black plastic eyeglasses. There's some gray in his dreadlocks. He asks me where I got his name and prisoner number. I reply: from a prison-watch group in Boulder that has close ties with political prisoners. Shakur is active in the Republic of New Afrika movement and was convicted of, among other things, complicity in a 1984 armed robbery that left two cops dead; the prosecution held him responsible under RICO statutes because the robbers had held meetings in his acupuncture clinic.

Shakur explains that he ended up in maximum security, first at Marion and now at ADX, because the warden at Lewisburg, Pennsylvania, where he was first confined, felt he had too much influence on young black men and too much outside contact. Shakur's message to me, in our too-brief interview, is that black men who have been in trouble with the law have guidance to offer their communities, and that the System locks them up to keep the country's black communities rudderless. "The prisons are placed in isolated areas around the country," he says. "People like myself who have a background in communities have a hard time feeling connected to the world. Imagine a kid who gets twenty-five years for a half ounce of crack cocaine: he's isolated. The potential for mental damage is tremendous."

Standing up to leave, Shakur asks me to send a copy of my story to his son. "Tupac Shakur," he says. "You know who that is."

I promise to get a copy to Tupac.

When Mr. Winn and I are alone again, he gives me a lecture. He says that ADX is being "completely open" with the media, and that he has no control over what I might make of my tour. (He cites, with a chuckle, the headline for the piece the London *Times* did on ADX: *America's Wild Men Jailed in "Tombs."*) However, he wishes I'd told him that I'd called the human-rights people in Boulder. "All you would have had to do was mention that," he says. "It would have helped me understand what you're doing."

I explain that I called Boulder only because I needed the names of inmates willing to talk. But by now his disappointment with me seems to have hardened into judgment.

Mr. Winn next announces that our tour must be finished by 3:30. It's now 2:15, the tour hasn't even started, and I have a second interview to do. What a shame, he says, that I didn't come in the morning. Then we'd have had all day.

"But I could have started any time you wanted," I say. "You asked me to pick a time. I said one o'clock off the top of my head."

He shakes his head sadly. He was under the impression that I couldn't come until one. He's a morning person, himself. If only he'd known . . .

Ray Luc Levasseur is a working-class French Canadian from Maine. He's powerfully built and well tattooed, and he exhibits the reined nervousness of a man who could smoke half a cigarette in a single drag. He has a mustache and eyebrows so broad and dark it's as if he has three mustaches.

From 1974 to 1984 Levasseur lived underground and worked with an organization that specialized in bombing the military and corporate enemies of the global working class. After a stint on the FBI's Ten Most Wanted list, he was captured in 1984.

"I watch very little TV, mostly news and an occasional ball game," he says. "When the radio is working—which it hasn't been for the past few weeks—I'll listen to NPR sometimes." The only time he sees a fellow prisoner is during his three weekly outdoor-recreation hours. He has a wife and three daughters whom he last touched in 1989.

Every prisoner in the federal system is expected to participate in some kind of rehabilitative "program"—drug or alcohol treatment, vocational training, factory work. To get out of ADX, a prisoner must not only follow the rules but do "programming" as well. Part of what makes Levasseur a "political" are his refusals. At Marion he refused to work in a factory that manufactured coaxial cable for the military. "They can step on me and keep me as long as they want," he tells me, "but I'm not making military or police-related equipment, period. Never." As for working in the furniture factory that recently opened at ADX: "I think using prisoners as indentured servants or slaves is fundamentally wrong."

I ask him about the guards at ADX.

"I haven't met one yet that's from this area," he says. "They're all imported. The good thing about that is that, unlike Marion, they don't have that good-old-boy network. It was terrible at Marion, everybody's working for their cousin, you know, and they would do some real brutal nasty shit to you and they knew they could get away with it. Here it's not so bad because they're all new here. My feeling is that, over time, that old-boy shit's going to settle in. I think prisons foster that kind of thing."

Mr. Winn, standing at my shoulder, is sighing at precise five-minute intervals.

I ask Levasseur whether he considers himself the worst of the worst.

"People like Robert McNamara," he says, "they've killed a hell of a lot more people than I have. That's the problem. If you want to define crime as somebody with a crack pipe, or somebody's B and E or something like that, it's always going to boil down to very black and very poor people. OK? But you get these monstrous crimes committed by somebody like McNamara. And Union Carbide, what they did in India, they killed eight thousand fucking people." He lowers his voice a little, reflectively. "Of course, I was convicted of bombing Union Carbide." He snickers and then, rubbing his face, regains his composure. "Small price to pay for the lives of those people." He points at Mr. Winn. "He probably *idolizes* somebody like Robert McNamara. He doesn't see what they do as a crime."

Mr. Winn takes this opportunity to say to me, coolly, "Do you have any final questions you'd like to ask?"

I shrug.

Levasseur shrugs.

I tell him I'll write to him.

Once he is gone, a guard releases us from our side of the contact visit room. We have twenty-five minutes left to tour ADX. Time enough to walk down a great many climate-controlled corridors; to inspect the cast-concrete indestructibility of the fixtures of an empty cell (the cell is gray, about seven by twelve feet, and it has an integrated sink-toilet-fountain, a concrete bed and desk, a built-in electric cigarette lighter, and a narrow window offering a fragment of blue sky); to drop in at one of the law libraries and the leisure library (mass-market paperbacks only; lots of Louis L'Amour and Robert Heinlein); and to have one brief conversation verging on the pleasant. I ask Mr. Winn how ADX has managed to attract the attention of CBS, ABC, NBC, CNN, NPR, the BBC, French TV, Yorkshire TV, *Der Spiegel*, the *New York Times*, the London *Times*, and *Details*. He replies that the attraction is partly the high-tech stuff but mainly "the mystique of Alcatraz"—the romance that inevitably surrounds whatever prison holds the worst of the worst.

Still hoping to win him over, I venture the opinion that romanticizing prisons is a sick thing. He nods. "Just work in one for a day," he says. "They're not happy places."

I'm moved by his sober tone, but only briefly. The violent political warfare which shook America in the sixties and seventies and which has lately resurfaced—in the Unabomber case, in Oklahoma City, in the Philadelphia of Mumia Abu-Jamal—is most active in the prisons that hold a million and a half people, almost all of them poor. That the vast majority of these people are unpolitical takes nothing away from the state of war. Rare is the war that is fought on principle; jailers and jailed are simply blood enemies. And the roots here are deep. Mr. Winn grew up on Army bases, whereas Shakur grew up in Jamaica, Queens, and Levasseur in a depressed mill town in Maine. Their war is hidden from public view by teal and salmon and phrases like "worst of the worst." Those who are losing it are, in the main, sociopaths. Those who are winning it wear nice suits and talk of sadness.

I'd like to believe I'm not implicated in this war.

TO FREMONT COUNTY, Colorado, prisons mean one thing and one thing only: dollars. The county seat, Cañon City, may have been the first community in America to recognize incarceration as a growth industry. In 1868, having supported Denver in its successful bid to become the permanent state capital, Cañon was offered its choice of payoff: the state prison or the state university. It took the prison.

More than a century later, the town and its environs have a lock on state corrections. Nine of Colorado's eighteen prisons are located within five miles of Cañon City's Wal-Mart. The Colorado Territorial Prison Museum, housed in a decommissioned cellblock at the west end of town, is a rallying point for Cañon's high society. In the yard outside the museum are picnic tables, a rusting octagonal gas chamber, and a pair of cells in which sunburned British tourists ham it up as desperate convicts. Prominent Cañonites contribute to the Museum Foundation at the Warden level (five to ten thousand dollars); lesser lights may choose, say, the Sergeant level (one hundred to five hundred dollars). To raise further money, there's an annual golf tournament and an occasional Big House Bash—a fancy-dress affair at which, a few years ago, arriving benefactors dropped their invitations into a plastic scale model of the gas chamber.

A few miles east of Cañon, on the banks of the Arkansas

River, is the one-stoplight town of Florence. Elks, Eagles, and Legionnaires call bingo here three nights a week. At the corner of the road to the FCC is a new Hardee's that everyone in town is proud of. Ranged along Main Street are one bank, one drugstore, one grocery store with a permanent-looking billboard welcoming the FCC, and a wealth of vacancies and For Sale signs. Here the mayor of Florence, Merle Strickland, a seventy-two-year-old Texan lady with diamond stud earrings and a white Ford pickup, liquidated her furniture store because she could make better money on Wall Street and (she quips) the stock is easier to carry.

Concrete-clad irrigation ditches line Florence's side streets, greening the cottonwood-shaded lawns of stuccoed pillbox houses and a few brick Victorians. Cyanide Street, on the western outskirts, dead-ends in a dismal RV park called Last Mile Estates. The Arkansas, roiling and bucking just beyond, is the color of steamed artichokes.

Florence was once a town of thirty thousand and the center of a booming extractive economy. Coal, oil, gold, limestone, gypsum, fuller's earth, and alabaster all were mined or processed here. Florence's No. 42, the country's oldest continuously producing commercial oil well, still draws four barrels a day. By the 1980s, however, most of Fremont County's mineral wealth was exhausted. Ruined hillsides and unnatural-looking gulches scarred the local landscape, and Florence's population had taken a free fall to three thousand.

"We were like a dry lakebed, an area of clay full of cracks," says Skip Dyer, the former executive director of the Fremont County Economic Development Corporation. "The money was the water, and the water had just disappeared. It was a rather desperate time for many, many people and many, many businesses."

To economically parched Fremont County, a federal correctional complex represented the terminus of a pipeline through which federal money, in the form of payrolls, could flow at upwards of fifty thousand dollars a day. There would also be one-time cash cloudbursts when facilities were built or renovated. Boosters of the prison envisioned thriving custom for their businesses, and a population rising to the critical mass that would draw new employers to the area.

Fremont County's tapping of the new federal resource began in 1986, when a local pencil salesman named Tom Schryver saw his chance to make a good old American killing. It happened that Schryver's brother worked for the BOP, and he mentioned to Schryver that the Fed was seeking troubled colleges, monasteries, and convents that might be convertible to minimum-security prisons. It happened, further, that Cañon City possessed just such a property: the Holy Cross Abbey. Holy Cross sat on 220 acres just outside the Cañon city limits, near the Wal-Mart, and was outfitted with dormitories and a dining hall that could feed three hundred. Its finances were rumored to be precarious.

There was abundant evidence, moreover, that Fremont County did not mind hosting inmates. On a Sunday morning after my visit to ADX, I pick up a Florence town councilman named Jimmie Lloyd who has promised to introduce me to Schryver. Lloyd, a retired air force lieutenant colonel, summarizes the Cañonite attitude toward prisons this way: "Escapees don't stick around, and who's going to burglarize a house that's potentially a prison guard's? You get caught and go to jail, you may wind up with the victim as your guard. You also run the risk of getting your head blown off. There's probably more guns in this area than in half the state."

Driving through the unincorporated town of Penrose,

Lloyd and I pass a house with ostriches in the back yard, and he offers his opinion that ostrich farms are a Ponzi scheme. On a dusty street where the house numbers follow no evident logic, we succeed in locating the modest one-story home of Tom Schryver.

Schryver is a good-natured man, his face open and smooth. He has a big belly but a slender man's handsome features. He meets us at his door in sandals and chocolate-colored polyester slacks. "I'm just an old hick," he tells me happily. "I was selling pencils when I met Steve Stewart."

Steve Stewart arrives moments later. He's a realtor and he looks it. He has the extra pounds, the trustable face, the ease in weekend wear. He has driven down from Colorado Springs and brought along three commemorative clocks for the coaches of his son's little league team. Tom Schryver has engraved brass nameplates for the clocks. "It's a sideline of Tom's," says Stewart.

Tom Schryver had met Stewart when he peddled personalized pencils and other commercial souvenirs to Stewart's agency. In late 1986, Schryver acquired a realtor's license and immediately paid a visit to the Holy Cross Abbey. The abbey's business manager confirmed that the monks were indeed prepared to sell. The manager and Schryver agreed on an asking price of 12.75 million dollars, and Schryver got exclusive rights to the property for seventy-five days. He began to petition the BOP's head of property acquisitions, a man named Jim Jones.

What finally swayed Jones was the twelve-minute video Schryver made. In Schryver's living room, drinking store-brand diet cola, the four of us watch the video. Schryver can't hide his pride in the zooms and pans and soundtrack. "It's not as easy as it looks to match up what you're saying with the pictures," he says. "When I wasn't talking, I turned up the volume of my stereo, and then I'd turn it back down when I had to talk."

The music sounds like Mantovani.

"It's a Reader's Digest record," Schryver says.

The video purports to be an overview of the abbey's buildings for any potential buyer. Schryver subtly geared it, however, to the Justice Department. "I make a joke about prisons," he says. "See if you can catch it. It's just a joke between me and my mind."

"Between you and your mind," Steve Stewart echoes in comic awe.

There are, in fact, several jokes. On the soundtrack, Schryver describes the abbey's gymnasium as "a very pleasant place to spend time." (He appeals to us gleefully: "Get it? *Spend time?*") He goes on to mention that the abbey's buildings are set back from Highway 50, thus providing "a buffer zone to the outside" ("Buffer zone! Hee-hee!") and he notes that the abbey's single entrance "can easily be outfitted with a gate to restrict access."

"This whole town has a lot in common with Dachau," Stewart remarks slyly.

"The last pan was especially hard because I had to do it from a car," Schryver says. "It came out beautifully. You see how there's a truck coming out just perfectly when I get to the entrance? This is a lot harder than you might think."

"'And now let's take a look at the crematorium,'" Stewart voice-overs.

In February 1987, Jim Jones flew to Florence and pronounced the abbey the best site he'd seen yet. More than a thousand Cañonites sent copies of a form letter urging the BOP to buy it. According to Stewart, Jones was overwhelmed by the response. He announced publicly that the Bureau was acquiring a property in Colorado.

"I was already counting the three hundred seventy-five thousand that was my share of the commission," Schryver says. "I was getting Mercedes-Benz literature."

"It was a done deal," Stewart says. "And then a week after the final appraisal I get up on a Saturday morning and there's a banner headline in the paper: DEAL OFF FOR ABBEY. That's how the exclusive agents for the property got their notice that the deal was off."

The monks at the abbey had held a final vote on the sale and changed their minds.

"I'd worked hard on that sucker," Schryver says. "I could have gotten all huffy and puffy when the deal fell through. But I let Steve do that."

Steve Stewart believed that since his agency had exclusive rights to represent the abbey and had found a ready, able, and willing buyer, the abbey still owed him the realtor's fee. He wrote to the Apostolic Delegate in Rome and placed a lien on the abbey. But no one in the Justice Department would confirm that the BOP intended to buy.

"Everybody's looking for their twenty minutes of fame," Jimmie Lloyd tells me on the way back to Florence. "Like most people, Tom Schryver didn't get his."

MY SECOND ATTEMPT to penetrate FCC Florence takes place at the medium-security Federal Correctional Institution. Like ADX, the FCI is a showcase. Among its notably humane features are a sweat lodge where Native Americans can practice their rites, six full-size pool tables, a painting studio, and a library whose holdings include *Gravity's Rain-*

bow in hardcover and Walter Kaufmann's study of Hegel. Footpaths crisscross a large central campus whose lush grass is push-mown by prisoners in khaki. Nearly half the inmates at the FCI are in for drug offenses.

My guide, Case Management Coordinator Denise Snider, gives me an exhaustive tour of the UNICOR furniture factory. UNICOR is a semiautonomous federal corporation, like the Postal Service. It runs the BOP's factories, selling exclusively to federal buyers. The products of FCI Florence are comfortable, personalityless chairs and sofas. Inmates working here earn between forty cents and a dollar and a quarter an hour. I see towers of foam rubber, air-powered drills and staplers attached to pendant yellow coils of tubing, an intriguing Gluing Room, and a whole lot of men in khaki.

UNICOR will train you for jobs on the floor—one of the program's stated purposes is to provide inmates with "marketable skills"—but to land a desk job in UNICOR's lovely late-model business office, you need prior experience in the outside world. At each desk, where the modern eye expects to see a braceleted young woman with padded shoulders and teased bangs, a bearded long-haired man in khaki is typing briskly. The effect is parodic or surreal.

For most of my visit to the FCI, Case Management Coordinator Snider remains profoundly unmoved by my efforts to charm and ingratiate. Her clothing and haircut are assertively sensible, and she's plainly counting the minutes till she's free of me. As I'm leaving, however, a few tiny chinks open in her professionalism.

"I was a psychology major in college," she says, explaining how she acquired two degrees in criminal justice. "A professor told me she thought I'd be perfect for criminology. It suits my nature. I like to find things out about people without their knowing that I'm doing it."

I ask her how many prison employees live in Florence or other nearby towns. I recall that Mr. Winn does not live in the area.

"We're encouraged to live close by," Snider says. "But the closest place I could find day care was in Pueblo. The administrators who are black might like to live close by, but they don't feel welcome in Florence or Cañon City, so they end up in Pueblo or Colorado Springs, with an hour commute. Our warden is black, for example. He can't live around here."

IN JUNE of 1987, after the abbey deal fell through, the Fremont County Economic Development Commission (FCEDC) learned from Jim Jones that the BOP had decided to build a new prison complex in the Western United States entirely from scratch. The FCEDC hastened to develop four potential sites in Fremont County, and Jones was particularly enthusiastic about a property owned by the Colorado Department of Corrections located between Cañon City and Florence. The FCEDC assured him he could have the land for free.

In May 1988, Jim Jones asked Skip Dyer, the FCEDC's executive director, what the community's response would be to a larger complex, one perhaps containing as many as three facilities. "They'd hug you a lot harder," Dyer replied.

Although the BOP was being wooed by depressed communities all over the West and was studying sites in at least five of them, Fremont County had the inside track. Just when it appeared that all systems were go, however, the

Colorado state legislature refused to authorize the gift of land to the Feds. "We'd had reasonable confidence that we'd get that state land," Dyer says. "When it fell through, we felt we had to strike while the iron was still hot."

The iron was struck by the owner of Jim's Clothing in Florence. Jim Provenzano is a heavy-set man with soft brown eyes and olive skin. His father, an Italian tailor, came to Florence in 1916 and built a business by taking the measurements of miners entering the local shafts, sewing while they mined, and delivering their suits when they emerged from their shift. Provenzano *fils* was a member of the countywide prison steering committee, and he knew that there was an alternate site, just south of Florence, that Jim Jones had deemed adequate. The asking price was a hundred thousand dollars. Provenzano told a friend at the Rocky Mountain Bank & Trust that he would put up a thousand dollars to buy the Florence property if the bank would put up a thousand, too.

"I could sooner put a man on the moon than afford a thousand dollars," Provenzano says. "But we only had two weeks, and I knew the Fed was interested in that property. So I said: Let's buy it. My main purpose was to bring our store into its seventy-fifth year. I hoped we could provide local employment and give our kids a place to work if they wanted it."

With Provenzano's impetus, the FCEDC quickly organized a fund-raising drive. "It was like a disease that everybody caught," Provenzano says. "It was like an auction. Everybody else was pledging; you had to pledge too." Within two weeks the FCEDC had eighty thousand dollars in the bank and another sixty thousand in pledges. By the summer of 1988, it was able to send the title for three hundred acres of desert to the BOP—thus fulfilling its promise of free land.

Ground was broken in Florence on July 14, 1990. Out-of-town dignitaries made appearances at a barbecue in the town park. A pickaxe commemorating the event now hangs on the wall at the Florence Chamber of Commerce. Also on the wall are framed watercolors of the four prisons in the complex. Twin garlands of steel are taped to the plywood paneling above the paintings. A calligraphed card identifies the garlands as RAZOR WIRE FROM FEDERAL PRISON.

FOR THE NATIONAL AND INTERNATIONAL MEDIA, ADX is the showcase of a new millennium, but just east of Cañon City there is a new Colorado State Penitentiary (CSP) that opened fifteen months earlier than the federal ADX, is identical in its principles, and is easily as carefully designed. You have to admire the Feds for persuading people that ADX is newsworthy.

My guide at the CSP, Administrative Officer Dennis Burbank, could hardly be more different from Louis Winn. Mr. Winn is a transfer to the area; Dennis is a local. Mr. Winn is smooth and well-spoken, a master at passing up obvious opportunities to volunteer information. Dennis expresses feelings, opinions. He's an individual who utilizes the words "utilize" and "individual" with an ease that makes them sound almost slangy. He can get all glowy on the topic of the federal ADX ("I *love* their isolation cells") and yet visibly shudder at the thought of corrections in Oklahoma ("a model of how not to do things"). When I meet him he's wearing a red-white-and-blue necktie of considerable hideousness. The tie bears a single word: LIBERTY.

As Dennis presents it, the CSP is designed to provide a kind of tough love: to be the stern, corrective parent that most of its residents presumably never had. If you follow the rules and learn to control your antisocial impulses, you proceed from the very unpleasant Level I (no privileges, a two-guard escort for a trip to the shower) to the less unpleasant Level III (more spending money, more personal freedoms) and finally, after six months or a year, back to a prison where you can interact with fellow prisoners. It's a theory of *in loco parentis*. What CSP sets out to do is to impress on the child-like, acting-out prisoner that the world around him is real and that he has responsibilities to it.

The staff at CSP devotes considerable ingenuity to tailoring "behavior management plans" to particular offenses. The punishment for throwing feces at a guard, for example, is to be deprived of the usual prison food. The thrower is put, instead, on a "special management diet": a squishy high-protein loaf that Dennis describes as "not very tasty." With as much delicacy as I can, I ask if the special management diet changes the nature of its consumers' feces. Dennis says no. The diet is simply a message: stop misbehaving, and we'll put you back on real food.

When I express uneasiness about the possibility of sensory deprivation disorders at CSP, Dennis has an expert paged, a social worker named Gene Espinoza, who tells me that prisoners are not, in fact, all that isolated. Besides the staff-intensive daily contacts, inmates also call to each other from their cells, tap on the walls, and, when they think no one's looking, fashion their bedsheets into "rat lines"—long cords that they push under the doors of their cells and attempt to snap like a whip and reach the doors of other cells with. If you've managed to "keister in" some tobacco (this is

Dennis's jolly phrase; it means "secrete in your rectum out of sight of a simple spread-your-cheeks check") and wish to sell it to a neighbor, the rat line is the preferred means of conducting the transaction.

My relationship with Dennis suffers a moment of awkwardness when I point out that the contacts which Mr. Espinoza calls a boon to mental health are in fact against the regulations and routinely punished. This is how Dennis resolves the paradox: "Inmates are not allowed to communicate with each other. Nevertheless, they communicate."

CSP is operating at full capacity. As of June, 486 men and thirteen women were imprisoned here. Each of CSP's four "units" has its own medical exam room and barber room (the latter doubles as a mental-health counseling area); the idea is to minimize the time an inmate spends outside his unit. At the center of the unit is a two-tiered control area from which eight "pods" radiate tangentially. The upper floor of the control area is glassed in and contains a couple of guards who oversee large color monitors controlling locks, lights, intercoms, water flow, and the like. Dennis says that the controls were originally touch-screen, but guards would find themselves opening up doors with a sneeze or the brush of a sleeve. Now they use trackballs and clickers.

Each pod has sixteen cells arranged on two tiers and looking out on a "day hall" with a waxed concrete floor. The first principle of a control unit is that no inmate should ever have direct contact with another inmate, and the electronics here serve an elaborate choreography of comings and goings. Prisoners at disciplinary Levels I and II must be cuffed and escorted by two guards whenever they leave their cells; the big carrot of Level III is being allowed to walk the fifty feet to the shower or exercise room or telephone without escort. Prisoners at the different levels are mixed together in each unit, so that the privileges of those in Level III are visible to all.

Eight or ten of the cells are quiescent at any given moment. Silently, behind glass, a blond-bearded inmate is working out in the lower-tier exercise room, whose equipment consists of a chin-up bar. In the upper-tier exercise room an inmate with a half-grown Afro can be seen with his face pressed to the window as he peers out at the late-afternoon nothing. (CSP has no outdoor recreation area.) One or two other inmates have their faces pressed to the windows of their cell doors. Yet another is showering. Through the glass door of the pod's narrow shower room I can see his head and torso not real clearly in honey-colored light. The water will run for no more than ten minutes before the pod computer turns it off. If he needs a razor, a guard brings it before the shower and takes it away after.

"It's still hard for me to get used to how quiet it is in this facility," Dennis says.

The cells themselves are seldom quiet. Television is important at CSP—so important that if an inmate arrives at CSP without a set of his own, he's given one as soon as he's out of Level I. CSP has its own station, broadcasting self-improvement programming and vocational training (Dennis mentions "janitorial work" as a vocation), as well as movies and devotional instruction. On Saturday nights, there's bingo. CSP's recreational therapist, Jim Gentile, focuses the closed-circuit camera on a spinning cage from which he draws numbered balls. He calls six games, and inmates with a winning card send him a Request for Interview slip. When he makes his rounds the next day he awards a candy bar to winners. Gentile says that if he takes a Saturday night off, he gets hate mail for three days.

The basement of CSP houses what's called Intake. Inmates arrive and depart here, wearing orange jumpsuits. When Dennis and I pay our visit, a face is pressed against the window of each holding cell. Newcomers. Everybody looks about twenty-eight. White, Hispanic, black; all of them in the pink. One of them calls to nobody: "Yo! How many phone calls a month do you get in Level I?"

I feel them looking at me and am careful not to meet their eyes. Lest: what? Lest some vertigo draw me to them? Lest they see my fear? Lest they implicate me in their war? Lest I have to register emotionally the fact that I am free and will soon be speeding along a highway through juniper and scrub pine toward dinner in Florence? In junior high I learned that by avoiding certain kids' eyes in the hallway I could sometimes escape notice, or at least escape being punched. Lowering one's eyes is a sign of deference—I learned this very early on. But it's also, of course, a way of not seeing.

One of the holding cells in Intake has a full window, not just a slit in the door. The black man with a shaved head who's inside it catches me looking at him. I avert my eyes and then look again, and he gives me a strange smirk—one that I don't think I'm reading too much into to say that it's a mockery of the kind of smile shared by two human beings but at the same time is a gesture of trust: that I might understand and share the mockery. I return the smirk, too widely. It falls off my face, and I avert my eyes.

FOR THE PRISON BOOSTERS who imagined the town blossoming under a shower of federal dollars, there appear to have been a few surprises. The major construction contracts for FCC Florence all went to big firms outside Fremont

County, and a lot of the Florentine men who had hoped for construction work failed the test of back strength. Instead of employment, the town got traffic, dust, and a lively bar trade. When it came time to staff ADX, the BOP, which was intent on maximizing the professionalism of its showcase facility, imported seasoned guards and administrators from elsewhere in the country. Most janitorial, laundry, lawn, and kitchen work at the complex is performed by prisoners, and for the locally filled positions, the maximum age for applicants turned out to be thirty-seven. This was an unwelcome revelation for a town of retirees; people at city hall refer to it as "the shocker."

Jim Provenzano had hoped that prison corrections officers would buy uniforms at his store. Unfortunately, he says, "they wanted me to sell boots at ten dollars below my cost; otherwise they'd use the regular government supplier. How am I going to compete with that?" Some FCC maintenance workers are buying uniforms from Provenzano, but he's seen little spillover demand for his stock of Western wear.

When Provenzano assesses the return on his thousand-dollar gamble, his sentences trail off into worried ellipses. "I don't mean to sound negative, but . . ." Although he believes that Florence will eventually prosper, he concedes that Jim's Clothing is not doing as well as he hoped. "I don't know if I'll be in business two years from now."

"I empathize with our merchants," says Merle Strickland, Florence's marketwise mayor. "They're trying to survive in what's primarily a service economy. I'd love to see a thriving business community, but they're going to have the same problems I had with my furniture store: people are going to buy where it's cheapest. If you want to be successful here, you have to make it in service."

Strickland takes me to see Florence's new nine-hole Bear Paw Golf Course, whose driving range and practice green afford a panorama of the FCC's northern perimeter. Bear Paw was built in part to appeal to prison bureaucrats, who were reputed to be keen linksmen, and in part to anchor a housing development. At the end of a rutted gravel road, several outsize model units offer nice views of electric fences.

According to Strickland, Florence has the water infrastructure to sustain a population of twenty thousand. Water is a big source of revenue for the town, which exacts a fifty percent markup from customers outside the city limits; the gross is about five thousand dollars a month from selling to the FCC. "Some of our councilmen are fond of saying that our town's biggest asset is its people," she says. "I happen to believe that the most valuable asset my constituents own is the water."

I tell Strickland that I don't see how exactly the prison has fed the new housing developments going up around town.

She gestures pooh-poohingly. "The growth isn't coming from the prison. It's coming from amenities like this golf course. It's part of the growth along the whole Front Range. Guards making twelve dollars an hour aren't going to find housing here. And I've heard a lot of prison administrators remark that they personally don't care to live that close to where they work."

Of the prison boosters, Strickland says: "They all think Santa Claus is coming. But there is no Santa Claus."

Just such a realization appears to have dawned on Jim Provenzano. He understands now, he says, that once employees leave work at the prison complex they want to go straight home, rather than stop and shop in Florence. He jokes that local businessmen ought to pay for radar traps on the roads to Pueblo and the Springs so that people can't get to the malls so quickly.

"People assume that because I'm the only store in a small town my prices must be higher," Provenzano says. "It's not true. But we've got a generation of kids who know nothing but Wal-Mart, who know nothing but malls."

Provenzano, who initially agreed to talk to me for "a few minutes," ends up chatting for an hour. When, on my way out, I show an interest in a pair of Levi's, he confirms what chain-store salesmen in my past have always vehemently denied: that 501s of the same marked size vary widely in their cut. He doesn't have the preshrunk 32×34s I want—his stock is not large—but he is able, with much measuring and comparing, to locate a pair of 33×34s cut small enough to fit me perfectly.

"I'm having problems with Levi," he says as he rings up the purchase. (The price is a chain-store price.) "They say I'm short on volume. We've been selling Levi's for sixty years, and now they say I'm short on volume."

After teasing me affably about my growing waist, and then asking me for my shirt size, he presents me with a T-shirt to wear with my new jeans. It's stenciled with a drawing of the Federal Prison Camp.

IF SHAKESPEARE'S RICHARD II HAD LIVED in Alcatraz in the 1930s, he might have noted the uniqueness of its design and setting, the splendor of the scenery around it, and the romance of its imperfect security. Richard II in ADX Florence would see perfect, anonymous utility in the middle of a blasted landscape. Comparing the prison where he lived unto the world of 1995, he couldn't miss seeing money. Dollars within, dollars without.

What's futuristic about ADX and CSP is not their high-tech accoutrements (you won't see the exoskeletal uniforms or blaster guns of sci-fi flicks) but the social context in which these facilities are coming on line. It isn't hard to extrapolate the logic of our political economy's solution to the crime problem. In many respects, the future is glimpsable in our not wholly unpleasant present. The murder rate is plummeting in New York City, for example, as New York State's prison population soars. Three-quarters of the inmates in the state system come from just seven impoverished neighborhoods in New York City. Apparently it's genuinely feasible simply to lock away the problem. Across the country, educational programs for inmates are on the wane, executions are mounting, and more and more legislators are clamoring to reduce recreation for prisoners and to extract greater revenues from prison labor.

The black or Latino youth whose father is in prison and whose neighborhood can offer no better job than bagging groceries commits a crime, is processed, and is then shipped to a warehouse in a rural white community. Between strikes one and three there's a cynical calculus: the imprisoned youth emerges from jail embittered and unemployable; inevitably, he commits another crime; inevitably, there are innocent victims. Residual crimes are the cost of doing business in this country, and even these pay the dividend of keeping the public's fear of crime ever fresh.

The social Darwinist may here ponder the beauties of our economy's evolution. The press covers crime (especially the relatively rare instances of random violence against white people) because crime sells—because the white audience loves to hear about it. Then the intensive, decontextualized, and highly salable coverage of crime becomes evidence of a Crime Epidemic; the Audience gets "sick and tired" of hearing about a thing that every marketer knows it actually never gets sick or tired of hearing about, and it empowers its elected representatives to Get Tough. Thus the criminal is demonized. The distance between Us and Him grows and grows, thereby ensuring that here in the country that invented the Western and the crime drama and the News at Eleven, in the country that celebrated the James brothers and Bonnie and Clyde, we will always be able to hear what we most don't want to hear, which is what we most want to hear. In enjoying and then punishing our murderers, we are continually trying to exorcise the contradictions that make us Americans. Our love-hate love affair with crime is the epos of the controlling dollar at war with the wild frontier.

Eventually, when the black or Latino youth whiffs at his third spitball, he's remanded for life to a system that maintains internal order and earns money by forcing its prisoners to do, for a dollar or less per hour, the menial work that as free men they refused to do for a minimum wage. For the men who won't cooperate, there's always a stint in dispensaries of benevolent discipline like ADX and CSP. At first hearing, Ray Levasseur's description of ADX as a "proto-techno-fascist's architectural wetdream" sounds like tired agitprop hyperbole. But consider fascism in its original (Italian) sense of getting government to work with the bloodless efficiency of a corporation; of making the trains run on time. Fascism's real essence is a patriotic corporatism that presents itself as beneficent and effective. In light of the future we are building in Fremont County, Ray Levasseur and Mutulu Shakur, whose claims of being "political" make them anomalies, are actually the system's most typical prisoners. It may be true that each of the individuals in our nation's prisons represents a story of personal irresponsibility. But the whole of a million and a half of these stories is greater than the sum of its parts. The whole is political, and Levasseur and Shakur are the voice of the statistics. They are saying, Let's think about what a million and a half men in jail might imply about the way we do business.

And here is the thing: the Feds aren't friendly to me, their reserve won't thaw. Whereas every Coloradan I speak to is a person of visible hopes, dreams, fears. It takes me only an hour to love them. They are not positive of anything. They seem at once freer and more captive than the federal functionaries who by day are sealed inside their compound and by twilight commute to Pueblo West. Free to be confused and suspicious, and captive to the perpetually self-perfecting mechanisms of control and cash flow that are stalking the last of America's traditional communities. Captive to the federal agency that allows a town to hope for construction jobs that don't materialize, promises three prisons and throws in an Alcatraz as an afterthought, hints at trade with local businesses but ends up using prearranged suppliers; captive to the inescapable efficiency of strip malls and tract housing. There's no conspiracy here, no conscious intent to deceive, no grand ironies. There's only, in this valley of erosional mesas and spent mines, the stepwise dwindling of an innocence. When Merle Strickland says that her community's greatest asset is its water rights and not its people, she's both exactly right and exactly wrong.

At night the prisons glow in the desert like a reactor, a launchpad, some latent federal thing. From miles away you can see that nothing's moving inside the wire.

[1995]

MR. DIFFICULT

OR A WHILE last winter, after my third novel came out, I was getting a lot of angry mail from strangers. What upset them was not the novel—a comedy about a family in crisis—but some impolitic remarks I'd made in the press, and I knew that it was a mistake to send more than bland one-sentence notes in reply. But I couldn't help fighting back a little. Taking a page from an old literary hero of mine, William Gaddis, who had long deplored the reading public's confusion of the writer's work and the writer's private self, I suggested that the letter writers look at my fiction rather than listen to distorted news reports about its author.

A few months later, one of the original senders, a Mrs. M—— in Maryland, wrote back with proof that she'd done the reading. She began by listing thirty fancy words and phrases from my novel, words like "diurnality" and "antipodes," phrases like "electro-pointillist Santa Claus faces." She then posed the dreadful question: "Who is it you are writing for? It surely could not be the average person who just enjoys a good read." And she offered this caricature of me and my presumed audience:

> the elite of New York, the elite who are beautiful, thin, anorexic, neurotic, sophisticated, don't smoke, have abortions tri-yearly, are antiseptic, live in lofts or penthouses, this superior species of humanity who read *Harper's* and *The New Yorker.*

The subtext seemed to be that difficulty in fiction is the tool of socially privileged readers and writers who turn up their noses at the natural pleasure of a "good read" in favor of the invidious, artificial pleasure of feeling superior to other people. To Mrs. M——, I was "a pompous snob, and a real ass-hole."

One part of me, the part that takes after my father, who admired scholars for their intellect and large vocabularies and was something of a scholar himself, wanted to call Mrs. M—— a few names in reply. But another, equally strong part of me was stricken to learn that Mrs. M—— felt excluded by my language. She sounded a little bit like my mother, a life-long anti-elitist who used to get good rhetorical mileage out of the mythical "average person." My mother might have asked me if I really had to use words like "diurnality," or if I was just showing off.

In the face of hostility like Mrs. M——'s, I find myself paralyzed. It turns out that I subscribe to two wildly different models of how fiction relates to its audience. In one model, which was championed by Flaubert, the best novels are great works of art, the people who manage to write them deserve extraordinary credit, and if the average reader rejects the work it's because the average reader is a philistine; the value of any novel, even a mediocre one, exists independent of whether people are able to enjoy it. We can call this the Status model. It invites a discourse of genius and art-historical importance.

In the opposing model, a novel represents a compact between the writer and the reader, with the writer providing words out of which the reader creates a pleasurable experience. Writing thus entails a balancing of self-expression and communication within a group, whether the group consists of *Finnegans Wake* enthusiasts or fans of Barbara Cartland. Every writer is first a member of a community of readers, and the deepest purpose of reading and writing fiction is to sustain a sense of connectedness, to resist existential loneliness; and so a novel deserves a reader's attention only as long as the author sustains the reader's trust. This is the Contract model. The discourse here is one of pleasure and connection. My mother would have liked it.

To an adherent of Contract, the Status crowd looks like an arrogant connoisseurial elite. To a true believer in Status, on the other hand, Contract is a recipe for pandering, aesthetic compromise, and a babel of competing literary sub-communities. With certain novels, of course, the distinction doesn't matter so much. *War and Peace, The House of Mirth*: you call them art, I call them entertainment, we both turn the pages. But the two models diverge tellingly when readers find a book difficult.

According to the Contract model, difficulty is a sign of trouble. In the most grievous cases, it may convict an author of violating the contract with his own community: of placing his self-expressive imperatives or his personal vanity or his literary-club membership ahead of the audience's legitimate desire for connection—of being, in other words, an asshole. Taken to its free-market extreme, Contract stipulates that if a product is disagreeable to you, the fault must be the product's. If you crack a tooth on a hard word in a novel, you sue the author. If your professor puts Dreiser on your reading list, you write a harsh student evaluation. If the local symphony plays too much twentieth-century music, you cancel your subscription. You're the consumer; you rule.

From a Status perspective, difficulty tends to signal excellence; it suggests that the novel's author has disdained cheap compromise and stayed true to an artistic vision. Easy fiction has little value, the argument goes. Pleasure that demands hard work, the slow penetration of mystery, the outlasting of lesser readers, is the pleasure most worth having; and if, like Mrs. M——, you can't hack it, then to hell with you.

The Status position is undeniably flattering to a writer's sense of importance. In my bones, though, I'm a Contract kind of person. I grew up in a friendly egalitarian suburb reading books for pleasure. Even as an adult, I consider myself a slattern of a reader. I have started (in many cases, more than once) *Moby-Dick*, *The Man Without Qualities*, *Mason & Dixon*, *Don Quixote*, *Remembrance of Things Past*, *Doctor Faustus*, *Naked Lunch*, *The Golden Bowl*, and *The Golden Notebook* without coming anywhere near finishing them. Indeed, by a comfortable margin, the most difficult book I ever voluntarily read in its entirety was Gaddis's 956-page first novel, *The Recognitions*.

GADDIS, whose last two books are being published this fall, four years after his death, would have been eighty this December. As much as any American writer of his generation, he frankly endorsed Status and disdained Contract. His methods were increasingly postmodern, but he had old-fashioned Romantic and high-modern notions of the artist as savior and the work of art as singular and sacred; the plight of both art and artist in a commercially mad America was at the center of his work. Which work is, itself, quintessentially difficult.

I read *The Recognitions* as a kind of penance, back in the early nineties. During the previous year, while my father, in a different time zone, was losing his mind, I'd written two treatments and four full drafts of an "original" screenplay. In lieu of actual dollar payments, I had the enthusiastic support of a Hollywood agent who, out of pity or negligence, never mentioned that my story bore a fatal resemblance to *Fun with Dick and Jane*, which I hadn't seen. My story had double and triple crosses and characters who used prosthetic makeup to impersonate other characters. I lived in that state of rage that comes of doing sustained work that you know to be shoddy and dishonest. By September, when I finally abandoned the project, one wall of my study was scuffed and dented from the pencils, scripts, shoes, and phone books I'd been throwing at it. I borrowed money and left Philadelphia to sublet a dark, underfurnished Tribeca loft (yes, Mrs. M——, a loft) whose silence was disturbed only by the shadowy traffic of pigeons in the airshaft. I'd been hoping to write some fiction, but I was sick of audience-friendly narrative, of well-made plots and lovable characters. One evening, in a state of grim distraction, like somebody going out to score hard drugs, I walked up Sixth Avenue and bought *The Recognitions* in a beautiful, newly reissued Penguin edition.

Every morning for a week and a half, I went from the breakfast table to a beige ultrasuede sofa module, turned on a lamp, and read nonstop for six or eight hours. I had some professional curiosity about Gaddis, but a few hundred pages of *The Recognitions* would have satisfied it. I sat and read the extra seven hundred pages in something like a fugue state, as if planting my feet on a steep slope, climbing. I was reluctant to leave my ultrasuede perch for any reason. The only way I could justify sitting there and spending borrowed money was to make a regular job, with regular hours, out of climbing the mountain.

There were quotations in Latin, Spanish, Hungarian, and six other languages to be rappelled across. Blizzards of obscure references swirled around sheer cliffs of erudition, precipitous discourses on alchemy and Flemish painting, Mithraism and early-Christian theology. The prose came in page-long paragraphs in which oxygen was at a premium, and the emotional temperature of the novel started cold and got colder. The hero, Wyatt Gwyon, was likable as a child ("a small disgruntled person"), but otherwise the author's satiric judgments and intellectual obsessions discouraged intimacy. It was a struggle to figure out what, or even who, the story was about; dialogue was punctuated with dashes and largely unattributed; Wyatt himself dwindled to a furtive, seldom-glimpsed pronoun ("he"); there came brutish party scenes, all-dialogue word-storms that raged for scores of pages. The only portable nourishment that might have helped sustain me on my climb was a familiarity with Gaddis's influences, maybe a nice pemmican of T. S. Eliot and Robert Graves, which I hadn't thought to bring. I was alone and unprepared on a steep-sided, frigid, airless, poorly mapped mountain. Did I already mention that *The Recognitions* has 956 pages?

But I loved it. At the novel's hidden pinnacle, behind its clouds of subsidiary symbolism, beyond its blind canyons of

Beat antinarrative, is a story about the loss of personal integrity and the difficult work of regaining it. Wyatt, a talented painter and former seminarian in his early thirties, is living in New York, unhappily married, and scraping by as a hired draftsman. He has abandoned his painterly ambitions, possibly because a corrupt French critic panned his early work, but more likely because he is incredibly earnest and has never found an adequate reply to the condemnation of art which a puritanical great-aunt issued in his boyhood: "Our Lord is the only true creator, and only sinful people try to emulate Him." One day, in New York, an American capitalist and art collector named Recktall Brown proposes a Faustian bargain: Wyatt will forge the work of Flemish Old Masters, and Brown will sell them for huge sums. Wyatt agrees to the deal, but after some early success he proves lacking in the necessary spinelessness. He considers resuming his religious studies, but when he goes home to New England he discovers that his father, a Protestant minister, has taken up Mithraism and lost his mind. Wyatt thereupon embarks on a long pilgrimage of sorts, first in New York, where he tries to expose his own forgeries, and later in Europe. He is last seen leaving a Spanish monastery, on page 900, intending "at last, to live deliberately." Having surmounted the American Protestant suspicion of art and survived the dangerous attractions of the American Protestant marketplace, he seems finally on his way to being a real painter.

At the time, on the mountainside, I wasn't conscious of clinging to the parallels between Wyatt's story and my own situation: our weirdly isolated lives in lower Manhattan, our failed attempts to sell out, our extremely earnest doubts about art, our craving for penance, our crazy fathers. I was just happy to have a good, hard book to read, and I was impressed with myself for managing it. Following Wyatt's pilgrimage became my own pilgrimage. The loft, for those ten days, in spite of the gurgling pigeons, was the quietest place I've ever been. It was profoundly, metaphysically quiet. By the time I reached the last page of *The Recognitions* I felt readier to face the divorce, deaths, and dislocations that were waiting for me out in the sunlit world. I felt virtuous, as if I'd run three miles, eaten my kale, been to the dentist, filed my tax return, and gone to church.

ONE PRETTY GOOD DEFINITION of college is that it's a place where people are made to read difficult books. Certainly, my own moments of peak collegiate learning occurred whenever I acquired new tools to unlock difficulty—when I was forced to figure out, all by myself, that Emily Dickinson sometimes meant the opposite of what her words said, or when my German professor asked us, with a mysterious grin, whether it was possible that Josef K. was *guilty*. To learn about irony, ambiguity, symbol, voice, and point of view, it made sense to read the most sophisticated texts.

Four years of sophistication had a cumulative effect. As a freshman, I thought it would be cool to make up stories for a living, to have that be my job, to see my name in print. By the time I was a senior, my ambition was to create literary Art. I took for granted that the greatest novels were tricky in their methods, resisted casual reading, and merited sustained study. I also assumed that the highest compliment this Art could be paid was to be taught in a university.

My parents didn't understand this. When I began to write my first book, after college, I could feel my father's skeptical eye on me, could hear him asking questions like "What are you contributing to society with your abilities?" In college I'd admired Derrida and the Marxist and feminist critics, people whose job was to find fault with the modern world. I thought that maybe now I, too, could become socially useful by writing fault-finding fiction. At the excellent public library in Somerville, Massachusetts, I identified a canon of intellectual, socially edgy, white-male American fiction writers. The same names—Pynchon, DeLillo, Heller, Coover, Gaddis, Gass, Burroughs, Barth, Barthelme, Hannah, Hawkes, McElroy, and Elkin—kept showing up together in anthologies and in the respectful appraisals of contemporary critics. Though various in their styles, they all seemed to take as a given that something was new and strange and wrong about postwar America. They shared the postmodern suspicion of realism, summarized by the critic Jerome Klinkowitz: "If the world is absurd, if what passes for reality is distressingly unreal, why spend time representing it?"

To prove to myself, if not to my father, that I was engaged in a serious professional pursuit, I tried to join this guild. I was one of those skinny young men in scary glasses and thrift-store clothes whom you see on Boston or Brooklyn subways, young men who look like they possess massive amounts of data about small-label rock bands or avant-garde literature or video technology, the very size of these data sets affording a kind of psychic protection. And Gaddis ought to have been my ideal. Gaddis, it was generally agreed, was the really smart, really angry, really forbidding Systems writer. *The Recognitions* was an ur-text of postwar fiction, both the granddaddy of difficulty and the first great cultural critique, which, even if Heller and Pynchon hadn't read it while composing *Catch-22* and *V.*, managed to anticipate the spirit of both. Gaddis was the original intense, thrift-store-clad, monster-data-set young man whose ambition, if he let it show in public, would have singed his fellow subway riders' eyebrows.

My problem was that, with a few exceptions, notably Don DeLillo, I didn't particularly *like* the writers in my modern canon. I checked out their books (including *The Recognitions*), read a few pages, and returned them. I liked the *idea* of socially engaged fiction, and I was at work on my own Systems novel of conspiracy and apocalypse, and I craved academic and hipster respect of the kind that Pynchon and Gaddis got and Saul Bellow and Ann Beattie didn't. But Bellow and Beattie, not to mention Dickens and Conrad and Brontë and Dostoevsky and Christina Stead, were the writers I actually, unhiply enjoyed reading. If Robert Coover's *Public Burning* and Pynchon's *Crying of Lot 49* moved me, it was mainly because I liked Coover's character Richard Nixon and Pynchon's Oedipa Maas. But postmodern fiction wasn't supposed to be about sympathetic characters. Characters, properly speaking, weren't even supposed to exist. Characters were feeble, suspect constructs, like the author himself, like the human soul. Nevertheless, to my shame, I seemed to need them.

It wasn't until the nineties, after I'd wasted a year on the screenplay, that I tried to rekindle my collegiate excitement about really hard books. I needed proof that I was a serious Artist, rather than the unwitting plagiarist of *Fun with Dick and Jane*; and *The Recognitions* was perfect for the task. Reading the whole thing would also confer bragging rights. If somebody asked me if I'd read *The Sotweed Factor*, I could shoot back: No, but have you read *The Recognitions*? And blow smoke from the muzzle of my gun.

In the event, nothing was as I'd expected. Not many people

in the nineties were asking if I'd read *The Sotweed Factor*. *The Recognitions*, on the other hand—whether because of its virtues or because of the circumstances of my reading it—bowled me over. Its characters weren't sympathetic, but the wit and passion and seriousness of their creator were. I titled my third novel partly in homage to it.

A few years after I conquered *The Recognitions*, I started Gaddis's second novel, *JR*. I again bought the handsome Penguin paperback, and I devoted an hour or two each evening to reading it. The novel, a massive comedy of modern American venality and social entropy, was just as brilliant as *The Recognitions*. Unfortunately, I no longer had the luxury or burden of entire days for reading. One night I gave up in the middle of a four-page paragraph, and for the next few nights I was out late, and when I opened *JR* again I was lost. I set it aside, hoping to pick up the threads some other night. Two months later, I quietly reshelved it. The bookmark, a sassy TicketMaster sleeve bearing an ad for "K-ROCK 92.3 FM (HOWARD STERN ALL MORNING / *CLASSIC ROCK 'N' ROLL ALL DAY*)," remained stuck on page 469, attesting to my defeat by *JR* or to *JR*'s defeat by my noisy life.

In Status terms, I'd simply failed as a reader. But I did have Contract on my side. I'd given the book weeks of evening reading, it still wasn't working for me, and now I was eager to read shorter, warmer books by James Purdy, Alice Munro, Penelope Fitzgerald, Halldór Laxness. Battling through *JR*, I'd wanted to grab Gaddis by the lapels and shout: "Hello! I'm the reader you want! I'm *looking* for a good Systems novel. If you can't even show *me* a good time, who else do you think is going to read you?"

But this only made it worse that I had quit. Precisely because I was well suited to read Gaddis, I felt as if I were personally betraying him, disappointing his expectations, by not finishing *JR*. From a Congregationalist childhood I'd gone straight to a collegiate worship of Art, without noticing the transition and without ever quite buying either faith. One day a secretary called from the Congregational Church to ask if I still wanted to be a member, and I said no, and that was that. But it's much harder to leave a small, embattled cult than a mainstream suburban church. Nothing in my Congregationalist experience had prepared me for the fanatical fervor, the guilt-provoking authority, of Mr. Difficult.

THERE'S SOMETHING medieval Christian about *The Recognitions*. The novel is like a huge landscape painting of modern New York, peopled with hundreds of doomed but energetic little figures, executed on wood panels by Brueghel or Bosch, and looking incongruously ancient beneath layers of yellowed lacquer. Even the blue skies in the book (the phrase "Another blue day" recurs as a despair-inducing leitmotiv) glow like oil-paint skies in an art museum beyond whose walls, forgotten, is the age of H-bombs and Army-McCarthy hearings in which the novel was written. The names dropped are Hans Memling, not Harry Truman; Paracelsus, not Elvis.

And yet the book is absolutely of the early fifties. Peel away the erudition and you have *The Catcher in the Rye*: a grim winter sojourn in a seedy Manhattan, a quest for authenticity in a phony modern world. Improvising on the theme of art forgery, Gaddis fills his novel with every conceivable variety of fraud, counterfeiter, poseur, and liar. Unlike Holden Caulfield, though, the main characters of *The Recognitions* participate in the phoniness themselves. The young literary poseur, Otto Pivner, is working on a play whose plot, he says, "still needs a little tightening up." The narrator glosses this lie in a tone that's fundamental to the novel, a tone at once unsparing and forgiving:

> (By this Otto meant a plot of some sort had yet to be supplied, to motivate the series of monologues in which Gordon, a figure who resembled Otto at his better moments, and whom Otto greatly admired, said things which Otto had overheard, or thought of too late to say.)

Wyatt Gwyon may be the romantic projection of the author's artistic aspirations ("How ambitious you are!" his wife, Esther, unhappily exclaims), but it's Otto who seems to embody Gaddis's own confusion, humiliations, and disappointments. Otto's biography overlaps with Gaddis's—both grew up fatherless, both spent time in Central America and returned to New York via banana boat with their arms, though uninjured, in picturesque slings—and I suspect that the book owes some of its mood of playful fabulation to Gaddis's implication in his own satire.

The one genuine artist in *The Recognitions* is a devoutly Catholic young composer named Stanley. Throughout the book, Stanley is working on a requiem for organ which he hopes to play in a fragile old church in northern Italy. In the very last pages, as the novel circles back to Europe, Stanley travels to the church and, failing to understand the caretaker's warning against playing anything dissonant or too heavy on bass, begins to perform the requiem. The church collapses and kills him, and *The Recognitions* closes with some of its best-known lines: "most of his work was recovered too, and it is still spoken of, when it is noted, with high regard, though seldom played."

The other well-known lines in *The Recognitions* are uttered by Wyatt after his wife, Esther, voices surprise that a certain popular poet (Auden, maybe) is homosexual. Rejecting her interest in "personal things about writers and painters" as a prurient distraction, Wyatt bursts out:

> What is there left of him when he's done his work? What's any artist, but the dregs of his work? the human shambles that follows it around. What's left of the man when the work's done but a shambles of apology.

Gaddis portrays Esther as a "vagina dentata" eager to sleep with male artists and "absorb the properties which had been withheld from her." Wyatt retreats from her into coldness and abstraction, and Gaddis retreats from readers in much the same way—as if, for him, intercourse with the public were a pleasure that threatened to taint the purity of his motives. What mattered to Gaddis, who avowedly strove to write literature that would "last," was not the weak and fleshly artist but the afterlife. Although he had a family, many friends, and a busy social life in which he enjoyed literary gossip, he consistently denied his person to the public. Strict prohibitions like this are a way in which threatened religious minorities resist the seductions of the majority culture, and Gaddis in the fifties had Norman Mailer and Truman Capote as examples of writers who had been seduced. He chose, instead, to be a purist of his faith. In his fifty-year career, he gave exactly one substantial interview, to *The Paris Review*. He published one brief autobiographical essay. He gave no public readings.

Not that an excess of media attention was ever a big problem. *The Recognitions* was published by Harcourt, Brace in 1955, with a marketing strategy of "Everyone is talking about this controversial book!" It received fifty-five reviews, an impressive number by today's standards, and, as William Gass notes in his introduction to the Penguin edition, "Only fifty-three of these notices were stupid." *The New Yorker* gave the book a brief, smirking dismissal ("words, words, words"); Dawn Powell, in the *New York Post*, offered up an error-riddled sneer. Sales were about five thousand in hardcover, not bad for a challenging first novel by an unknown writer. But the only prize the book won was for its design, and it quickly disappeared from public sight.

"I almost think that if I'd gotten the Nobel Prize when *The Recognitions* was published I wouldn't have been terribly surprised," Gaddis told *The Paris Review* in 1986, adding that the book's reception had been "sobering" and "humbling." Maybe if the novel had met with greater acclaim Gaddis would have relaxed a little; maybe Wyatt's "what is it they want" tirade, like his other puritanisms, would have been revealed as a skinny-young-man attitude to be outgrown. I doubt it, though. The book is *about* the everyday world's indifference to the superior reality of art. Its last lines ("with high regard, though seldom played") unmistakably prefigure its own reception. Nurturing the hope that your marginal novel will be celebrated by the mainstream—the Cassandra-like wish that people will thank you for telling them unwelcome truths—is a ritual way of ensuring disappointment, of reaffirming your own world-denying status, of mortifying the flesh, of remaining, at heart, an angry young man. In the four decades following the publication of *The Recognitions*, Gaddis's work grew angrier and angrier. It's a signature paradox of literary postmodernism: the writer whose least angry work was written first.

SOME OF GADDIS'S RAGE appears to have been built-in. Born in 1922, he grew up with his mother in an old house in Massapequa, Long Island, and at a small Connecticut boarding school that he attended from the ages of five to thirteen. Five is young for boarding school. Five strikes me as a vital figure in Gaddis's biography. In *JR*, an alter ego of Gaddis, an angry drinker named Jack Gibbs who was likewise sent to boarding school at the age of five, speaks of having "been in the way since the day I could walk," and he describes the loneliness of boarding school:

> End of the day alone on that train, lights coming on in those little Connecticut towns stop and stare out at the empty street corner dry cheese sandwich charge you a dollar wouldn't even put butter on it, finally pull into that desolate station scared to get off scared to stay on [. . .] school car waiting there like [. . .] a God damned open hearse think anybody expect to grow up.

Gaddis as a young man was a rowdy, a drinker. Kept out of the war by a kidney ailment, he studied English at Harvard and became president of the *Lampoon*, but in his senior year he was expelled without a degree after a run-in with the Cambridge police. He then bounced around Europe, Latin America, and New York during the seven somewhat shadowy years he was at work on *The Recognitions*. In the year of its publication, he married an actress, Pat Black, with whom he soon had two children. Here the mood of his biography abruptly changes, the foreign locales giving way to fifties commerce and suburban life with kids. Like Melville a century before him, Gaddis went to work for a living in lower Manhattan. He did public-relations writing for IBM, Eastman Kodak, Pfizer, and the United States Army, among others. (An evaluator of his work at IBM, recommending a "simpler style" for one of his projects, complained that "the whole of the text is perhaps too much an impenetrable mass.") For twenty years, even as the country's literary tastes were swinging from the realism dominant in the fifties to the zanier modes of *Portnoy's Complaint* and *Catch-22*, Gaddis essentially dropped out of sight. He started and abandoned a "novel on business" and a play about the Civil War. He smoked a lot and drank a lot. His first marriage ended when he was living in Croton-on-Hudson. Not until the end of the sixties did he scrape together enough grant money to return full-time to the novel about business.

By the time the book was published, in 1975, the country's mood had caught up with him. *JR* received major and admiring review attention and won the National Book Award. The chunky paperback edition with its chunky title lettering was, like Patti Smith LPs and the *Moosewood Cookbook*, a common sight in the secondhand stores and student-slum apartments of my college years. The spine of *JR* was often suspiciously uncracked, however, or a strangely low used price was penciled inside the cover, or the bookmark, which might be a sheet of rolling paper or a Talking Heads ticket stub, could be found on page 118, or 19, or 53, because Gaddis's fiction was, if anything, more difficult than ever. *JR* is a 726-page novel consisting almost entirely of overheard voices, with nary a quotation mark, a "he said," or a "she said," no conventional narration of any kind, no "later that same evening," no "meanwhile in New York," not a single chapter break, not even a section break, but thousands of dashes and ellipses, another cast of dozens, and a laughably complicated plot based on Wagner's *Ring* and centered on a multimillion-dollar business empire owned and operated by an eleven-year-old Long Island schoolboy named J R Vansant.

J R is the grubby kid you have to laugh at because he's not old enough to hate, the preadolescent whose entire being is devoted to wanting stuff and to trading it for other, better stuff. First he does it with a classmate:

—Boy, what crap. That's all you've got is crap. What's this.

—It's this club you can join if I recommend you.

—What kind of club.

—It's this club, see? You step inside and suddenly excitement surrounds you! You enter a world highlighted by the soft, flickering glow of open-hearth fireplaces . . . the attentive rustle of beautiful Bunnies—

Soon enough, he's trading with captains of industry. Early in the novel, J R's sixth-grade teacher takes the class to Wall Street to buy one share of Diamond Cable stock and "learn how our system works." While the class's new stock is losing ten percent of its value in a few hours, and brokers and corporate officers are engaging in vile manipulations of markets and senators and foreign governments, and a corporate PR flak is laying on the smarm ("you and your other fellow Americans no longer play a passive part in our nation's great economy"), J R is studying the bylaws of Diamond Cable, asking dead-on questions like "What's a warrant?" and "What's that minus sign two and an eighth?" and ascertaining that the class's share of stock entitles it to file a shareholder's lawsuit. Within weeks, by threatening such a suit and accepting a cash settlement, J R, who conducts his business on a pay phone at the elementary school, acquires his working capital. He buys a million and a half Navy-surplus wooden picnic forks, a bankrupt textile mill in upstate New York, and then an outward-spiraling galaxy of dubious concerns—a brewery, a printer, a publisher, a nursing home, a mortuary. Like his creator, J R is an obsessive. (Also like Gaddis, J R has no visible father. His mother is a busy nurse.) He pursues what his country teaches him is worth pursuing. He's devoid of charm, compassion, and scruples, but he doesn't know any better, and so you root for him against the novel's many corporate and legal sharks, who should know better but behave just as badly. *JR* anticipates Jonathan Lebed, the alleged teenaged market manipulator in New Jersey. It predicts the S&L crises and corporate raiders of the eighties ("Because like what good is this here pension fund doing just sitting there," J R wonders, "if we can like put it to work for them to get this here acquisition, you know?"), and it nicely demolishes George W. Bush's claim that Wall Street greed was an anomaly of the nineties.

The most sincere adult in the novel is, again, a young composer, a sweetheart named Edward Bast, whom J R dragoons into serving as the front man for his conglomerate. While Bast spends his days helping other characters (nobody, of course, helps him), the opera that he wants to compose is gradually scaled back to a cantata, to a piece for small orchestra, and finally to a piece for solo cello. The novel's maddening distractions recall the frustrations of Kafka's fiction; you can sense an author nightmarishly unable to find a quiet space to work. Bast tries to compose music in a Manhattan pied-à-terre that's a bitter cartoon of entropy; two broken faucets spew hot water day and night, the only clock runs backward, the rooms are piled high with boxes of unidentified crap, a never-located radio dribbles nonsense, and bushels of junk mail keep arriving for J R, who has sent Bast a mechanized envelope opener that slices letters in half. In another part of town, Thomas Eigen, a PR writer for Diamond Cable who once wrote an "important" literary novel, comes home from the office too tired to work on his new opus. The apartment is a mess, his wife is angry, and his little boy insists that he play a board game:

—You got in the Heffalump's trap. Mama Papa got in the Heffalump trap. Mama?
—She can't hear you David. Don't shout.
—If I get red now I'll, yellow. I got yellow too look, I always win look, now look where I am and . . .
—David you don't always win, nobody . . .
—I won Mama four times today. Mama?
—Stop shouting David . . . He held the bag down, —and I . . . got . . .
—Black! You peeked. Papa you peeked!
—Peeked?

JR is written for the active reader. You're well advised to carry a pencil with which to flag plot points and draw flow charts on the inside back cover. The novel is a welter of dozens of interconnecting scams, deals, seductions, extortions, and betrayals. Between scenes, the dialogue yields briefly to run-on sentences whose effect is like a blurry handheld video or a speeded-up movie. The images that flash by are of denatured, commercialized landscapes—trees being felled, fields paved over, roads widened—which recall to the modern reader how aesthetically shocking postwar automotive America must have been, how dismaying and portentous the first strip malls, the first five-acre parking lots.

Indeed, one defense of Gaddis and his difficulty is that conventional fiction, driven by substantial characters and based on a soul-to-soul contract between reader and writer, was simply inadequate to the social and technological crises that twentieth-century writers saw developing all around them. Both the moderns and the postmoderns resorted to a kind of literature of emergency. The moderns employed new, self-conscious methods to address the new reality and preserve the vanishing old one. The postmodern enterprise was even more radical: to resist absorption or co-optation by an all-absorbing, all-co-opting System. Closure was the enemy, and the way to avoid it was to refuse to participate in the System. For Pynchon this meant flight and paranoia; for Burroughs it meant transgression. For Gaddis it meant being very angry—so angry that, at a certain point, he stopped making sense. But in avoiding formal closure Gaddis risked a blunter sort of closure: exhausted readers closing his books. I was halfway through *JR* when I bailed out. Even then, though, his anger made me wonder: had he betrayed me, or had I betrayed him?

FICTION IS THE MOST fundamental human art. Fiction is storytelling, and our reality arguably consists of the stories we tell about ourselves. Fiction is also conservative and conventional, because the structure of its market is relatively democratic (novelists make a living one copy at a time, bringing pleasure to large audiences), and because a novel asks for ten or twenty hours of solitary attentiveness from each member of its audience. You can walk past a painting fifty times before you begin to appreciate it. You can drift in and out of a Bartók sonata until its structures dawn on you. But a difficult novel just sits there on your shelf unread—unless you happen to be a student, in which case you're forced to turn the pages of Woolf and Beckett.

This may make you a better reader. But to sign on with the postmodern program, to embrace the notion of formal experimentation as a heroic act of resistance, you have to believe that the emergency that Gaddis and his fellow pioneers were responding to is still an emergency five decades later. You have to believe that our situation as suburbanized, gasoline-dependent, TV-watching Americans is still so new and urgent as to preempt old-fashioned storytelling. You have to be some kind of critic. And once a literature and its criticism become codependent, the fallacies set in.

There's the Fallacy of Capture, as in the frequent praise of *Finnegans Wake* for its "capturing" of human consciousness, or in the justification of *JR*'s longueurs by its "capture" of an elusive "postwar American reality"; as if a novel were primarily an ethnographic recording, as if the point of reading fiction were not to go fishing but to admire somebody else's catch. There's the Fallacy of the Symphonic, in which a book's motifs and voices are described as "washing over" the reader in orchestral fashion; as if, when you're reading *JR*, its pages just turn themselves, words wafting up into your head like arpeggios. And the Fallacy of Art Historicism, a pedagogical convenience borrowed from the moneyed world of visual art, where a work's value substantially depends on its novelty; as if fiction were as formally free as painting, as if what makes *The Great Gatsby* and *O Pioneers!* good novels were primarily their technical innovations. And the epidemic Fallacy of the Stupid Reader, implicit in every modern "aesthetics of difficulty," wherein difficulty is a "strategy" to protect art from co-optation and the purpose of this art is to "upset" or "compel" or "challenge" or "subvert" or "scar" the unsuspecting reader; as if the writer's audience somehow consisted, again and again, of Charlie Browns running to kick Lucy's football; as if it were a virtue in a novelist to be the kind of boor who propagandizes at friendly social gatherings.

It's unfortunate for Gaddis that so many of his friends, scholars, and defenders participate in these fallacies. Joseph Tabbi, the editor of Gaddis's essays and a true believer in subversive difficulty, believes that the Apocalypse—the death of the individual, the triumph of the System—is not merely imminent, it has already occurred without your even realizing it, so don't blame the orphic Gaddis for his inaccessibility. Tabbi's apologies are a nice example of five-alarm avant-gardism:

> Gaddis's audience has been limited in part because readers trained on nineteenth-century realism miss in his work those signs and conventional symptoms by which characters may be recognized, too readily, as rounded and whole. Such conventional characters are agents within a bourgeois and industrial world that is now, in the United States, largely historical.

If you're having a good time with a novel, you're a dupe of the postindustrial System; if you still identify with characters, you need to retake Postmodernism 101. William Gass, in his introduction to *The Recognitions*, referring to a "we" that I suspect he doesn't really think includes William Gass, names the childish thing that it's time to put behind us: "Too often we bring to literature the bias for 'realism' we were normally brought up with." Gass's defense of difficulty complements Tabbi's, but with greater sophistry and alliteration. "If the author works at his work," Gass writes, "the reader may also have to, whereas when a writer whiles away both time and words, the reader may relax and gently peruse." Gaddis's fiction could have used fewer friends like this and better enemies. Even Steven Moore, a Gaddis scholar whose criticism is a model of clarity and intelligent advocacy, lets his enthusiasm get the better of him. *JR*, for Moore, is a "lean and economical" book, because its inferential, all-dialogue form forces readers to supply missing descriptions and information; the purpose of a novel being, what, to capture and efficiently store data?

My small hope for literary criticism would be to hear less about orchestras and subversion and more about the erotic and culinary arts. Think of the novel as lover: Let's stay home tonight and have a great time; just because you're touched where you want to be touched, it doesn't mean you're cheap; before a book can change you, you have to love it. Or the novelist as cook who prepares, as a gift to the reader, this many-course meal. Not just ice cream but broccoli rabe as well.

Difficult fiction of the kind epitomized by Gaddis seems to me more closely associated with the lower end of the digestive tract. His detractors refer to his "logorrhea," but it's more accurate to characterize him as retentive—constipated to the point of being unreadable, sometimes even unintelligible. Edmund Wilson, in his Freudian phase, identified the playwright Ben Jonson as a classic anal-retentive writer, obsessed with excretion, money, lists, seedy underworlds, arcane words, obscure references. Wilson suggested that the best writers trust their talents, and he contrasted Jonson's cramped output with that of his friend and rival Shakespeare, whose "open and free nature" Jonson himself praised. *The Alchemist,*

Jonson's peculiar play about a London con man posing as a transmuter of gold, reads like Renaissance Gaddis. Both writers stuff way too many swindles into their plots, and for both of them money is the world's shit ("Recktall Brown"!), at once fascinating and repellent.

If I'm sounding a little Freudian myself, it's because the first lines of page 523, the terminus of my second reading of *JR*, look so much like impacted excreta:

> across smalltite traces and has Nonny put in for a mineral
> depletion allowance tipped his hand to the FDA coming
> down hard on cobalt safety levels now Milliken jumps in
> to protect home industry only thing they had besides sheep
> and Indians till he suddenly gets the idea his state is

Lean and economical? *JR* suffers from the madness it attempts to resist. The first ten pages and the last ten pages and every ten pages in between bring the "news" that American life is shallow, fraudulent, venal, and hostile to artists. But there never has been and will never be one single reader who is unpersuaded of this "news" on page 10 but persuaded on page 726. The novel becomes as chilly, mechanistic, and exhausting as the System it describes. Its world is ruled by corporate white men who pursue their work with pleasureless zeal, casually sideline women and minorities, and invent difficult insider languages to discourage newcomers: how oddly like the book itself! (And how odd that Gaddis and his academic admirers reject Christian puritanism only to demand that his readers renounce the sinful pleasures of realism and cultivate a selfless and pure love of Art!) Even the fascination of JR Vansant wanes by mid-novel. JR is an avatar of Bart Simpson, but Bart is incomparably better suited to our cultural environment than JR is. The genre for effective and entertaining Systems satire is the half-hour weekly television cartoon, not the literary novel. Even the best gags in *JR* wear you out before you're done with them. On *The Simpsons*, the gags hit their target, the target feels pain, and next week there's a new episode.

The curious thing is that I suspect Gaddis himself would rather have watched *The Simpsons*. I suspect that if anyone else had written his later novels, from *JR* onward, he would not have wanted to read them, and that if he had read them he would not have liked them. Gaddis developed a style that his disciples believe ought to have transformed the way Americans read fiction, but his own tastes were notably conservative. He had particular disdain for modern art. For the cover of his fourth novel, *A Frolic of His Own* (1994), he chose an abstract painting by his daughter, Sarah, without mentioning on the jacket that she'd painted it when she was five: "See, any child *can* paint like that." Steven Moore, no doubt with the best of intentions, has assembled an impressive list of what Gaddis did and didn't like to read. Basically, he didn't like art fiction. He had, Moore reports, "little interest" in the contemporaries with which he was associated, including Pynchon. "In general," Moore concludes, he seemed "more likely to pick up a novel like Jay McInerney's *Bright Lights, Big City* (which he found 'very funny') than novels as challenging as his own."

To serve the reader a fruitcake that you wouldn't eat yourself, to build the reader an uncomfortable house you wouldn't want to live in: this violates what seems to me the categorical imperative for any fiction writer. This is the ultimate breach of Contract.

IF *JR* IS DEDICATED to the proposition that America basically sucks, the message of Gaddis's third novel, *Carpenter's Gothic* (1985), is that it really, really, really sucks. Gaddis himself conceded that the book was "an exercise in style," and its content is strictly paint-by-numbers. A telegenic Southern preacher turns out to be—a dangerous, venal hypocrite! A United States senator turns out to be—corrupt! The book is a husk. Unlike *The Recognitions*, it was handsomely reviewed.

Gaddis's last real novel, *A Frolic of His Own*, rambles on for nearly six hundred pages in illustration of how a system designed to create order (American law) can end up sponsoring disorder. The book is ideal for graduate study. It makes a banal but unexceptionable social point (we litigate too much in America), it's riddled with motifs, quotations, stories-within-stories, and countless allusions to Gaddis's own earlier works and other famous texts (better brush up on your Plato and Longfellow), and its only aesthetic weakness, really, is that much of it is repetitive, incoherent, and insanely boring. This novel, of course, got the warmest reviews of any of Gaddis's books, and was given one of those unofficial lifetime-achievement National Book Awards.

The best parts of *Frolic* are the legal opinions and some of the characterizations. Creating a character entirely through dialogue is like boxing with one arm behind your back, and I'm not persuaded by the Gaddistic argument that straining our imaginations makes a character any realer to us. (In fact, the work of reading Gaddis makes me wonder if our brains might even be hard-wired for conventional storytelling, structurally eager to form pictures from sentences as featureless as "She stood up.") Still, his inferentially drawn characters can be vivid. Oscar Crease is a fifty-something amateur playwright and part-time professor in whose disorderly person a comically large number of lawsuits intersect. He lives in the large old house of his childhood on Long Island, hopelessly surrounded by a lifetime's worth of miscellaneous papers: another cartoon of entropy. Functionally, Oscar is a baby. He spends much of the novel in a wheelchair, forever pawing at his girlfriend's blouse, trying to get his hands and mouth on her breasts, and sucking down wine day and night.

In *The Recognitions*, a son grows up and vanishes. *Carpenter's Gothic*, the book without children, is a book without hope. At the center of the other two novels is a very large child. In *Frolic*, it's the selfish, unreasonable, self-pitying, incapable, insatiable Oscar, a pig in the role of king, a suffering artist who (ha ha!) happens to have little talent. Oscar claims your sympathy only to abuse it. His long play about the Civil War is obviously and unfunnily bad, but a hundred pages are devoted to reproducing the manuscript and another fifty to endless jawing about its relation to art, justice, and order. The novel is an example of the particular corrosiveness of literary postmodernism. Gaddis began his career with a modernist epic about the forgery of masterpieces. He ended it with a pomo romp that superficially resembles a masterpiece but punishes the reader who tries to stay with it and follow its logic. When the reader finally says, Hey, wait a minute, this is a mess, not a masterpiece, the book instantly morphs into a performance-art prop: its fraudulence is the whole point! And the reader is out twenty hours of good-faith effort.

Regarding Gaddis's two posthumous books, I feel the way I did when my father was in a nursing home. Unless you're a very good old friend, it's better not to see him suffering like this. The title of his last novel, *Agapē Agape* (2002), comes from a tonally arch and intellectually dubious essay that he once tried to write about player pianos and mechanization in the arts. The book is mainly a free-form rant, however, *with the sentences, yes, run the sentences, run together, make it choppy, even easier than it looks but no what no, what matters is the art.* An unnamed novelist lies dying, his body a wreck that has betrayed his spirit. He reproaches himself for his failures, denounces the populist "herd" for misunderstanding him, and worries that he's perceived as a mere "cartoon." But a cartoon is what *Agapē Agape* is: one opaque, obsessive, citation-riddled, solipsistic paragraph deifying "the work" as "the only refuge" from one's painful humanity. I counted almost every one of *Agapē Agape*'s ninety-six pages as I read them. The novel did manage to stab me with its final note, a note reminiscent of Gaddis's early dreams of a Nobel prize—

> That was Youth with its reckless exuberance when all things were possible pursued by Age where we are now, looking back at what we destroyed, what we tore away from that self who could do more, and its work that's become my enemy because that's what I can tell you about, that Youth who could do anything

—but I was moved for the very reasons that Gaddis denigrated throughout his career: because I was touched by the human shambles. I was thinking of the artist, not the art.

If you're still wondering if you missed something, some key to Gaddis that will unlock his difficulty, you can set your mind at rest by reading *The Rush for Second Place*, a slender collection of his essays and occasional writings. Here you'll learn that Gaddis can't finish even a short nonfiction piece without breaking into a rant. You'll find essays consisting of strung-together quotes that you have to read carefully, twice, before you conclude that no argument (or, indeed, logic) is hidden in the string. You'll see that, sure enough, literary difficulty can operate as a smoke screen for an author who has nothing interesting, wise, or entertaining to say. You'll find not one reference to the pleasure of reading fiction. You'll learn, rather, that Gaddis believed that novels should improve the world—that good fiction is not about "the way things are" but about "the way things should be." You'll learn that the phrase "agapē agape" refers to his belief that the world of Contract, the American world of dollars and machines, has ripped apart the charitable love (agapē) to which early-Christian communities aspired.

Or something like that—it's a little unclear. I imagine Gaddis's disciples wagging their fingers at me, telling me I'm another Stupid Reader, explaining that the essays subvert my expectations of clarity, of pleasure, of edification; that I haven't got the joke yet. They have postmodern apologies for his difficulty, such as this one by Gregory Comnes:

> The narrative enactment of this epistemology shows readers how hard work is a necessary precondition for having meaning in narrative by forcing readers to participate actively in the construction of narrative meaning, requiring them to bring information to the text to read what was never written.

They tell me, in other words, that I just need to *work a little bit harder*. To which I can only reply that there is no headache like the headache you get from working harder on deciphering a text than the author, by all appearances, has worked on assembling it; and that I'm beginning to get that headache.

———

AND BEGINNING, as well, to sound like Mrs. M——?

Like many other Contract-minded Americans, like the literary societies of a hundred years ago, like the book clubs of today, I understand that the Contract sometimes calls for work. I know the pleasures of a book aren't always easy. I expect to work; I *want* to work. It's also in my Protestant nature, however, to expect some reward for this work. And, although critics can give me pastoral guidance as I seek this reward, ultimately I think each individual is alone with his or her conscience. As a reader, I seek a direct personal relationship with art. The books I love, the books on which my faith in literature rests, are the ones with which I can have this kind of relationship. *The Recognitions*, to my surprise, turned out to be a book like this.

After *The Recognitions*, however, something happened to Gaddis. Something went haywire. Whether it's true or not, I tell myself a story about a five-year-old boy who was "in the way," about a skinny young man who, like Hamlet inscribing his stepfather's villainy on his brain, assembled an encyclopedia of phoniness unparalleled in literature. He confided his faith and hope to a 956-page-thick vault, and he gave the grownup world one chance to recognize him. When the world, inevitably, failed this test, he took his talent to the archetypically phony work of corporate PR, as if to say: "You'll never catch me hoping again." The modern cry of pain became the postmodern bitter joke. The corporate PR work was vile, but at least he was conscious of its vileness. Indeed, the essence of postmodernism is an adolescent celebration of consciousness, an adolescent fear of getting taken in, an adolescent conviction that all systems are phony. The theory is compelling, but as a way of life it's a recipe for rage. The child grows enormous but never grows up.

I think there's a good story in this. To the extent that I believe it's the story of Gaddis himself, it softens my anger with him, dissolves it in sadness. A Gaddis like this is not remotely a cartoon, and a story like this would never fit into a *Simpsons* format. A story like this, where the difficulty is the difficulty of life itself, is what a novel is for.

[2002]

BOOKS IN BED

I N THE EROTIC BROADSHEETS of the *New York Times*, which every morning lies on my breakfast table, silently awaiting my attentions, there recently appeared what seemed to me a wholly reasonable op-ed piece by Adam Hochschild on the horror of airport television. "At gates cursed with the TV's," Hochschild wrote, "most of the passengers are trying to talk, work or read. But the penetrating TV noise needles itself into the conversations and onto the pages." His complaint soon brought replies from the Refiners, Resonators, and Rebutters who typically write letters to the *Times*. One Refiner suggested that airport TVs might play silently with captions. One Resonator wrote movingly of the kindred horror of "smelling and hearing popcorn" in movie theaters; another invited readers to "try spending a night in any moderately priced hotel without enduring the buzz-muffle of televised talk." (The rage palpable in the word "buzz-muffle"! Nothing more reliably bolsters my faith in humanity than the dyspepsia of letters to the *Times*.) There was also, however, a classic Rebuttal from the president of Turner Private Networks, who claimed, bizarrely, that airport TV is "not intrusive" and, more persuasively, that Hochschild is "more alone than he might think." Apparently, Nielsen surveys show that ninety-five percent of air travelers believe that television enhances the airport environment, and eighty-nine percent believe that "it makes the time spent in an airport more worthwhile." I pitied Hochschild when I read this. Here he is, trying bravely to give voice to a silent majority of sufferers, hoping to incite communal outrage, when along comes somebody with a figure—*ninety-five percent*—to knock his legs out from under him. He's mugged by a norm.

This business of norms, which are a fixture of the information age—as friends or as tyrants, depending on how normal you are—was on my mind this winter when I embarked on a survey of contemporary popular sex books and was confronted with evidence that I am one of the few heterosexual men in America who's not turned on by elaborate lingerie. In bookstores, pop-sex books are usually shelved under Health (a topic of such importance to the culture that every book now published, including novels, could arguably be shelved there), and, since sexual "health" is impossible to define objectively, they offer the reader a uniquely rich array of normative pronouncements. "Matching lacy bra and panties, garter belt and stockings, bustiers, G-strings, and teddies—most men can't get enough of this stuff," Sydney Biddle Barrows, the Mayflower Madam, writes in *Just Between Us Girls*. She later adds: "Whatever the reason, bustiers and merry widows seem to be almost universally popular garments." Dr. Susan

Block, in *The 10 Commandments of Pleasure*, commands the female reader, "Wear lingerie," and explains that "men who love sex love a woman who thinks about it, dresses up for it." Susan Crain Bakos, the author of *Sexational Secrets*, concurs: "Men love it when you come to bed in high heels, bustier, and stockings." Lest these generalizations seem unscientific, the authors of *Sex: A Man's Guide* report that, according to their survey of *Men's Health* readers, lingerie is "without a doubt . . . the U.S. male's favorite erotic aid."

I have no objection to a nice bra, still less to being invited to remove one. But brothelwear of the kind sold at Frederick's of Hollywood seems to me scarcely less hokey than a Super Bowl halftime show. What I feel when I hear that the mainstream actually *buys* this stuff is the same garden-variety alienation I feel on learning that Hootie & the Blowfish sold thirteen million copies of their first record, or that the American male's dream date is Cindy Crawford. In a sense, I'm proud of not being like everybody else. Like everybody else, though, I'm anxious about sex, and with sex the recognition that I'm not like everybody else leads directly to the worry that I'm not as good as—or, at any rate, not having as much fun as—everybody else.

Sexual anxiety is primal; physical love has always carried the risk that one's most naked self will be rejected. If Americans today are especially anxious, the consensus seems to be that it's because of "changing sex roles" and "media images of sex" and so forth. In fact, we're simply experiencing the anxiety of a free market. Contraception and the ease of divorce have removed the fetters from the economy of sex, and, like the citizens of present-day Dresden and Leipzig, we all want to believe we're better off under a regime in which even the poorest man can dream of wealth. But as the old walls of repression tumble down, many Americans—discarded first wives, who are like the workers displaced from a Trabant factory; or sexually inept men, who are the equivalent of command-economy bureaucrats—have grown nostalgic for the old state monopolies. What are *The Rules* if not an attempt to reregulate an economy run scarily amok?

Until the Rules become universal, though, such comfort as can be found in the market economy comes principally from norms. Are you worried about the size of your penis? According to *Sex: A Man's Guide*, most men's erections are between five and seven inches long. Worried about the architecture of your clitoris? According to Betty Dodson, in the revised edition of her *Sex for One: The Joy of Selfloving*, the variations are "astounding." Worried about frequency? "Americans do not have a secret life of abundant sex," the researchers of *Sex in America* concluded. Worried about how long it takes you to come? On average, says Sydney Barrows, it takes a woman eighteen minutes, a man just three.

The problem with relying on norms for comfort, however, is not only that you may fail to meet them but that you may meet them all too well. Who really wants to be sexually just like everybody else? Isn't the bedroom where I expect, rather, to feel special? Unique, even? The last thing I want is to be reminded of the vaguely icky fact that across the country millions of other people are having sex. This is the conundrum of the individual confronting masses about which he can't help knowing more than he'd like to know: I want to be alone, but not too alone. I want to be the same but different.

POPULAR SEX BOOKS are only a part of the sex industry, but one could argue that they're the most representative wing, in that they are books. If a sexual fetish is understood as a displacement of genital energies, then language, even more than lingerie, is by far the most prevalent paraphilia in the country today. You can't show a bare breast on network television, but there's no limit to the backdoor prurience of talk about rape, incest, and sexual harassment. Cybersex and phone sex are vastly more popular ways of avoiding intimate fluids than is the worship of, say, knees or feet.

Although our pop sex writers seem to recognize the ascendance of language, they don't trust their readers to know how, or even when, to use it. In *Sex: A Man's Guide* we learn that lovers can be encouraged to talk dirty by making lists of "clinical" and "dirty" terms and comparing them. Dr. Block reels off forty-five possible pet names for a penis, including "peenie-weenie," "dipstick," and "lovepump," and commands her readers: "Take your pick." (More adventurous souls are urged to "make up something special" to suit their "very special wonder worm.") Susan Bakos cues Tantric lovers to the appropriate moment for "whispered terms of endearment," and she suggests that women who want to learn to talk dirty rent some video porn and study it carefully. "Once you are comfortable saying the words as a scriptwriter wrote them," she tells us, "you can personalize them to make it sound more like you speaking."

Reading a book of expert sexual instruction must rank near the bottom on the scale of erotic pastimes—somewhere below peeling an orange, not far above flossing. One problem is that, although the intention is precisely the opposite, these books collectively and individually make the world of sex seem very small. Never mind that there are only so many ways to fit body parts together or that Alex Comfort has already said and said well, in works that have sold better than eight million copies, pretty much all there is to say about it. There seems, in general, to be far too little lore to go around. Author after author derives the etymology of "cunnilingus," stresses the importance of doing "kegel" exercises to strengthen the pubococcygeal muscles, and quotes Shakespeare on the topic of alcohol. ("It provokes the desire, but takes away the performance.") Author after author insists that men are "visual creatures" and that the size of a penis matters less than what its owner does with it. When the lore runs out, the advice turns bleakly otiose. Dr. Susan Block commands lovers: "Use babytalk, or at least 'pet names.'" In *Sexational Secrets*, whose subtitle promises "exotic advice your mother never told you," Susan Bakos instructs masturbating men to use, "in various combinations," the Slow Single Stroke, the Fast Single Stroke, the Slow Two-Hand Stroke, the Fast Two-Hand Stroke, the Cupped Hand, the Finger Stroke, the Wrist Pump, the Slap, the Beat, the Rub, the Squeeze Stroke, the Open-Hand Stroke, and the Vagina Simulator Stroke; instructions for each are provided.

The italicized cheerfulness with which pop-sex authors convey the useless and the banal is identical to that of the newscasters on airport TV, whose most striking talent is the ability to summon (or to fake, like an orgasm) fresh wonderment over the latest wrinkle in automobile safety. Trying to make fascinating and new what is neither, the authors tirelessly coin neologisms. They toss off "sexation," "primemate," "soulgasm," and "partnersex" with the supreme self-assurance that American audiences now demand from professional exhibitionists. Dr. Block, who calls herself an "erotic philosopher," illustrates her commandments with glimpses of her husband and herself in bed: "Max grunts like a bonobo chimp when he wants to go down on me, then moans and coos and tells me I'm delicious as he slurps away." For people who have never shared a fantasy with their lovers but "would like to try," the philosopher has this advice: "Watch the *Dr. Susan Block Show* together—that'll stimulate your fantasies!"

Not every pop-sex book points to television quite this literally, but all the books seem bent on enmeshing sex (formerly life's one free pleasure) in the web of consumer spending. The reader is relentlessly exhorted to buy erotic videos, high-quality lingerie, candles, champagne, incense, oils, vibrators, perfumes, bath-bubble mix. Betty Dodson, Ph.D., sounds less like a prophet of an autoerotic utopia than like an infomercial host; she twice gives readers an address from which her videos may be ordered. Sydney Barrows suggests that renting luxury cars, wearing full-length fur coats, and taking expensive vacations will spice up the deadliest marriage. In *Sexational Secrets*, Susan Bakos sets out to gather for the presumably impecunious reader the rarefied sexual know-how that members of the moneyed classes spend thousands to obtain. Apparently, the best sex is being had today by a lucky international elite who can afford $625 for multiple-orgasm workshops. Whether Bakos is interviewing "beautiful French courtesans" or a master of Kundalini yoga, she goes out of her way to stress the demographics of their clientele. They are "sheiks," they live in "secluded" suburban homes, they wear "business suits" and drink "flavored coffees."

As for the benefits of better sex, Betty Dodson reports that after attending one of her lectures on the vulva a woman asked for a raise at work "—and got it!" (Dodson attributes the woman's enhanced self-esteem to becoming "cunt positive.") And a raise at work is small potatoes compared to these authors' promises, expressed and implied, for the sexually liberated society as a whole. We can look forward to the disappearance of "prejudice and bigotry, heartache and misery, loneliness and violence"; the obsolescence of guns and missiles; the release of "the spirit of creativity" and the renewal of "the joy of living." Here is Dodson's "futuristic fantasy" of liberation:

> It's New Year's Eve, 1999. All the television networks have agreed to let me produce "Orgasms Across America." Every TV screen will be showing high-tech, fine-art porn created by the best talent this country has to offer. At the stroke of midnight, the entire population will be masturbating to orgasm for World Peace.

It was Mao's nasty inspiration that for a revolution truly to succeed it must never stop, and our own culture's version of nonstop revolution is collected and distilled in pop-sex books: a ceaseless propaganda of self-congratulation wedded to a ceaseless invocation of the still-powerful Enemy. If victory in the Sexual Revolution should ever be declared, people might no longer seek instruction and guidance from commercial sources. Consequently, our experts fill their books with reminders of how much better off we all are than our grandparents. They laud the science of Alfred Kinsey and Masters and Johnson; they gleefully puncture the myth of the Freudian "mature" vaginal orgasm; they ridicule, under such banners as "The Annals of Ignorance," the hopeless stupidity of human beings a century ago. But the running dogs of sexual repression still hunt in packs outside our doors. One author blames "narrow, paternalistic 1950s-style family values" and our "sex-negative, genital-shaming upbringing," while another blames "traditional marriage" and "anti-porn activists who are intent on preserving their romantic illusions." Absolutely everyone blames religion. To hear the experts tell it, we live in a sexually repressed nation, under the dark thrall of Catholicism, fundamentalism, and ignorance.

I wonder what planet these experts are on. They seem blind to the way today's fifteen-year-olds act and dress, oblivious to the atmosphere of sexual license of which they themselves are the direct beneficiaries, and wholly ignorant of the large body of recent scholarship, by Peter Gay and others, that has revealed beneath the veneer of Victorian "repression" a universe of sexual experience as richly ramified as our own. There doubtless still exist a few American teenagers who choose to give greater weight in their lives to religious scruples than to pop culture. But who is Dr. Susan Block to tell these kids they've chosen badly? As for the overwhelming majority of young people who pay more attention to *Baywatch* than to the Bible, they are indeed lucky to live in a time when it's common knowledge, for example, that women have orgasms and that few, if any of them, are vaginal. It's worth pointing out, though, that what made this knowledge common was the growing power of women, rather than the other way around.

However manfully I resist nostalgia, Victorian silences appeal to me. Dr. Block, in an uncharacteristic fit of wisdom, observes, "The irony of creating a taboo is that, once something is forbidden, it often becomes very interesting." Sex in a time of ostensible repression at least had the benefit of carving out a space of privacy. Lovers defined themselves in opposition to the official culture, which had the effect of making every discovery *personal*. There's something profoundly boring about the vision that is promulgated, if only as an ideal, by today's experts: a long life of vigorous, nonstop, "fulfilling" sex, and the identical story in every household. Although it pains me to remember how innocent I was in my early twenties, I have no desire to rewrite my life. To do so would eliminate those moments of discovery when whole vistas of experience opened out of nowhere, moments when I thought, So *this* is what's it's like. Just as every generation needs to feel that it has invented sex—"Sexual intercourse began / In nineteen sixty-three / (Which was rather late for me)" was Philip Larkin's imperfectly ironic lament—we all deserve our own dry spells and our own revolutions. They're what make our lives good stories.

Unfortunately, stories like these are easily lost amid the slick certitudes of our media culture: that a heavy enough barrage of information produces enlightenment, and that incessant communication produces communities. Susie Bright and Susan Block and Dr. Ruth are loud and cable-ready. You can turn them on, but you can't turn them off. They yammer on about the frenulum, the perineum, the G-spot, the squeeze technique, bonobo chimpanzees and vibrators, teddies and garter belts, "eargasms" and "toegasms." Their work *creates* the bumbling amateur. Their discovery of sexual "technique" *creates* a population bereft of technique. The popular culture they belong to thus resembles an MTV beach party. From the outside, the party looks like fun, but for passive viewers its most salient feature is that they haven't been invited to it. "Are some people having multiple orgasms . . . electrifying oral experiences, incredible and emotionally intense love-making sessions that last for hours?" Susan Bakos asks the reader. "Unbelievable as it may sound—yes. Why not you?" A lonely reader could be forgiven for replying: Because there's a television in my bedroom.

THE TERM "PARAPHILIA" connotes perversion, something unhealthy. But, while there's little doubt that our culture promotes a paraphiliac displacement from the genital to the verbal, this displacement is not intrinsically diseased. The reason that reading a sex book can assuage loneliness (at least momentarily) is that sex for human beings is easily as much imaginative as it is biological. When we make love, we forever have in our heads an image of ourselves making love. And, although substituting a hot text for a warm body may be nothing but a way of tricking our genitals, what's remarkable is that the trick so often works. When I was fourteen I canvassed and recanvassed my *Webster's Collegiate* for words like "intercourse." Scouring *Ann Landers Talks to Teenagers About Sex* for the dirty bits, I was excited to learn that the mere sight of a "girl in a tight sweater" is sufficient to arouse a teenage boy.

For the person who seeks such written thrills but lacks the resources to compile his own supply of frisson-inducing texts, there now exists *The Joy of Writing Sex: A Guide for Fiction Writers*, a kind of para-paraphiliac volume, by the novelist Elizabeth Benedict. This new *Joy* consists mainly of sex scenes excerpted from the work of contemporary fiction writers and framed by Benedict's own chirpy, sanitizing glosses. Whatever subversive thrills *Portnoy's Complaint* might provide are unlikely to survive an analysis like this: "Roth manages to turn the cliché of the teenage boy's first visit to a whore into a rich, sidesplittingly funny scene that leads us back again to the themes of the novel, the struggle between being a good Jew and a good Jewish son and being as naughty as your libido begs you to be." Benedict confides that a big attraction of writing the manual was that she could "read sexy books and think for long periods of nothing but sex." That she considers this an enviable circumstance may explain the deep kinship—the quite striking parallels—between her product and the products of pop-sex authors. Its price sticker is its destiny.

Like the pop-sexers, Benedict congratulates our age on its enlightenment and congratulates her readers on their good fortune in having come of age after the publication of *Fear of Flying*. She alludes to the "incalculable tragedies of self-censorship" that befell authors in the dark ages before 1960, and she hints at the evil forces (Puritanism, fundamentalists, sexually repressive governments) that threaten our precarious liberty. Although she, like Dr. Block, briefly acknowledges the excitement that taboo generates ("Now that we can say anything, what else is there to say?"), pursuing this argument would undermine her project, and so she doesn't. Similarly uneasy is her recognition that divorcing sex-scene technique from the larger challenges of writing good fiction is as useless as divorcing sexual technique from the challenge of loving someone. Good sex writing, it turns out, is a lot like good fiction writing in general. It has, she says, "tension, dramatic conflict, character development, insights, metaphors and surprises." These qualities are the Slow and Fast One- and Two-Handed Strokes to which Benedict returns, in various combinations, throughout the book. Avoid clichés, she advises—or at least "give them a unique twist." Try to "make the writing interesting." Don't forget: "You need not be explicit but you must be specific." And if it doesn't fit, you must acquit.

Although Benedict believes that she can liberate the reader from the "demons" of self-censorship, she's vague on exactly how this occurs. At one point, she implies that liberation is simply a matter of gumption: "**Question**: Who are your censors and how do you silence them? **Answer**: Just do it." But a book that intends to give us "permission to indulge" new possibilities requires an exemplary performer, and, as with Betty Dodson, whose *Sex for One: The Joy of Selfloving* mainly retails the professional triumphs of Betty Dodson, the work that most interests Benedict is her own. She includes four substantial excerpts from her fiction, and she praises them with charming artlessness. ("These are emotionally complex scenes . . .") At the same time, she takes care to remind us that *her* skills didn't come from any manual. In her own work, she says, she didn't "consciously try to create conflict or to inject surprises"—although, sure enough, she now realizes "how important those elements are."

The fraud of *The Joy of Writing Sex* is meaner than the fraud of sex manuals, since every man can be a king in bed and every woman a queen but not everyone can be a successful novelist. Nietzsche said, "Books for all the world are always foul-smelling books; the smell of small people clings to them." The truth, of course, may be that I'm no larger than the next man. But who wants to know a truth like this? Just as every lover at some level believes that he or she makes love as it's made nowhere else on the planet, so every artist clings for dear life to the illusion that the art he or she produces is vital, necessary, and unique.

Aesthetic elitism, sexual snobbery: these are not the reprehensible attitudes that our culture makes them out to be. They're the efforts of the individual to secure a small space of privacy within the prevailing din. All people should be elitists—and keep it to themselves.

THE ONE WELCOME SERVICE that Benedict performs in *Joy* is her surgical removal of sex scenes from their context. The more sincerely explicit a novel's dirty bits, I think, the more they beg to be removed. When I was a teenager, novels were Trojan horses by means of which titillation could sometimes be smuggled into my sheltered life. Over the years, though, I've come to dread the approach of sex scenes in serious fiction. Call it the orgasmic collapse: the more absorbing the story, the more I dread it. Often the sentences begin to lengthen Joyceanly. My own anxiety rises sympathetically with the author's, and soon enough the fragile bubble of the imaginative world is pricked by the hard exigencies of naming body parts and movements—the sameness of it all. When the sex is persuasively rendered, it tends to read autobiographically, and there are limits to my desire for immersion in a stranger's biochemistry. A few geniuses—Philip Roth may be one of them—have the skill or bravado to get away with explicit sex, but in most novels, even otherwise excellent ones, the corporeal nomenclature is hopelessly contaminated through its previous use by writers whose aim is simply to turn the reader on.

Jacques Derrida once demonstrated, in his sublimely contortionist essay "White Mythology," that language is such a self-contained system that even a word as basic as "sun" cannot be proved, by anyone using language, to refer to an objective, extralinguistic Sun. A candle is *like* a small sun, but the sun is *like* a large candle; examined closely, language turns out to operate through the lateral associations of metaphor, rather than through the vertical identifications of naming. So what is "sex"? Everything is like it, and it's like everything—like food, like drugs, like reading and writing, like deal-making, like war, like sport, like education, like the economy, like socializing. In the end, however, every orgasm is more or less the same. This may be why writing *about* sex is at once effective and boring. Language of the nominal, hot-slippery-cunt-ramrod-straight-dick variety both aims for and achieves its own closure. The orgasm is a kind of consumer purchase, and, one way or another, the language that attends it always remains a kind of ad copy.

Language *as* sex, on the other hand, is fraught with the perils of an open-ended eros. When I'm in bed with a novel, I hope its author will be faithful to me. Right now I'm reading Nick Hornby's *High Fidelity*, an enjoyable sendup of male anxiety in which the narrator's girlfriend leaves him for his upstairs neighbor, a man he now remembers was "something of a demon" in bed:

> "He goes on long enough," I said one night, when we were both lying awake, staring at the ceiling. "I should be so lucky," said Laura. This was a joke. We laughed. Ha, ha, we went. Ha, ha, ha. I'm not laughing now. Never has a joke filled me with such nausea and paranoia and insecurity and self-pity and dread and doubt.

When a full-blown sex scene finally looms on the narrative horizon, a hundred pages into a novel that's almost entirely about sex, my distaste at the prospect of orgasmic collapse is mitigated by a rare circumstance: I'm actually finding both the female love object (an American folk-rock singer) and the setting (a barren flat in a barren London neighborhood) quite sexy. Though I'm not looking forward to the hardened nipples and spurted semen that seem likely to follow, I'm prepared to forgive them, maybe even enjoy them. But when, after one last eight-page delay for awkward negotiations and precoital anxiety, Hornby gets his lovers into bed, the narrator abruptly declares: "I'm not going into all that other stuff, the who-did-what-to-whom stuff." Facing a choice between fidelity to "what happens" and fidelity to his reader, Hornby doesn't let the reader down. In one simple, curtain-dropping sentence he proves to me that he himself, at some point in his reading, has experienced the same uncomfortable suspense that I have just experienced, and for a moment, though I'm alone in bed with a book, I don't feel alone. For a moment, I belong to a group neither as big as a statistically significant sample nor as small as the naked self. It's a group of two, the faithful writer and the trusting reader. We're different but the same.

[1997]

MEET ME IN ST. LOUIS

ON A CHILLY MORNING in late September, by the side of a truck-damaged road that leads past brownfields to unwholesome-looking wholesalers, a TV producer and his cameraman are telling me how to drive across the Mississippi River toward St. Louis and what, approximately, I should be feeling as I do so.

"You're coming back for a visit," they say. "You're checking out the skyline and the Arch."

The cameraman, Chris, is a barrel-chested, red-faced local with a local accent. The producer, Gregg, is a tall, good-looking cosmopolitan with fashion-model locks. Through the window of my rental car, Gregg gives me a walkie-talkie with which to communicate with him and the crew, who will be following me in a minivan.

"You'll want to drive slow," Chris says, "in the second lane from the right."

"How slow?"

"Like thirty-five."

In the distance I can see commuter traffic, still heavy, on the elevated roadways that feed the Poplar Street Bridge. There's a hint of illegality in our plotting by the side of a road here, in East St. Louis wastelands suitable for dumping bodies, but we're doing nothing more dubious morally than making television. Any commuters we might inconvenience won't know this, of course, but I suspect that if they did know it—if they heard the word "Oprah"—most of them would mind the inconvenience less.

After I've tested the walkie-talkie, we drive back to a feeder ramp. I've spent the night in St. Louis and have come over the bridge for no other reason than to stage this shot. I'm a Midwesterner who's been living in the East for twenty-four years. I'm a grumpy Manhattanite who, with what feels like a Midwestern eagerness to cooperate, has agreed to pretend to arrive in the Midwestern city of his childhood and reexamine his roots.

The inbound traffic is heavier than the outbound was. A tailgater flashes his high beams as I brake to allow the camera van to pull even with me on the left. Its side panel door is open, and Chris is hanging out with a camera on his shoulder. In the far right lane, a semi is coming up to pass me.

"We need you to roll down your window," Gregg says on the walkie-talkie.

I roll down the window, and my hair begins to fly.

"Slow down, slow down," Chris barks across the blurred pavement.

I ease up on the gas, watching the road empty in front of me. I am slow and the world is fast. The semi has pulled up squarely to my right, obscuring the Gateway Arch and the skyline that I'm supposed to be pretending to check out.

Chris, leaning from the van with his camera, shouts angrily, or desperately, above the automotive roar. "Slow down! Slow down!"

I have a morbid aversion to blocking traffic—inherited, perhaps, from my father, for whom an evening at the theater was a torment if somebody short was sitting behind him—but I obey the shouted order, and the semi on my right roars on ahead of me, unblocking our view of the Arch just as we leave the bridge and sail west.

Over the walkie-talkie, as we reconnoiter for a second take, Gregg explains that Chris was shouting not at me but at his assistant, who is driving the van. Every time I slowed down, they had to slow down further. I feel sheepish about this, but I'm happy that nobody got killed.

For the second take, I stay in the far right lane and poke along at half the legal speed limit, trying to appear—what? writerly? curious? nostalgic?—while the trucker behind me looses blast after blast on his air horn.

In front of St. Louis's historic Old Courthouse, where the Dred Scott case was tried, Chris and his helper and I wait in suspense while Gregg reviews the new footage on a handheld Sony monitor. Gregg's beautiful hair keeps falling in his face and has to be shaken back. East of the Courthouse, the Arch soars above a planted grove of ash trees. I once wrote a novel that was centered on this monitory stainless icon of my childhood, I once invested the Arch and the counties that surround it with mystery and soul, but this morning I have no subjectivity. I feel nothing except a dullish anxiousness to please. I'm a dumb but necessary object, a passive supplier of image, and I get the feeling that I'm failing even at this.

My third book, *The Corrections*—a family novel about three East Coast urban sophisticates who alternately long for and reject the heartland suburbs where their aged parents live—will soon be announced as Oprah Winfrey's latest selection for her televised Book Club. A week ago, one of Winfrey's producers, a straight shooter named Alice, called me in New York to introduce me to some responsibilities of being an Oprah author. "This is a difficult book for us," Alice said. "I don't think we're going to know how to approach it until we start hearing from our readers." But in order to produce a short visual biography of me and an impressionistic summary of *The Corrections* the producers would need "B-roll" filler footage to intercut with "A-roll" footage of me speaking. Since my book-tour schedule showed a free day in St. Louis the following Monday (I was planning to visit some old friends of my parents), might it be possible to shoot some B-roll in my former neighborhood?

"Certainly," I said. "And what about filming me here in New York?"

"We may want to do that, too," Alice said.

I volunteered that between my apartment and my studio in Harlem, which I share with a sculptor friend of mine, there was quite a lot of visual interest in New York!

"We'll see what they want to do," Alice said. "But if you can give us a full day in St. Louis?"

"That would be fine," I said, "although St. Louis doesn't really have anything to do with my life now."

"We may want to take another day later and do some shooting in New York," Alice said, "if there's time after your tour."

One of the reasons I'm a writer is that I have uneasy relations with authority. The only time I've ever worn a uniform was during my sophomore year in high school, when I played the baritone for the Marching Statesmen of Webster Groves High School. I was fifteen and growing fast; between September and November I got too big for my uniform. After the last home game of the Statesmen's football season, I walked off the field and passed through crowds of girl seniors and juniors in tight jeans and long scarves. Dying of uncoolness, I tugged down my tuxedo pants to try to cover my ridiculous spats. I undid the brass buttons of my orange-and-black tunic and let it hang open rebelliously. I looked, if anything, even less cool this way, and I was spotted almost immediately by the band director, Mr. Carson. He strode over and spun me around and shouted in my face. "Franzen, you're a Marching Statesman! You either wear this uniform with pride or you don't wear it at all. Do you understand me?"

When I accepted Winfrey's endorsement of my book, I took to heart Mr. Carson's admonition. I understood that television is propelled by images, the simpler and more vivid the better. If the producers wanted me to be Midwestern, I would try to be Midwestern.

On Friday afternoon, Gregg called to ask if I knew the owners of my family's old house and whether they would let a camera crew film me inside it. I said I didn't know the owners. Gregg offered to look them up and get their permission. I said I didn't want to go in my old house. Well, Gregg said, if I could at least walk around outside it, he would be happy to get permission from the owners. I said I wanted nothing to do with my old house. I could tell, though, that my resistance displeased him, and so I offered some alternatives that I hoped he might find tempting: he could shoot in my old church, he could shoot in the high school, he could even shoot on my old street, provided he didn't show my family's house. Gregg, with a sigh, took down the names of the church and the high school.

After I hung up, I became aware that I'd been scratching my arms and legs and torso. I seemed, in fact, to be developing a full-blown bodywide rash.

By now, on Monday morning, as I stand in the shadow of an Arch that means nothing to me, the rash has coalesced into a flaming, shingles-like band of pain and itching around the lower right side of my torso. This is an entirely unprecedented category of affliction for me. The itching has abated during the excitement of filming on the bridge, but while we wait for Gregg to sign off on the footage I want to claw myself savagely.

Gregg at last looks up from his little monitor. Though visibly dissatisfied with the second take, he announces that a third take won't be necessary. Chris, the cameraman, grins like a hunting dog whose instincts have been vindicated. He's wearing jeans and a corduroy shirt; he looks as if he'd listened to the Allman Brothers and Lynyrd Skynyrd in his youth. Gregg, for his part, seems like a person to whom the Smiths and New Order were important. As he and I drive west out of the city, I wait for him to ask me questions about St. Louis or to joke with me about the tedium and artificiality of what we're doing, but he has messages to return on his cell phone. He has an expensive crew, a marginally cooperative actor, and seven hours of daylight left.

TO FREE UP MONDAY for shooting, I did my socializing on Sunday at the home of my parents' old next-door neighbors, Glenn and Irene Patton. The Pattons had foreseen better than I the difficulty of visiting too many people sequentially, and they'd called me in New York to offer to host a small reception.

I pulled into my old street, Webster Woods, at three o'clock, approaching the Pattons' from the direction that didn't take me past my family's house. A light rain of no season, neither summer nor fall, was coming down; a gang of crows was cawing in some tree. Although Glenn had recently had both of his knees replaced and Irene had just recovered from a genuine case of shingles, the two Pattons looked happy and healthy when they met me at their door.

Through the windows of their kitchen, where I made ineffectual gestures of helping with refreshments, I could see the back of my old house. Irene spoke warmly of the young couple who lived in it now. She told me what she knew of their lives and of their improvements to the house in the two years since my brothers and I had sold it. Our tiny back yard was now a parking lot for a medium-sized boat and a tremendous SUV. The grass appeared to have been paved over, but I couldn't tell for sure, because I couldn't stand to look for more than a second.

"I told them you were coming," Irene said, "and they said you're more than welcome to come over and see the house, if you'd like."

"I don't want to see it."

"Oh, I know," Irene said. "Ellie Smith, when I called to invite her for today, said she hadn't driven down this street since you boys sold the house. She says it's just too painful for her."

The Pattons' doorbell began to ring. We'd invited four other couples who had known my parents well and whom I hadn't seen since my mother died. There was something of

the miracle now in watching them arrive two by two and settle in the Pattons' carpeted living room, in seeing all of them
so alive and so much themselves. They were close to my parents' age—in their seventies and eighties—and my memories
of some of them were as old as my oldest memories of my
parents. If you really *get* the death of a person you love, as I
had finally and reluctantly *got* the death of my parents, then
you know that the first and most fundamental fact of it is
that you will never again see the person as a living, smiling,
speaking body. This is the mysterious basic substance of the
loss. To put my arms around women with whom my mother
had played bridge for much of her life, to shake the large
hands of men with whom my father had cleared brush or
found fault with Ronald Reagan's presidency, was to feel loss
and its contrary simultaneously. Any of these couples could
have been my parents, still one hundred percent alive, still
making light of their ailments, still accepting from Glenn
Patton one of his famously well-poured drinks, still loading
up small plates with raw vegetables and assorted dessert bars
and baked Brie with a sweet tapenade. And yet they weren't
my parents. There was an altered house next door to prove
it. There was a boat and a bloatational SUV in the back
yard.

By the time the party had ended and I sat down to watch
some Rams football in the Pattons' family room, a big au-
tumn wind was picking up outside, drying the street and
lightening the sky. I thought of the last page of *Swann's Way*:
the wind that "wrinkled the surface of the Grand Lac in little
wavelets, like a real lake." The great oak trees that helped
Marcel "to understand how paradoxical it is to seek in reality
for the pictures that are stored in one's memory, which must
inevitably lose the charm that comes to them from memory

itself and from their not being apprehended by the senses."
And his conclusion: "The reality that I had known no longer
existed."

This was a lesson I'd absorbed long before my mother
died. Visiting her at home, I'd been disappointed again and
again by the thinness, the unvividness, of rooms that in my
memory were steeped in almost magical signficance. And
now, I thought, I had even less cause to go seeking the past
in that house. If my mother wasn't going to come walking
up the driveway in her housecoat with her hands full of the
crabgrass she'd pulled or the twigs she'd picked up off the
lawn, if she wasn't going to emerge from the basement with
an armload of wet sheets that she'd been waiting to hang on
the clothesline once the rain stopped (she'd always liked the
smell of sheets that had hung outside), the scene in the Pattons' windows didn't interest me. As I sat watching football
and listened to the barren wind, I believed that the reason I
couldn't stand to look at my old house was that I was done
with it: that I didn't want to feel the inevitable nothing when
I went inside it, I didn't want to have to blame an innocent
house for still existing after its meaning had been emptied
out.

BUT THE SHOW MUST GO ON! We shoot four takes of me
making a left turn into Webster Woods, Gregg stopping
us after each so that he can examine it on his monitor. We
do multiple takes of me driving very slowly toward my old
house. Over the walkie-talkie one of the men suggests that
I look around curiously, as if I haven't been here in a while.
We reshoot the same scene with Chris in the passenger seat,
capturing my point of view through the windshield and then

wedging himself against the door to capture me looking around curiously, as if I haven't been here in a while.

By one o'clock, we're parked at the bottom of the little hill on which my old house sits. The new owners have built a retaining wall across the incline up which I used to struggle to push a lawn mower. The wall is pink—the effect is of a Lego fortress—but maybe there's a long-term plan to let ivy grow and cover it.

After a moment I have to look away. The sky and sun are brilliant, the local trees still green. Three small kids are playing outside the only new house, an ugly stuccoed box, that's been built on the street since I lived here. Gregg is asking the children's mother for permission to film them. I don't know the mother. I used to know everybody in Webster Woods, but now I only know the Pattons.

For half an hour, while the crew films generic American children romping on generic grass, I sit in the sun on a triangular traffic island across the street from the Pattons. I try not to claw myself where I itch. Behind me is a young oak tree that my family planted after my father died. My father had left no instructions for his burial or cremation—had refused all his life to discuss the matter—and so we decided to plant a tree on this island where he'd cut grass and raked leaves for nearly thirty years. We scattered some of his ashes around the tree and installed a small marble marker engraved IN MEMORY OF EARL FRANZEN. I have a feeling that this tree would interest Gregg, and I don't quite understand my resolve not to tell him about it. Certainly, if I'm protecting my privacy, it's perverse of me to be annoyed that the crew is lavishing attention on someone else's children.

After Gregg has run to my car to get a release form for the mother to sign, I am summoned to stroll down the street while Chris, shooting, backs away from me. Gregg asks me to say a few words about Webster Woods, and I deliver a short paean to the place, my happiness in growing up here, my affection for the public schools and the Congregational Church.

Gregg is frowning. "Something more specifically about this neighborhood."

"Well, obviously, it's a suburban neighborhood."

"Something about what kind of people live here."

My feeling about the people who live here now is that they're not the people who used to live here, and that I hate them for this. My feeling is that I would die of rage if I had to live on this street where I once lived so happily. My feeling is that this street, my memory of it, is *mine*; and yet I patently own none of it, not even the footage being shot in my name.

So I deliver, for the camera, a brief sociology lecture on how the neighborhood has changed, how the homes have been expanded, how much more money the new families have. The truth content of this lecture is probably near zero. Irene Patton has come out of her house and waves to me from her front yard. I wave back as to a stranger.

"Are you sure we can't shoot you in front of your house?" Gregg says. "Just in front of it, not inside it?"

"I'm really sorry," I say, "but I don't want to." And then, because I don't understand what it is that I'm protecting, I have a spasm of regret for being so difficult. I tell Gregg that I'll give him a picture of the house in the winter with snow on it. "You can show the picture," I say.

Gregg tosses his hair back. "And you'll definitely give us that."

"Definitely."

But Gregg still seems unhappy with me, and so I find myself offering him the tree. I explain to him about the tree, I tell the story, but the effect isn't what I hoped for. He seems only mildly interested as I lead the crew back to the triangle and point out the marble marker. Irene Patton is still in her yard, but I don't even look at her now.

For another half-hour we shoot me and the tree from many angles and distances. I walk slowly toward the tree, I stand in front of the tree contemplatively, I pretend to contemplate the inscription at the base of the tree. The itching on my torso reminds me of the scene in *Alien* where the newly hatched alien erupts through the space traveler's chest.

Apparently I'm failing to emote.

"You're looking up at the tree," Gregg coaches. "You're thinking about your father."

My father is dead, and I, too, am feeling dead. I remember and then make myself forget that some of my mother's ashes were scattered here as well. While Chris zooms and pans, I am mainly registering the configuration of oak twigs on my retina, trying to remember the size of the tree when we planted it, trying to calculate its annual growth rate; but part of me is also watching me. Part of me is imagining how this will play on TV: as schmaltz. Rendering emotion is what I do as a writer, and this tree is my material, and now I'm helping to ruin it. I know I'm ruining it because Gregg is frowning at me the way I might frown at a faulty ballpoint pen. That my belly and back are itching so insanely is almost a relief, because it distracts me from the shame of failing to do justice to my father and his tree. How I wish I hadn't offered Gregg this tree! But how could I not have offered *something*?

I am failing as an Oprah author, and the team and I are finishing up some final strolling footage, well into our third hour in Webster Woods, when I complete the failure. Five words come bursting from my chest like a hideous juvenile alien. I say: "This is so fundamentally bogus!"

Chris, to my surprise, raises his face from his eyepiece and laughs and nods vigorously. "You're right!" His voice is loud with merriment and something close to anger. "You're right, it is totally bogus!"

Gregg, stone-faced, merely looks at his watch. Time is short, and the author is being difficult.

FROM WEBSTER WOODS we drive out through the western reaches of the county to the Museum of Transportation, a glorified track siding to which railroads have delivered obsolete rolling stock, perhaps taking charitable tax deductions for their trouble. I have no particular fascination with trains and I've never been to the museum, but a transportation museum makes a cameo in *The Corrections*, and one of the novel's main characters is a railroad man. So my job is to stand or walk near trains and look contemplative. I do this for an hour.

When it's time for me to leave for the bookstore where I'm reading and signing tonight, I shake Gregg's hand and say I hope he got some footage he can use. In the gloom of his reply I recognize a fellow perfectionist and worrier, whose retakes are the equivalent of my rewrites.

"I guess I'll find some way to make it work," he says.

Borders Bookstore in Brentwood is crowded when I arrive. One of my publisher's publicists, a St. Louis native named Pete Miller, has flown in and has brought to the reading his sister, his girlfriend, and a bottle of single-malt Scotch for me to drink on my tour. Seeing him now, after a day with strangers, I feel among family again. It's not simply that I've worked with the same smallish publisher for fourteen years, or that Pete and his colleagues feel more like friends than like business associates. It's that Pete and his girlfriend have just come from New York and New York is the city, of all the cities in the world, that feels to me like the home I grew up in. My parents had me late in life, and my most typical experience as a child was to be left to my own devices while adults went to work and had parties. That's what my New York is.

Homesick, I nearly throw my arms around Pete. Only after I've given my reading does the full scope of my connection to this other home, this St. Louis, become apparent. In the signing line are scores of acquaintances—former classmates, parents of my friends, friends of my parents, Sunday school teachers, fellow actors in school plays, teachers from high school, coworkers of my father's, bridge partners of my mother's, people from church, near and distant old neighbors from Webster Woods. The new owner of my family's house, the man I've been hating all day, has driven over to greet me and to give me a relic from the house: a brass door knocker with my family's name on it. I take the knocker and shake his hand. I shake everybody's hand and drink the Scotch that Pete has poured me. I soak up the good will of people who demand nothing from me, who've simply stopped by to say hello, maybe get a book signed, for old times' sake.

From the bookstore I head straight for the airport. I'm due to take the evening's last flight to Chicago, where, in the morning, Alice and I will tape ninety minutes of interview for *Oprah*. Earlier today, while I was doing my best to look contemplative for the camera, Winfrey publicly announced her selection of my book and praised it in terms that would have made me blush if I'd been lucky enough to hear them. One of my friends will report that Winfrey said the author had poured so much into the book that "he must not have a thought left in his head." This will prove to be an oddly apt description. Beginning the next night, in Chicago, I'll encounter two kinds of readers in signing lines and in interviews. One kind will say to me, "I like your book and I think it's wonderful that Oprah picked it"; the other kind will say, "I like your book and I'm so sorry that Oprah picked it." And because I'm a person who instantly acquires a Texas accent in Texas, I'll respond in kind to each kind of reader. When I talk to admirers of Winfrey, I'll experience a glow of gratitude and good will and agree that it's wonderful to see television expanding the audience for books. When I talk to detractors of Winfrey, I'll experience the bodily discomfort I felt when we were turning my father's oak tree into schmaltz, and I'll complain about the Book Club logo. I'll get in trouble for this. I'll achieve unexpected sympathy for Dan Quayle when, in a moment of exhaustion in Oregon, I conflate "high modern" and "art fiction" and use the term "high art" to describe the importance of Proust and Kafka and Faulkner to my writing. I'll get in trouble for this, too. Winfrey will disinvite me from her show because I seem "conflicted." I'll be reviled from coast to coast by outraged populists. I'll be called a "motherfucker" by an anonymous source in *New York* magazine, a "pompous prick" in *Newsweek*, an "ego-blinded snob" in the *Boston Globe*, and a "spoiled, whiny little brat" in the *Chicago Tribune*. I'll consider the possibility, and to some extent believe, that I am all of these things. I'll repent and explain and qualify, to little avail. My rash will fade as mysteriously as it blossomed; my sense of dividedness will only deepen.

But this is all still in the future as I speed north on I-170, veering through the underlit lanes, my stomach empty, my head a little woolly with Scotch. The brass door knocker has upset me. I've left it in Pete Miller's care because I don't want to have it. (It will resurface months later in my editor's desk.) I don't want to hold the knocker, don't even want to look at it, for the same reason that I've been averting my eyes from my old house. Not because it reminds me of how empty of meaning the house is now, but because the house is perhaps not so empty after all. The distant past may live only in my head, and my memories of it may merely be mocked by the sterile present, but there are much more recent and much more painful memories that I haven't touched at all: memories that I've tried to leave behind me in the house.

For example, there's the little Pyrex dish of canned peas that I found in the refrigerator the last time my mother was in the hospital. My mother had long ago reconciled herself to staying in the house while her children fled to the coasts. We invited her to move to one of the coasts herself, but the house was her life, it was what she still had, it was not so much the site of her loneliness as the antidote to it. But she was often very alone there, and I was always at pains, in New York, not to remember this aloneness. Generally I managed to forget it pretty well, but when I flew into town on the day of her last surgery I found unavoidable reminders in the house: a soiled towel soaking in a bucket in the basement, a half-finished crossword by her bed. For the last week or so before she was hospitalized, my mother couldn't keep any food down, and by the time I arrived her refrigerator was empty of almost everything but ancient condiments and delicacies. On the top shelf there was just a quart of skim milk, a tiny can of green peas with a square of foil on top, and, next to this can, a dish containing a single bite of peas. I was ambushed and nearly destroyed by this dish of peas. I was forced to imagine my mother alone in the house and willing herself to eat a bite of something, anything, a bite of peas, and finding herself unable to. With her usual frugality and optimism, she'd put both the can and the dish in the refrigerator, in case her appetite returned.

The last day I was ever in the house, three months later, I worked with one of my brothers to make last-minute repairs and to box my old belongings. We'd been going at it twelve and fourteen hours a day that week, and I was packing furiously up to the moment I went to fetch a rental truck. I didn't have time to feel much of anything but the pleasure of getting the boxes labeled, the truck loaded up; and then suddenly it was time for me to leave. I went looking for my brother to say goodbye to him. I happened to pass my old bedroom, I found myself stopping in the hallway to look inside, and it occurred to me that I would *never see this room again*; a wave of grief rose up in me. I ran down the stairs, breathing heavily through my mouth, not seeing well. I clapped my arms around my brother and ran, just ran, from the house and hopped in the truck and drove too fast down the driveway, ripping a branch off a tree in my hurry to get on the road. I think I made myself be done then. I think the implicit promise I gave myself that afternoon, the promise I would have broken if I'd gone back inside the house today, was that I had left for the last time and I would never have to leave again.

Promises, promises. I'm speeding toward the airport.

[2001]

INAUGURATION DAY, JANUARY 2001

A COUPLE OF SATURDAYS AGO, lacking any better invitation, you might have got up at 5:30 and left your silk scarves and your cashmere coat in the closet, put on your beat-up Red Wings and several layers of old wool, and cabbed up to the Harlem State Office Building, on 125th Street, where twenty young socialists, a shoal of fellow-traveling Fordham students, and two stray Barnard seniors who'd been drinking all night at the Village Idiot were waiting for transportation to Washington.

The transportation, when it came, rather late, proved to be two antique yellow school buses. David Schmauch, a member of the Harlem branch of the International Socialist Organization, was in charge of the operation. Schmauch, who resembles a clean-shaven Kenneth Branagh, was wearing duck boots, a nylon parka, and a goofy stocking cap. He'd paid fifteen hundred dollars out of his own pocket for the buses, and he'd sold nowhere near fifteen hundred dollars' worth of tickets. One contingent of sympathizers, he said, had backed out when it learned that the buses had no bathrooms. You might have been tempted to sneer at this objection, at the bourgeois primness of it, but after your very slow bus, slowed further by rain and fog, had made a bathroom stop at every service area along the New Jersey Turnpike—each stop dilating into cigarette break and extended snack opportunity—you might have wished, yourself, for a motor coach with self-contained amenities.

On the other hand, the more time you'd sat on a warm, dry bus reading your copy of the *Socialist Worker*, the less time you'd have had to stand in the mud at Stanton Square, behind the Supreme Court, where the only shelters were the dope-scented porta-potties and the plastic-shrouded gazebo from which warmup speakers for the Reverend Al Sharpton were fishing for cheers in a sea of four or five thousand wet non-Republicans. Worse weather was imaginable: it could have been raining harder. If you'd lucked onto the slower bus and arrived very late, only your smaller fingers might have been frozen by the time Sharpton took charge of the mike and stirred you, against your will, with the brevity and force of his denunciations. There in the rain, among the wilting placards ("Hail to the Thief!" and "The People Have Spoken—All Five of Them") and the rain-beaded lenses of Bertolt Brecht eyewear, you might even have warmed to Sharpton's cheaper shots—his challenge to Dubya "to do more than get messy with Jesse," for example, or his calculated stuttering of "Clarence T—Tom—Thomas."

The crowd was all smiles as it formed a column and marched slowly up Maryland Avenue to surround the

Supreme Court. If you'd been there, you might have been stirred by the ceaseless chanting of

> *Racist, sexist, anti-gay,*
> *GEORGE BUSH, go away!*

and

> *Hey, Dubya, what do you say—*
> *How many votes did you steal today?*

even if you didn't actually believe that George Bush was a bigot or that he'd stolen any votes that day. Maybe, long ago, you felt similarly divided at high-school pep rallies. Maybe, although the cheerleaders in this crowd wore dreadlocks and leather pants and those burdensome-looking collections of buttons (those rosarylike skeins of explicit ideology), rather than letter sweaters and pleated skirts, you'd have once again found yourself simultaneously thrilled and repelled. But when the sidewalk surrounding the Supreme Court was fully occupied by drenched protesters, and the chant had shifted to a conga beat of

> *THIS is what dem-oc-racy looks-like,*
> *THAT is what hyp-oc-risy looks-like*

with hundreds of wet arms pointing at the Court on every shout of "*THAT*," your irritation with the self-congratulation of the THIS might have been swept away by a sudden, over-powering resentment of the THAT: the marble courthouse that loomed, silent, unlighted, unresponsive, behind a line of cops in riot helmets. You might have been glad you came down here.

But then, as the line moved on and you rounded the south-east corner of the Court, you might have had the deeply weird experience of seeing yourself seeing yourself. There, in the Florida House on the other side of Second Street, behind tall windows hung with patriotic bunting, were men and women waiting for the party to commence, wearing the kind of suits and shoes that you'd left at home, eating the kind of food that you'd eaten in restaurants almost every night the week before, drinking the eighty-proof kind of drink for which you were suddenly thirsting, and peering out with a mix of curiosity and fear and satisfaction at the sodden line of marchers of which you were at least somewhat, if only for a moment, and yet not entirely reluctantly, a living part.

The trip back took seven hours. The young socialists—an installer for Verizon, a bartender who was formerly a soccer star at Brown, a first-year schoolteacher—compared cell phones, read Marx in abridgment ("It saves reading three volumes of *Capital* for two years"), unanimously praised *Friends*, and split, along strict gay/straight lines, over the merits of *Xena, Warrior Princess*. Few pleasures compare with that of riding on a bus after dark, hours behind schedule, with people you violently agree with. But finally, inevitably, you get dumped back in the city. Rain is freezing on the ground, snow covering the slush. You may still be one version of yourself, the version from the bus, the younger and redder version, as long as you're waiting for the subway and riding home. But then you peel off the thermal layers, still damp, of the long day's costume, and you see a wholly different kind of costume hanging in your closet; and in the shower you're naked and alone.

[2001]